STO

ALLEN COUNTY PUBLIC LIBRARY

ACPL ITE
DISCARDED

Y0-BYA-258

Ar
780.973
F489c

Finell,J.G.   comp.
Amer.Music Center
Contemporary music performance
directory:a listing of American
performing ensembles,sponsoring
organizations,performing facilities,
concert series,and festivals of 20th
century music

1897332,

THE CONTEMPORARY MUSIC
PERFORMANCE DIRECTORY

THE

CONTEMPORARY MUSIC

PERFORMANCE

DIRECTORY

A Listing of American Performing Ensembles, Sponsoring Organizations, Performing Facilities, Concert Series and Festivals of 20th Century Music

Compiled by

Judith Greenberg Finell

American Music Center
250 West 57th Street
Suite 626-7
New York, New York 10019

This Directory was made possible with public funds from the New York State Council on the Arts and the National Endowment for the Arts in Washington, D.C., a Federal Agency.

This Directory was also made possible with funds from the Fromm Music Foundation at Harvard.

© 1975 by The American Music Center

Library of Congress Catalog Number 75–24697
ISBN 0–916052–01–X (paper)
ISBN 0–916052–03– 6 (cloth)

All rights reserved

Printed in the United States of America

1897332

Contents

American Music Center

The American Music Center was established in 1940 by a small group of composers including Marion Bauer, Aaron Copland, Howard Hanson, Otto Luening, and Quincy Porter. They believed that they and their fellow composers were handicapped in their struggle toward recognition by the lack of a central information center for contemporary American music. Thus they founded the AMC "to foster and encourage the composition of contemporary music and to promote its production, publication, distribution, and performance."

Since then, AMC membership has grown to more than 750 members. While most members are composers, publishers, scholars, performers, and students, others who support the aims of the AMC have joined as well. In 1962, the AMC was designated by the congressionally chartered National Music Council as the "Official United States Information Center for Music," and its place among other national music centers was confirmed.

The AMC is a unique source of information about American composers and their music. A bi-monthly newsletter informs subscribers of premieres, contests, new publications, new recordings, relevant legislation, and any other news of concern to the American composer.

Up-to-date biographical files of composer members are maintained and the Center is thus able to provide otherwise unavailable information. A steady flow of inquiries, by phone and by mail, is handled by the Center's Library and increasingly, the AMC is becoming an information center for foreign inquiries about American composers.

The AMC aims to serve as the spokesman for the American composer by issuing press releases on sensitive and important issues, by organizing conferences, and by offering programming possibilities and suggestions to performers and conductors.

The Library

The AMC Library houses an unusual collection of published and unpublished scores, records, and tapes of works by American composers. Holdings deposited by Center members include works for solo instruments, chamber ensemble, band, orchestra, voice, and chorus. In order to promote the performance of American music, the Center intends to publish catalogs in all categories of its collection.

A librarian is available to assist performers in locating composers, obtaining performance materials, programming, researching previous performances, and applying for sponsorship. Library materials are available to AMC members and qualified individuals who wish to perform or study them.

Board of Directors

Officers

Ezra Laderman, President
Martin Bookspan, Vice-President
Oliver Daniel, Vice-President
Claire Brook, Secretary
Arthur Cohn, Treasurer

Past Presidents:
Otto Luening
Quincy Porter
Mel Powell
Hugo Weisgall

Jack Beeson
Martin Bookspan
Claire Brook
Elliott Carter
Arthur Cohn
Chou Wen-Chung
David Cooper
Oliver Daniel
Charles Dodge
Stephen Fisher
Robert Freeman
Miriam Gideon
David Hamilton
James Harrison
Mrs. Ernest Heller
Leighton Kerner
Leo Kraft

Ezra Laderman
Robert Hall Lewis
Ursula Oppens
W. Stuart Pope
Seymour Shifrin
Harvey Sollberger
Robert Starer
Louise Talma
Joan Tower
Lester Trimble
George Walker
Theodore Weiler
Henry Weinberg
Arthur Weisberg
Hugo Weisgall
Thor Wood
Charles Wuorinen

Toni Greenberg, Executive Director

Preface

The once isolated community of living composers and musicians devoted only to their music is vanishing. Today, contemporary music is increasingly a part of the standard repertoire. There are few concert series or performing ensembles that do not present some works of this century. Performance competitions once reserved for 19th century virtuoso pieces now also require the rendition of modern works. Musicians who previously performed only pre-20th century works have broadened their repertoires to include contemporary pieces.

There is a richness of contemporary music activity in America today as never before. Performances of modern music are taking place not only in metropolitan cultural centers and universities, but in suburban and rural communities as well. The public is expressing an unprecedented interest in having direct contact with composers and performers by sponsoring musician residencies, attending lecture-concert demonstrations, and devoting time and resources to contemporary music events.

Much contemporary music is presented and supported in non-traditional ways. Since many modern compositions are written for chamber ensemble, performances are often held in intimate settings such as churches, community centers, museums, and libraries as well as larger, more formal concert halls. Musicians also perform in schools, parks, hospitals, and homes for the elderly. In turn, increasing support for music has come from business, government, and civic groups as well as the universities and foundations that have traditionally supported the arts. Many organizations also donate performing facilities and services such as publicity, administration, and booking.

This Directory identifies these new performing and sponsoring opportunities for musicians by listing funding and presenting organizations, concert series, festivals, and performing facilities. In addition, the listing of performing ensembles here will enable sponsors to locate groups whose musical interests coincide with theirs, and will help composers find ensembles whose instrumentation meets their needs.

This Directory was compiled from January 1974 through July 1975. Over 10,000 questionnaires were sent to composers, performers, concert managers, artist representatives, administrators, and educators. Requests for information were placed in newpapers and performing facilities. The response was overwhelming. Most of the organizations listed here sent repertoire sheets, biographical information, brochures, reviews, performance schedules, and funding guidelines. This information and subsequently acquired address and personnel changes is being maintained at the American Music Center and is available upon request. Please contact the Center if you wish assistance in reaching the organizations listed here.

Those who wish to be included in future editions should complete the form in the back of this book.

J.G.F.

New York
September 1975

Acknowledgments

This Directory was compiled from information supplied by thousands of individuals and organizations. Many state and local arts councils and arts service organizations willingly offered descriptions of activities and performing ensembles in their area. In addition, most of those listed completed detailed questionnaires and generously supplied supplemental literature.

Certain individuals offered crucial information and advice. Arthur Bloom and LuRaye Crandall of the New York State Council on the Arts were extremely informative concerning the activities and resources of New York State. Ralph Rizzolo of the National Endowment for the Arts and Paul Fromm of the Fromm Music Foundation at Harvard also contributed essential information and support.

Many individuals not listed in this book selflessly gave information for the benefit of others. Cheri Fein of Poets and Writers gave invaluable advice on all aspects of this project. Concerning computerization, Barry Brook and Murray Ralph were helpful, as were Joseph Kulin and Richard Serota of the Foundation Center. Joseph Boonin, Randell Croley, and the late Frederick Freedman gave advice on publication and distribution. Those offering information concerning musical activities throughout the United States included Montgomery Byers, Jacob Druckman, Isabelle Fisher, Hannelore Hahn of the New York City Parks, Recreation, Cultural Affairs Adminsitration, Christopher Pavlakis, Gregory Reeve of the Center for New Music in New York, and Nolanda Turner of Handel Publications.

The individuals who provided publicity and the mailing lists of their organizations were: Raymond Ericson of the New York Times, David Cooper and Rosalie Calabrese of the American Composers Alliance, Robert Carver and Ted Dreher of the American Federation of Musicians, Sandra Dilley and Robert Triplett of the Associated Councils of the Arts, Carla Bley of the Jazz Composers Orchestra Association, Craig Short of the College Music Society, Daniel Gustin and Janet Gulotta of the Berkshire Music Center, Gerald Born of the American Library Association, and William Dawson of the Association of College, University, and Community Arts Administrators.

Many American Music Center Board members provided essential guidance. Claire Brook, David Hamilton, Leighton Kerner, Leo Kraft, Ezra Laderman, and Thor Wood were particularly helpful. The staff of the American Music Center, especially Toni Greenberg, Executive Director, and MaryLou Francis gave valuable advice and support.

Finally, the dedicated Directory staff, who devoted an extraordinary amount of time and energy to this project, deserve special thanks: Joan Antelman, Darlene Gaughan, Gary McGee, and David Wakefield.

State Abbreviations

Alabama	AL	Montana	MT
Alaska	AK	Nebraska	NE
Arizona	AZ	Nevada	NV
Arkansas	AR	New Hampshire	NH
California	CA	New Jersey	NJ
Canal Zone	CZ	New Mexico	NM
Colorado	CO	New York	NY
Connecticut	CT	North Carolina	NC
Delaware	DE	North Dakota	ND
District of Columbia	DC	Ohio	OH
Florida	FL	Oklahoma	OK
Georgia	GA	Oregon	OR
Guam	GU	Pennsylvania	PA
Hawaii	HI	Puerto Rico	PR
Idaho	ID	Rhode Island	RI
Illinois	IL	South Carolina	SC
Indiana	IN	South Dakota	SD
Iowa	IA	Tennessee	TN
Kansas	KS	Texas	TX
Kentucky	KY	Utah	UT
Louisiana	LA	Vermont	VT
Maine	ME	Virginia	VA
Maryland	MD	Virgin Islands	VI
Massachusetts	MA	Washington	WA
Michigan	MI	West Virginia	WV
Minnesota	MN	Wisconsin	WI
Mississippi	MS	Wyoming	WY
Missouri	MO		

Performing Ensembles

Performance of contemporary music was the requisite for inclusion of performing ensembles in this Directory. All ensembles listed perform some 20th century chamber or choral music, jazz, new or experimental music, multi-media works, or electronic music. Some include modern works in repertoires spanning several centuries, while others perform contemporary music exclusively.

Unless otherwise noted, ensemble members are professional musicians.

The groups range in size from duos to chamber orchestras. No soloists or full orchestras are listed. Artists who do not permanently belong to a group, but perform on a free-lance basis, were not included.

The information on these ensembles was compiled from November 1974 through July 1975. Since addresses and personnel change frequently, contact the American Music Center if you have difficulty in locating a group.

In addition to the information listed here, many ensembles have also sent us repertoire sheets, biographical information, brochures, reviews, and performance schedules. The American Music Center will provide this information upon request. Questions concerning fee schedules should be addressed to the performing organizations directly.

Alabama

Judson Ensemble
Jeanne E. Shaffer, Director
Judson College
Division of Fine Arts
Marion, AL 36756
(205) 683-2011 Ext. 44
Variable number of student performers. Singers accompany themselves on guitar, flute, piano, and percussion.
20th century choral music. Performs contemporary works throughout the Southeast, particularly in schools and churches.

NAD
Ladonna Smith, Davey Williams, Directors
1505 4th Avenue
Tuscaloosa, AL 35401
(205) 758-0145
Ladonna Smith, electronic keyboards, microphones, mixer, voice, percussion, viola, piano; Davey Williams, acoustic guitar, electric guitar, percussion, saxophones, clarinets.
New and experimental music. Performs live electro-acoustic duets and electronic improvisations.

Transcendprovisation
Ladonna Smith, Davey Williams, Directors
1505 4th Avenue
Tuscaloosa, AL 35401
(205) 758-0145
Theodore Bowen, contrabass, saxophone, flute; Adrian Dye, organ, percussion, voice; Anne LeBaron, harp, percussion, viola; Timothy Reed, flutes, trombone, recorders, percussion, voice; Ladonna Smith, keyboards, viola, voice, electronics, percussion, accordion, trumpet; Davey Williams, guitars, violoncello, saxophones, clarinets, electronics, balalaika.
New and experimental music, improvisatory music. Is concerned with three concepts: (1) transcending its 6-player format by forming subgroups, (2) transcending common instrumentation by exploring unusual instrumental combinations, (3) transcending standard instrumental techniques by evoking new sounds from standard instruments.

USA Percussion Ensemble
John J. Papastefan, Director
University of South Alabama
Department of Music
Mobile, AL 36688
(205) 460-6136(7)
Variable number of student performers, ranging from 6 to 12.
20th century chamber music, new and experimental music, jazz. A course in percussion ensemble performance.

1

Alaska

Alaska Chamber Trio
Dr. Rose-Marie Johnson, Director
University of Alaska
Music Department
Fairbanks, AK 99701
(907) 479-7555
Theodore De Corso, clarinet, saxophone; James Johnson, piano, harpsichord; Rose-Marie Johnson, violin, viola d'amour.
Chamber music. Performs trios of all eras in free school concerts, workshops. Presents master classes.
Group members teach at the University of Alaska.

The Anchorage Symphony String Quartet
Maurice Bonney, Director
3200 La Touche, Apartment G-2
Anchorage, AK 99504
(907) 274-7827
Maurice Bonney, viola; Ruth Jefford, violin; Elizabeth Leffingwell, violoncello; Paul Rosenthal, violin.
Chamber music. Performs string quartets of all eras. Performs sextets and octets with guest artists.
Alternate address:
Anchorage Symphony Orchestra
P.O. Box 2131
Anchorage, AK 99501
(907) 272-8805.

Anchorage Symphony Woodwind Quintet
Maurice Bonney, Director
3200 La Touche, Apartment G-2
Anchorage, AK 99504
(907) 274-7827
Chamber music. Performs works of all eras.
Alternate address:
Elaine B. Nelson, Tour Manager
2542 Loussac Drive
Anchorage, AK 99503
(907) 274-6250 or 274-1645 Ext. 232.

The Arctic Chamber Orchestra
Gordon B. Wright, Director
P.O. Box 666
Fairbanks, AK 99707
(907) 479-7555
30 performers.
Chamber orchestra music. Performs works of all eras.

Sitka Festival Ensemble
Paul Rosenthal, Director
P.O. Box 907
Sitka, AK 99835
(907) 747-8745
Christiaan Bor, violin, viola; Yukiko Kamei, violin, viola; Nathaniel Rosen, violoncello; Paul Rosenthal, violin, viola; Jeffrey Solow, violoncello; Doris Stevenson, piano; Milton Thomas, viola. Guest artists included.
Chamber music.

Arizona

Arizona State University Cello Ensemble
Takayori Atsumi, Director
Arizona State University
Music Department
Tempe, AZ 85281
(602) 965-3298
Variable number of student, amateur, and professional performers, ranging from 8 to 24.
20th century chamber music, new and experimental music. Promotes interest in performing and listening to violoncello music. Intends to acquire a library of violoncello literature.

Arkansas

Henderson State College Lab Band
Earl Hesse, Director
Henderson State College
P.O. Box 2901
Arkadelphia, AR 71923
(501) 246-7622 or 246-5511 Ext. 209
Student ensemble of 20 performers. Instrumentation: 5 trumpets, 5 trombones, 5 saxophones, percussion.
A course in contemporary jazz performance.

California

Alive Ensemble
Larry Stein, Director
23138 Davey Avenue
Newhall, CA 91321
(805) 259-4080 or 255-1050
Ray Kalanquin, mime; Larry Stein, percussion, synthesizer; Ron Stein, guitar, flute; Sam Woodhouse, actor.
New and experimental music, multi-media. Presents works for music, dance, theater, and film

in classrooms. Commissions works by young composers, film makers, dancers, and playwrights which demonstrate the interrelationship of the arts.

Alma Trio
c/o Mariedi Anders Artists Management, Inc.
535 El Camino del Mar
San Francisco, CA 94121
(415) 752-4404
William Corbett Jones, piano; Gabor Rejto, violoncello; Eudice Shapiro, violin.
Chamber music. Performs piano trios of all eras. In residence at the University of Southern California, Los Angeles.

Amadeus Quartet
c/o Mariedi Anders Artists Management, Inc.
535 El Camino del Mar
San Francisco, CA 94121
(415) 752-4404
Norbert Brainin, violin; Martin Lovett, violoncello; Siegmund Nissel, violin; Peter Schidlof, viola.
Chamber music. Performs string quartets of all eras.

The Arriaga Quartet
11627 Mayfield Avenue
Los Angeles, CA 90049
(213) 826-2952
Connie Kupka, violin; Carole Mukogawa, viola; Barry Socher, violin; David Speltz, violoncello.
Chamber music. Performs string quartets of all eras, including neglected works of the past and present.
Agent: Anne J. O'Donnell Management, Inc.
353 West 57th Street
New York, NY 10019
(212) 581-1184.

Arts Circus
Larry Stein, Director
23138 Davey Avenue
Newhall, CA 91321
(805) 259-4080 or 255-1050
Edwin Brown, dancer; Roberta Friedman, film maker; Ray Kalanquin, mime; Toby Keeler, video; Anselm Rothschild, piano; Larry Stein, percussion, synthesizer; Ron Stein, guitar, flute; Sam Woodhouse, actor. Programs range from solo workshops and performances to programs involving 10 or more players, depending on finances, distance, and audience.

New and experimental music, multi-media. Combines music, dance, theater, and film. Commissions works by young composers, film makers, dancers, and playwrights which demonstrate the interrelationship of the arts.

Berkeley Contemporary Chamber Players
Edwin Dugger, Richard Felciano, Olly Wilson, Directors
University of California
Music Department
Berkeley, CA 94720
(415) 642-2678
Variable number of performers, with a core group of 10.
20th century chamber music, new and experimental music.

Biome
Frank McCarty, Allen Strange, Directors
222 Johnson Avenue
Los Gatos, CA 95030
(408) 354-1591
Frank McCarty, woodwinds, percussion, electronics; Allen Strange, guitar, bass, electronics; Pat Strange, violin, electronics; Steve Whealton, electronics, film, slides.
20th century chamber music, new and experimental music, multi-media. Performs live electronic works and multi-media theatrical works. Offers concerts and workshops in electronics and new instrumental techniques. Members act as consultants in studio design and new music programs.

Cal Arts Percussion Ensemble
John Bergamo, Director
California Institute of the Arts
24700 McBean Parkway
Valencia, CA 91355
(805) 255-1050 Ext. 317
Variable number of performers, ranging from 1 to 20.
20th century chamber music, new and experimental music. Emphasizes music for percussion, adding other instruments when needed. Functions as a cooperative with members contributing to purchase of music and instruments.

California New Music Ensemble
Louis Goldstein, Director
California Institute of the Arts
24700 McBean Parkway
Valencia, CA 91355
(805) 255-1050 Ext. 525
Jeanne Clausson, violin; Dean Drummond, conductor; John Fitzgerald, percussion; Louis Goldstein, piano; Rogers Lott, percussion; Ed Meares, double bass; David Rosenthal, percussion; Alan Solomon, clarinet; Stephani Starin, flute.
20th century chamber music, new and experimental music. Performs new works by contemporary Americans, emphasizing California composers. Commissions works.
In residence at California Institute of the Arts.

California State University Brass Choir
John P. Browne, Jr., Director
California State University
Music Department
Chico, CA 95926
(916) 895-5260
Variable number of student performers. Instrumentation: 4 French horns, 4 trumpets, 4 trombones, 2 baritones, 2 basses, percussion.
20th century chamber music, new music. Performs concerts and lecture-demonstrations at schools and music educators conferences.

California State University Northridge Jazz Ensemble
Joel Leach, Director
California State University
18111 Nordhoff Street
Northridge, CA 91324
(213) 885-3152
20 to 21 student performers. Instrumentation: woodwinds, brass, percussion.
Performs big band jazz locally and on tour.

Cal State Sonoma Concert Jazz Ensemble
Walter Oster, Director
California State University, Sonoma
Music Department
Rohnert Park, CA 94928
(707) 795-2416
Variable number of student performers, ranging from 17 to 21. Instrumentation: 5 trumpets, 4 trombones, 5 saxophones, double bass, percussion, piano, woodwinds when needed.
Jazz. Performs at campus and community

functions. All music performed is written or arranged by Walter Oster, Director.

Dominican College Performing Ensemble
Ted Blair, Director
Dominican College
San Rafael, CA 94901
(415) 457-4440
Variable number of student and professional performers.
Chamber music.

+ Ensemble
See Plus Ensemble

The ♀ Ensemble
Pauline Oliveros, Director
1602 Burgundy Road
Leucadia, CA 92024
(714) 753-7400
Bonnie Barnett, voice; Lin Barron, violoncello; Stuart Dempster, trombone; Joan George, bass clarinet; Ron George, percussion; Pauline Oliveros, composer.
New and experimental music. Works on modes of attention and awareness necessary for the performance of sonic meditations. Transmits these modes to others through workshops and programs in order to encourage audience participation and involvement.

Faculty Artist Trio
c/o Clayton Wilson
University of California
Santa Barbara, CA 93106
(805) 961-3261
Burnett Atkinson, flute, piccolo; Emma Lou Diemer, piano, harpsichord, organ; Clayton Wilson, oboe, English horn.
Chamber music. Performs trios of all eras at campus concerts.

The ♀ Ensemble
See Ensemble, The ♀

Festival Players Of California
Dr. Dorye Roettger, Director
3809 De Longpre Avenue
Los Angeles, CA 90027
(213) 665-6444
Michael Artega, trumpet; David Atkins, clarinet; Suzanne Balderston, harp; Timm Boatman, percussion; David Camesi, trumpet; Patricia Garside, flute; Joseph Glaser, guitar; Hyman Goodman, violin; Ronald Grun, bassoon; Karen

Henderson, violoncello; John T. Johnson, tuba; Robert Laurel, violin; Stanley Manolakas, French horn; Helen McComas, soprano voice; Mildred O'Donnell, viola; Ellen Perrin, recorders; Dorye Roettger, oboe; James Sawyer, trombone; Susanne Shapiro, harpsichord; Renee Vanasse, piano; Dale Ziegler, tenor voice.
Chamber music. Performs works of all eras.

Francesco Trio
David Abel, Director
1659 16th Avenue
San Francisco, CA 94122
(415) 664-5828
David Abel, violin; Bonnie Hampton, violoncello; Nathan Schwartz, piano. John Graham often included on viola.
Chamber music, new music. Performs piano trios of all eras. Commissions works, tours extensively.
Agent: June Kingsely Artists Management
2221 Baker Street
San Francisco, CA 94115
(415) 931-2574.

Fullerton College Brass Ensemble
Richard H. Cruz, Director
Fullerton College
321 East Chapman
Fullerton, CA 92634
(714) 871-8000 Ext. 88 or 89
Variable number of student performers.
20th century chamber music. Performs contemporary brass trios, quartets, and quintets, emphasizing local composers.

Hartnell Sinfonietta
Nathan Koblick, Director
Hartnell College
Salinas, CA 93901
(408) 422-9606
19 student and professional performers.
Chamber orchestra music. Performs works of the 19th and 20th centuries.

Hollywood Chamber Players
Ella M. Good, Director
2461 Cheremoya Avenue
Los Angeles, CA 90068
(213) 463-3846
Delores Ackrich, violoncello; Ella M. Good, clarinet; Lloyd Hildebrand, bassoon; John Jensen, piano; Gordon MacKinnon, oboe; Patricia Mathews, viola; Mary Ann Ringgold, violin.
Chamber music.

Freddie Hubbard Sextet
Freddie Hubbard, Director
10901 Whipple Street, Number 8
North Hollywood, CA 91602
(213) 877-1929
Carl Burnett, drums; George Cables, electric piano; Buck Clarke, conga drums, various percussion; Henry Franklyn, double bass; Freddie Hubbard, trumpet, flugelhorn; Carl Randall, tenor saxophone.
Jazz. Performs modern works in the tradition of Louis Armstrong.

I.S.C.M. Ensemble
See New Muse, California.

Karr-Lewis Duo
Gary Karr, Director
c/o Mariedi Anders Artists Management, Inc.
535 El Camino del Mar
San Francisco, CA 94121
(415) 752-4404
Gary Karr, double bass; David Harmon Lewis, harpsichord, organ, piano.
Chamber music, new and experimental music. Performs double bass and keyboard duos of all eras. Premieres American works. Tours extensively. Presents lecture-demonstrations.

Daniel Kobialka-Machiko Kobialka Duo
Daniel Kobialka, Director
28260 Beatron Way
Hayward, CA 94544
(415) 538-1512
Daniel Kobialka, violin; Machiko Kobialka, piano.
Chamber music, new music. Performs duos of all eras. Commissions and premieres works by American composers.
Agent: Lee McRae
2130 Carleton Street
Berkeley, CA 94704
(415) 848-5591.

Los Angeles Chamber Orchestra
Neville Marriner, Director
1017 North La Cienega
Los Angeles, CA 90069
(213) 657-5883
Instrumentation: 8 first violins, 6 second violins, 4 violas, 4 violoncellos, 2 double basses, winds as needed.
Chamber orchestra music. Performs works of all eras. Commissions new works to be presented in

campus workshops, in a subscription series, and on tour.

Los Angeles Percussion Ensemble And Chamber Players
William Kraft, Director
3681 Alomar Drive
Sherman Oaks, CA 91403
(213) 872-1073 or 990-1124
Percussionists: Dale Anderson, Larry Bunker, Walter Goodwin, Mitchell Peters, Tom Raney, Barry Silverman, Ken Watson, Robert Winslow. Guest instrumentalists and vocalists often included.
20th century chamber music, new and experimental music.

Los Angeles Saxophone Quartet
c/o Victor Morosco
23054 Oxnard Street
Woodland Hills, CA 91364
(213) 346-1397
Roger Greenberg, tenor saxophone; Larry McGuire, baritone saxophone; Victor Morosco, soprano saxophone; James Rotter, alto saxophone. Chamber music, new and experimental music, jazz. Performs saxophone quartets of all eras, including transcriptions of Baroque works. Composers have written works for the group.

The Love Brothers Band
Harry Babasin, Roy Harte, Directors
6232 Santa Monica Boulevard
Hollywood, CA 90038
(213) 467-3288
Harry Babasin, bass; Del Bennett, trumpet, flugelhorn; Roy Harte, drums; Bill Hood, reeds; Newcombe Rath, reeds; David Wheat, guitar; Jimmy Wyble, guitar; Barry Zweig, guitar.
New and experimental music, jazz.

Lyric Wind Quintet
c/o David Sprung
California State University
Music Department
Hayward, CA 94542
(415) 881-3135
Roberta Brokaw, flute; Jerry Dagg, bassoon; Leland Lincoln, oboe; David Sprung, French horn; William Wohlmacher, clarinet. Pianist often included.
Chamber music, new and experimental music. Performs at campus and community concerts, emphasizing 20th century music.

In residence at California State University, Hayward.

The Modern Brass Quintet
Donald Waldrop, Director
1940 Hollyvista Avenue
Los Angeles, CA 90027
(213) 664-4124
Josef Kruger, French horn; Malcolm McNab, trumpet; Roy Poper, trumpet; James Sawyer, trombone; Donald Waldrop, bass trombone, tuba. Chamber music. Performs brass quintets of all eras, emphasizing contemporary music and neglected works of the past.
Agent: Peter Christ
Artists' Alliance
P.O. Box 65833
Los Angeles, CA 90065
(213) 257-6787.

The Montagnana Trio
John Gates, Director
906 Kagawa Street
Pacific Palisades, CA 90272
(213) 459-3656
John Gates, clarinet; Delores Stevens, piano; Caroline Worthington, violoncello.
Chamber music. Performs trios of all eras. Commissions many works.
Agent: Nancy Tuttle
Columbia Artists Management, Inc.
165 West 57th Street
New York, NY 10019
(212) 397-6932.

Music For Clarinet And Friend
Barney Childs, Phil Rehfeldt, Directors
University of Redlands
School of Music
Redlands, CA 92373
(714) 793-2121
Barney Childs, piano, percussion, electronics; Phil Rehfeldt, clarinet, percussion.
20th century chamber music. Performs newly commissioned works for clarinet and various accompanying media. Lectures on composition and performance.

New Beginnings
Sarah Lutman, Peter Tomita, Directors
624 East 17th Street
Oakland, CA 94606
(415) 763-4419
Jon Aymong, trumpet; Michele Burr, double bass;

David Cann, violin; Jim de Corsey, French horn; Andy Erhenpfort, tuba; Joan Gallegos, cymbalom, piano; Vernell Hampton, viola; Sally Kell, conductor; Angela Koregolos, flute; Katie Kyme, violin; Herb Lashner, oboe; Larry London, clarinet; Sarah Lutman, bassoon; Norman Peck, percussion; Peter Tomita, trombone; John Trujillo, trumpet.
20th century chamber music. Presents community concerts, emphasizing California composers.

New Muse
William Kraft, Leonard Rosenman, Directors
3681 Alomar Drive
Sherman Oaks, CA 91403
(213) 990-1124
20th century chamber music, new and experimental music.
Formerly the I.S.C.M. Ensemble.

The New Music Company
Dr. Lloyd Rodgers, Director
California State University
Music Department
Fullerton, CA 92634
(714) 870-3511
Variable number of student and faculty performers. Permanent instruments: violin, violoncello, piano.
20th century chamber music, new and experimental music.

New Music Ensemble
Dr. Justus Matthews, Director
California State University
Music Department
Long Beach, CA 90840
(213) 498-4891
Variable number of student performers.
A course in contemporary music performance.

New Music Ensemble
Dr. Byong-kon Kim, Director
California State University
Music Department
Los Angeles, CA 90032
(213) 224-3448 or 224-3462
Variable number of student performers, with maximum of 25.
20th century chamber music, new and experimental music, chamber orchestra music.

New Music Ensemble
Dr. Daniel Kessner, Director
California State University
Music Department
Northridge, CA 91324
(213) 885-3181
Variable number of student instrumentalists and vocalists, ranging from 20 to 40. Basic instrumentation: 1 to 2 woodwinds and brass, keyboard, percussion, harp, violin, viola, violoncello, double bass.
20th century chamber music, new and experimental music. A course in contemporary music performance. Performs chamber works, emphasizing pieces by students at California State University, Northridge.

New Music Ensemble
Richard Saylor, Director
California State University
Music Department
San Bernardino, CA 92407
(714) 887-6311
Variable number of student and faculty performers.
New and experimental music. Performs music that combines acoustic instruments and electronic sounds.

New Music Ensemble
Herbert Bielawa, Director
California State University
Music Department
San Francisco, CA 94132
(405) 469-1431
Variable number of student performers.
20th century chamber music, new and experimental music. A course in contemporary music performance.

New Music Ensemble
John Adams, Director
San Francisco Conservatory of Music
1201 Ortega
San Francisco, CA 94122
(415) 564-8086
Variable number of student performers, ranging from 1 to 20.
A course in new music performance. Performs experimental music with instruments and electronics, locally and on tour. Commissions and records new works.

New Music Ensemble
Barney Childs, Phillip Rehfeldt, Directors
University of Redlands
School of Music
Redlands, CA 92373
(714) 793-2121 Ext. 252
Variable number of student performers, ranging
from 8 to 18.
New and experimental music. A course in
contemporary music performance for students at
the University of Redlands and Johnston College.

Novaj Kordoj
Pat Strange, Director
222 Johnson Avenue
Los Gatos, CA 95030
(408) 354-1591
Crispin Cambell, violoncello; Lorrie Hunt, viola;
Pat Strange, first violin; Esteban Zapiain, second
violin.
20th century chamber music, new and
experimental music. Performs 20th century string
quartets exclusively. Performs compositions using
amplification, electronics, and theater, as well as
more conventional pieces.

Anthony Ortega Jazz Ensemble
Anthony Ortega, Director
5445 Conwell Avenue
Azusa, CA 91702
(213) 969-1454
Variable number of performers. Instruments used
in various combinations are: flute, oboe,
saxophone, clarinet, electric bass, piano.
Jazz, new and experimental music.

Pacific Percussion Ensemble
Thomas Raney, Director
3804 Chandler Boulevard
Burbank, CA 91505
(213) 848-0043
Percussionists: Timm Boatman, Todd Miller,
Thomas Raney, Barry Silverman, Wally Snow.
Performs percussion works of all eras.

**Alexandra Pierce-Louanne Fuchs Long, Duo
Pianists**
Alexandra Pierce, Director
University of Redlands
School of Music
Redlands, CA 92373
(714) 793-2121
20th century piano music. Performs works of all

eras, emphasizing the 20th century. Seeks new
works to perform.
Members teach at the University of Redlands.

+ Ensemble
William Brooks, Gordon Mumma, Directors
University of California
Music Board
Santa Cruz, CA 95064
(408) 429-2292
William Brooks, piano, voice; Chris Brown, piano;
Roger Emanuels, violoncello; Carl Fravel, oboe,
electronics; James Langdell, clarinet; Gordon
Mumma, French horn, trumpet, electronics.
New and experimental music.

Prima Materia
Roberto Laneri, Director
University of California at San Diego
Music Department
La Jolla, CA 92037
(714) 452-2230
Vocalists: Alvin Curran, Susan Gormlie, Michiko
Hirayama, Roberto Laneri, John Mizelle, Ron
Nagorca, Manuela Renosto, Pamela Sawyer.
New and experimental music. Uses sound as a
vehicle for meditation in performing vocal
improvisation. Intends to serve a a 'resonator for
the universal vibration.'
Agent: Hugues Wahnon Management
P.O. Box 6378
San Diego, CA 92106
(714) 222-2572.

Salon Ensemble No. 1
Rudy Cipolla, Director
430 Judah Street
San Francisco, CA 94122
(415) 731-8061
Laurel Bice, flute; Rudy Cipolla, mandolin,
mandocello; Frank Denke, piano; Ernest
Michaelian, violin.
Chamber music, new music. Performs in churches,
community centers, and schools.

Salon Ensemble No. 2
Rudy Cipolla, Director
430 Judah Street
San Francisco, CA 94122
(415) 731-8061
Bob Black, mandola; Bob Bruen, mandolin; Louis
Chicca, accordion; Rudy Cipolla, mandolin; Chick
Gandell, violin; David Grisman, mandocello; Jack
Reynolds, mandola.

8

Chamber music, new music. Performs in churches, community centers, and schools.

San Andreas Fault
Daniel Lentz, Director
67 La Vuelta Road
Santa Barbara, CA 93108
(805) 969-2093
16 vocalists. Instrumentalists added as needed.
Choral chamber music. Performs works by Harold Budd, Don Carlo Gesualdo, Lou Harrison, and Daniel Lentz.

San Bernardino Chamber Orchestra
Richard Saylor, Director
California State University
Music Department
San Bernardino, CA 92407
(714) 887-6311
20 to 30 student performers.
A course in chamber orchestra music performance, in which some new and experimental music is performed.

San Francisco Chamber Orchestra
Edgar J. Braun, Director
907 Keeler Avenue
Berkeley, CA 94708
(415) 433-3000
Instrumentation: 2 flutes, 2 oboes, 2 clarinets, 2 bassoons, 2 French horns, 2 trumpets, percussions, 10 violins, 4 violas, 3 violoncellos, double bass.
Chamber orchestra music. Performs works of all eras.

San Francisco Contemporary Music Players
Marcella DeCray, Jean-Louis Le Roux, Directors
2874 Washington Street
San Francisco, CA 94115
(415) 921-6852
Variable number of performers, ranging from 2 to 12. Permanent members: Marta Bracchi-Le Roux, piano; Marcella DeCray, harp; Jean-Louis Le Roux, oboe.
New and experimental music. Performs contemporary works in a Bring Your Own Pillow (BYOP) Concert Series. Tours nationally.
Agent: Irene Vacchina
Arn-Vacchina Associates
1050 North Point
San Francisco, CA 94109
(415) 776-7798.

Steiner-Berfield Trio
Dr. Frances Steiner, Director
30525 La Vista Verde Drive
Rancho Palos Verdes, CA 90274
(213) 833-3442
David Berfield, piano; Diana Steiner, violin; Frances Steiner, violoncello.
Chamber music. Performs trios of all eras.

Trio Concertante
Daniel Kobialka, Director
28260 Beatron Way
Hayward, CA 94544
(415) 538-1512
Paul Hersh, viola, piano; Daniel Kobialka, violin; Laszlo Varga, violoncello.
Chamber music.
Agent: Lee McRae
2130 Carleton Street
Berkeley, CA 94704
(415) 848-5591.

201 New Music Ensemble
Keith Humble, Thomas Nee, Directors
University of California at San Diego
La Jolla, CA 92037
(714) 453-3230
Variable number of graduate student and faculty performers, ranging from 4 to 20.
20th century chamber music, new and experimental music. A graduate course in contemporary composition and performance. Performs contemporary works, including contemporary electronic and theatrical pieces.

University Chamber Players
c/o David Sprung
California State University
Music Department
Hayward, CA 94542
(415) 881-3135
Tom Acord, tenor voice; Edwin Barlow, baritone voice; Beverly Bellows, harp; James Bertram, guitar; Roberta Brokaw, flute; Anthony Caviglia, trumpet; Eleanor Cohen, soprano voice; Floyd Cooley, tuba; Jerry Dagg, bassoon; Denis deCoteau, viola; Allen Gove, violoncello; Leland Lincoln, oboe; Daniel Livesay, trombone; Kenneth Mansfield, organ; Daniel Montoro, percussion; Jerome Neff, percussion; Jeffrey Neighbor, bass; Marvin Nelson, trumpet; Nathan Rubin, violin; Donald King Smith, piano; David Sprung, French horn; Ellen Wasserman, piano;

9

Harold Whelan, violin, viola; William Wohlmacher, clarinet.
Chamber music. Performs works of all eras, emphasizing the 20th century. Premieres works, some by local composers, in the annual California State University, Hayward Chamber Music Series. Members are on the University music faculty.

The Western Arts Trio
c/o Pietro Menci, Director
International Artists Agency
1564 18th Avenue
San Francisco, CA 94122
(415) 661-1962
Brian Hanly, violin; Werner Rose, piano; David Tomatz, violoncello.
Chamber music. Performs contemporary works, primarily by American composers. Premieres and commissions works. Tours extensively.
In residence at Wyoming State University, Laramie.

Westwood Wind Quintet
Peter Christ, Director
c/o Artists' Alliance Management
P.O. Box 65833
Los Angeles, CA 90065
(213) 257-6787
David Atkins, clarinet; Peter Christ, oboe; Ronald Grun, bassoon; Marni Robinson, French horn; Gretel Shanley, flute.
Chamber music. Performs woodwind quintets of all eras, emphasizing the 20th century. Performs in concerts, clinics, and seminars locally and on tour. Presents children's concerts in schools.

The ♀ Ensemble
See Ensemble, The ♀

Bob Zieff Ensemble
Bob Zieff, Director
2461 Cheremoya Avenue
Hollywood, CA 90068
(213) 463-3846
Dick Collins, trumpet; Pat Mathews, viola; Jay Migliore, clarinet, saxophone; Ray Pizzi, piccolo, saxophones; Fred Seykora, violoncello; Bob Tricarico, alto clarinet, contrabassoon; Jimmy Wyble, guitar; Bob Zieff, conductor.
Jazz. Performs improvisatory works and gives lecture-demonstrations concerning the historical background of the music performed.

Colorado

The Pablo Casals Trio
c/o Carl H. P. Dahlgren
Dahlgren Arts Management, Inc.
330 Albion Street
Denver, CO 80220
(303) 320-4851
Jurgen De Lemes, violoncello; Oswald Lehnert, violin; Paul Parmelee, piano.
Chamber music. Performs trios of all eras on tour, in lecture-demonstrations and in workshops.
In residence at the University of Colorado.

The Colorado College New Music Ensemble
Stephen Scott, Director
The Colorado College
Music Department
Colorado Springs, CO 80903
(303) 473-2233 Ext. 236
Variable number of student performers.
20th century chamber music, new and experimental music. Intends to increase the knowledge and support of new music in the campus community.

Colorado State University Musica Nova
Dr. Dave R. Harman, Director
Colorado State University
Music Department
Fort Collins, CO 80521
(303) 491-5570
Variable number of student performers.
20th century chamber music. Provides performing ensemble experience for advanced university music students concerned with contemporary music.

Denver Symphony Extensions
William L. Roberts, Director
1615 California Street
Denver, CO 80202
(303) 292-1580
Bob Andreasen, trumpet; Ron Arentz, trombone; Jim Carroll, electric bass; Gordon Close, electric guitar; Jerry Endsley, trumpet; John Keene, French horn; Dave Murchie, electric piano, violin; Wilke Renwick, French horn; Bill Roberts, drums; Milt Stevens, trombone.
Chamber music. Performs contemporary arrangements of works of all eras. Presents public school concerts. Familiarizes students with serious music by presenting it in jazz-rock arrangements.

Most members belong to the Denver Symphony Orchestra.

Rocky Mountain Brass Quintet

c/o William Pfund
University of Northern Colorado
School of Music
Greeley, CO 80631
(303) 351-2226

Edwin Baker, trombone; Ron Fuller, trumpet; James Miller, French horn; William Pfund, trumpet; Jack Robinson, tuba.

Chamber music. Performs brass quintets of all eras in concerts and workshops throughout the U.S.A.

In residence at the University of Northern Colorado.

Connecticut

Advent

Anthony C. Davis, Director
80 Sherman Avenue, Apartment 6
New Haven, CT 06511
(203) 562-5248

Wes Brown, bass; Anthony C. Davis, piano; Gerry Hemingway, percussion; Hal Lewis, alto saxophone, soprano saxophone; Leo Smith, trumpet, flugelhorn; Steve Wald, guitar.

Jazz. Introduces creative black music to new audiences. Features compositions by group members, and jazz masters including Duke Ellington, Charles Mingus, and Thelonious Monk.

The Berkshire Quartet

Urico Rossi, Director
Music Mountain
Falls Village, CT 06031
(203) 824-7126

Theodore Israel, viola; Michael Kuttner, violin; Fritz Magg, violoncello; Urico Rossi, violin.

Chamber music.

Genevieve Chinn And Allen Brings, Duo-Pianists

c/o Allen Brings
199 Mountain Road
Wilton, CT 06897
(203) 762-5186

Chamber music, new and experimental music. Performs works of all eras. Presents neglected contemporary pieces, and commissions works.

The Contemporary Saxophone Quartet

Philip DeLibero, Director
780 Farmington Avenue
West Hartford, CT 06119
(203) 232-2491

Philip DeLibero, soprano saxophone; George Kirck, alto saxophone; Gary Lai-Hipp, tenor saxophone; Richard Wells, baritone saxophone.

Chamber music, new and experimental music. Performs standard repertoire and contemporary pieces, including electronic and multi-media works. Encourages composers to write for the ensemble.

Music Of South India

David B. Reck, Director
Wesleyan University
Music Department
Middletown, CT 06457
(203) 347-7659

Ramnad V. Raghavan, mridangam; C. Reck, tambura; David Reck, veena; L. Shankar, violin.

South Indian Music. Explores improvisatory forms and procedures, such as ragas and talas, derived from contemporary and traditional South Indian Music.

Bobby Naughton Units

Bobby Naughton, Director
Kettletown Road RFD 4
Southbury, CT 06488
(203) 264-8968

Randy Kaye, percussion; Bobby Naughton, vibraphone, piano; Perry Robinson, clarinet; Mark Whitecage, reeds; Richard Youngstein, bass.

New and experimental music, jazz. Performs improvisatory and newly composed music.

New Dalta Ahkri

Leo Smith, Director
P.O. Box 102
New Haven, CT 06510
(203) 934-9383

Anthony Davis, piano, vibraphone; Leonard Jones, bass; Leo Smith, trumpet, flugelhorn, piccolo trumpet, percussion.

Creative black music. Functions as a showcase for improvisational black music.

The New England Contemporary Ensemble
Richard Moryl, Director
Shirley Court
Brookfield, CT 06804
(203) 775-3747
Joseph Celli, oboe; Sara Cutler, harp; Joanne
Moryl, keyboard; Richard Moryl, soprano
saxophone; Richard Palanzi, technical design;
Nancy Savin, soprano; David Smith, percussion.
20th century chamber music, new and
experimental music. Performs works by
contemporary composers in concerts and
workshops. Often combines electronics, film, and
dance.

The New York Brass Quintet
Robert Nagel, Director
Broadview Drive
Brookfield, CT 06804
(203) 775-1358
Allen Dean, trumpet; Thompson Hanks, tuba;
Paul Ingraham, French horn; Robert Nagel,
trumpet; John Swallow, trombone.
Chamber music, new and experimental music.
Performs brass quintets of all eras. Commissions
works, appears with symphony orchestras, tours,
and gives master classes at universities.
Agent: Nancy Tuttle
Columbia Artists Management, Inc.
165 West 57th Street
New York, NY 10019
(212) 397-6900.

Organic Oboe
Joseph R. Celli, Director
Turner Street
Ridgefield, CT 06877
(203) 792-2032
Joseph R. Celli, oboe, English horn, electronics;
Richard Palanzi, sound environmentalist.
New and experimental music, multi-media.
Combines contemporary oboe and English horn
music, film, live electronics, slides, theater.
Presents programs in open settings, such as
sculpture gardens. Encourages audience
involvement.

Winter Consort
Paul Winter, Director
RD 1, Pine Tree Road
West Redding, CT 06896
(203) 938-2035
Tigger Benford, tabla, bongo and conga drums,
traps, other percussion; Ben Carmel, timpani, bass
marimba, Brazilian surdos; Robert Chappell,
harpsichord, regal, harmonium, organ, guitar;
David Darling, violoncello, electric 8-string
violoncello, voice; Paul Winter, soprano
saxophone, alto saxophone, contrabass
sarrusophone.
20th century chamber music, new and
experimental music. Performs works combining
elements of jazz, African, Brazilian, and Indian
music. Combines written and improvised music
reminiscent of Elizabethan consort playing.
Available for concerts, workshops, residencies,
and tours.
Agent: Torrence/Perotta Management
1860 Broadway
New York, NY 10023
(212) 541-4620.

Xylophonia
Bob Becker, Director
Wesleyan University
Music Department
Middletown, CT 06457
(203) 347-9411 Ext. 235
Bob Becker, xylophone, bones; Steve Gadd,
percussion; Mike Holmes, piano, effects; Tony
Levin, bass, saw.
Jazz. Performs works featuring xylophone written
from 1900 to 1940. Presents classical overtures,
ragtime pieces, and dance music.

Delaware

Satori Woodwind Quintet
Charles Holdeman, Director
University of Delaware
Cultural Programs-Continuing Education
Division
Newark, DE 19711
(302) 738-2000
Charles Holdeman, bassoon, recorders; Patricia
Valley Holdeman, flute, alto flute, piccolo,
recorder; Robert Kendel, oboe, English horn;
Timothy Maloney, clarinets, soprano saxophone,
alto saxophone; Scott Temple, French horn.
Chamber music. Performs works of all eras,
emphasizing the 20th century, in concerts, clinics,
and workshops.
In residence at the University of Delaware.
Alternate address:
Charles Holdeman
P.O. Box 144
New London, PA 19360
(215) 869-9572.

University Of Delaware String Quartet
c/o Patricia Kent
University of Delaware
Cultural Programs-Continuing Education
Division
Newark, DE 19711
(302) 738-2893
Janice Baty, second violin; Walter Cogswell, viola;
James Holesovsky, violoncello; Daniel Roslin, first
violin.
Chamber music, new and experimental music.
Performs works of all eras.
In residence at the University of Delaware.

District of Columbia

Theater Chamber Players
Leon Fleisher, Dina Koston, Directors
2312 Tracy Place, N.W.
Washington, D.C. 20008
(202) 667-4470
Ronald Barnett, percussion; Phyllis Bryn-Julson,
soprano; Pina Carmirelli, violin; Frank Cohen,
clarinet; Leon Fleisher, conductor; Patricia
Grignet, oboe; Lois Howard, harpsichord; Hyo
Kang, violin; Dina Koston, piano; Jaime Laredo,
violin, viola; Ellen Mack, piano; Albert Merz,
percussion; William Montgomery, flute; Sharon
Robinson, violoncello; Berl Senofsky, violin;
Robert Sheldon, bassoon; David Starobin, guitar;
Donald Sutherland, harpsichord, organ; Karen
Tuttle, viola; Jeannette Walters, soprano.
Chamber music, new and experimental music.
Performs works of all eras, emphasizing
contemporary pieces. Attempts to relate new
music to its antecedents.

Florida

Pierre Mande String Ensemble
Pierre Mande, Director
2485 Trapp Avenue
Miami, FL 33133
(305) 858-0942
Daniel Gottlieb, percussion; Richard Karl, violin;
Marilyn Klinger, violoncello; Pierre Mande,
violin; Mimi Retskin, piano; Doris Richard, harp;
Louis Sarantos, clarinet; Nicolas Von Der None,
double bass; Maxine Wechsler, bassoon.
Chamber music. Performs works of all eras in
community concerts.

Stage Band One
Gene A. Lawton, Director
Central Florida Community College
Music Department
Ocala, FL 32670
(904) 237-2111
25 student performers.
A course in jazz performance.

Georgia

Atlanta Brass Quintet
Steven Winick, Director
Georgia State University
Art and Music Building, Room 509
Atlanta, GA 30303
(404) 658-2979
Richard Brady, trombone; Don Day, second
trumpet; Jeff Jacobsen, French horn; Michael
Puckett, tuba; Steven Winick, first trumpet.
Chamber music, new and experimental music.
Performs works of all eras, emphasizing the 20th
century.

Atlanta Brass Trio
Steven Winick, Director
Georgia State University
Art and Music Building, Room 509
Atlanta, GA 30303
(404) 658-2979
Jeff Jacobsen, French horn; Harry Maddox,
trombone; Steven Winick, trumpet.
Chamber music. Performs works of all eras.
Available for clinics and workshops in schools
throughout the Southeast.
In residence at Georgia State University.

Columbus College Jazz Band
Paul J. Vander Gheynst, Director
Columbus College
Columbus, GA 31907
(404) 568-2239
Variable instrumentation and personnel available
from a group of 25 student performers.
Jazz, new and experimental music.

Experimusica
Dr. David Mathew, Director
Georgia Southern College
Music Department
Statesboro, GA 30458
(912) 681-5600 Ext. 396
Variable number of student performers.

New and experimental music. Performs works combining electronic sounds and other media.

Georgia State University Brass Ensemble
William H. Hill, Director
Georgia State University
University Plaza
Atlanta, GA 30303
(404) 658-2982
Variable number of student performers, ranging from 1 to 25 brass, percussion, and keyboard players.
Chamber music. Performs works of all eras. Tours extensively. Participates in symposiums and conferences.

Songbirdsongs
John Adams, Director
Route 1, P.O. Box 44
Stockbridge, GA 30281
(404) 633-2381
John Adams, percussion, composer; Anne McFarland, piccolo.
New and experimental music. Performs music exclusively from *Songbirdsongs*, by John Adams. Performances include slides, descriptive notes, and, if requested, a discussion of birds, and the composer's music and philosophy. Available nationally.

University Of Georgia Woodwind Quintet
Ronald L. Waln, Coordinator
University of Georgia
Music Department
Athens, GA 30602
(404) 542-7531
James Burton, bassoon; John Corina, oboe, English horn, recorder; Theodore Jahn, clarinet, flute, oboe, bassoon, saxophone; David Pinkow, French horn; Ronald L. Waln, flute, bassoon.
Chamber music, new and experimental music. Performs woodwind quintets of all eras throughout the Southeast.
Members are on the faculty of the University of Georgia.

Hawaii

International Strings
Polly Jane Kella, Director
3672 Loulu Street
Honolulu, HI 96822
(808) 988-4387
Carla Birnbaum, harp; Fred Heilman, double bass; Kathleen Kella, viola; Polly Jane Kella, violin.
Chamber music, new and experimental music. Performs works of all eras in community centers, homes for the elderly, and correctional institutions.

Idaho

The Muhlfeld Trio
H. James Schoepflin, Director
Idaho State University
Music Department
Pocatello, ID 83209
(208) 236-2225 or 236-3636
Horatio Edens, violoncello; H. James Schoepflin, clarinet; Judith A. Schoepflin, piano.
Chamber music. Performs trios of all eras, emphasizing the 20th century.
In residence at Idaho State University.
Agent: Interwest Concerts
1664 Monte Vista
Pocatello, ID 83201
(208) 236-3636 or 232-4986.

Northwest Wind Quintet
Richard Hahn, Director
University of Idaho
School of Music
Moscow, ID 83843
(208) 885-6231
Cecil Gold, clarinet; Richard Hahn, flute; Ronald Klimko, bassoon; Bruce Matthews, French horn; Robert Probasco, oboe.
Chamber music, new and experimental music. Performs works of all eras in concerts and clinics throughout the U.S.A.
In residence at the University of Idaho.

Illinois

Blackearth Percussion Group
c/o Garry Kvistad
Northern Illinois University
Music Department
DeKalb, IL 60115
(815) 753-1551
Percussionists: James Baird, David Johnson, Garry Kvistad, Allen Otte.
New and experimental music. Performs new works for percussion ensemble, and multi-media pieces for percussion, electronics, visual elements, and theater. Commissions pieces, and performs works by group members. Also performs works by

Larry Austin, Herbert Brun, John Cage, Lukas Foss, Lou Harrison, and Frederic Rzewski.
In residence at Northern Illinois University.

Chicago Chamber Orchestra
Dieter Kober, Director
323 South Michigan Avenue
Chicago, IL 60604
(312) 256-5575
Chamber orchestra music. Performs 35 free annual concerts of music from all eras.

Chicago Contemporary Dance Theatre
Maggie Kast, Director
5320 South University Avenue
Chicago, IL 60615
(312) 643-8916
8 permanent dancers, variable number of musicians. Philip G. Winsor, resident composer.
New and experimental music. Presents multi-media theater pieces involving dance.
Agent: Beryl Zitch
The Contemporary Forum
2528A West Jerome
Chicago, IL 60645
(312) 764-4383.

The Chicago Saxophone Quartet
Walker L. Smith, Director
918 Noyes Street
Evanston, IL 60201
(312) 491-0075
Robert Black, soprano saxophone; James Kasprzyk, baritone saxophone; Richard Kennell, alto saxophone; Walker L. Smith, tenor saxophone.
Chamber music. Performs works of all eras, specializing in contemporary American and French compositions.

Chicago Symphony String Quartet
Victor Aitay, Director
220 South Michigan Avenue
Chicago, IL 60604
Victor Aitay, first violin; Frank Miller, violoncello; Edgar Muenzer, second violin; Milton Preves, viola.
Chamber music. Performs string quartets of all eras.

Contemporary Chamber Group Of The University Of Chicago
Ralph Shapey, Director
University of Chicago
5835 South University
Chicago, IL 60637
(312) 753-2617 or 753-2613
22 performers who are graduate and post-graduate Fellows of the University of Chicago Department of Music. Chicago-area performers also participate under contract as associate artists. Instrumentation: woodwinds, brass, percussion, harp, piano, celesta, string quintet. Soprano soloist often included.
20th century chamber music, new and experimental music. Repertoire of nearly 250 works by contemporary composers.

Dungill Family
Harriette Dungill, Director
1708 West Steuben Street
Chicago, IL 60643
(312) 233-8281
Alexander Dungill, drums, trombone, baritone voice; Charles Dungill, drums, baritone voice; Doyle Dungill, piano; Elaine Dungill, trumpet, guitar, mezzo-soprano voice; Evette Dungill, saxophone, tambourine, voice; Gloria Dungill, bass guitar, tuba, contralto voice; Harriette Dungill, saxophone, guitar, soprano voice; Melody Dungill, vibraharp, tambourine, contralto voice.
New and experimental music, original African music and drumming. Presents music of numerous races and nationalities.

Electric Stereopticon
J. B. Floyd, Al O'Connor, Directors
Northern Illinois University
Music Department
DeKalb, IL 60115
(815) 753-1551
J. B. Floyd, keyboards, electronics, composer; Al O'Connor, vibraphone, percussion, electronics, composer; Norm Magden, cinematographer, photographer; Dave Merrifield, percussion; Jeff Paull, cinematographer, photographer; Jeff Steele, electric bass, keyboard.
New and experimental music, jazz, multi-media. Performs works combining jazz, rock music, improvisation, film, light, transparencies, and electronics. Performs compositions by group members, and Larry Austin, John Cage, Donald Erb, Lejaren Hiller, David Rosenboom, Karlheinz

Stockhausen, and Morton Subotnick. Commissions works.

William Ferris Chorale
William Ferris, Director
75 East Harris Avenue
La Grange, IL 60525
(312) 482-8791
Approximately 35 singers. Instrumental ensembles included when necessary.
Choral-instrumental music. Presents concerts of Renaissance and contemporary choral music.

Illinois Wesleyan University Collegiate Chamber Singers
David Nott, Director
Illinois Wesleyan University
Bloomington, IL 61701
(309) 556-3076 or 556-3061
12 to 14 student singers: 4 sopranos, 3 altos, 3 tenors, 4 basses.
20th century choral chamber music.

Ineluctable Modality
Edwin London, Director
University of Illinois
School of Music
Urbana, IL 61801
(217) 333-0635 or 333-2620
Variable number of student and professional performers, ranging from 12 to 24, occasionally expanding to 45.
20th century choral and vocal chamber music. Performs new multi-media works, chamber operas, live electronic works, and masterpieces from the early 20th century. Is available with or without the University of Illinois Contemporary Chamber Players for concerts, lecture-demonstrations, clinics, and residencies.

Israelievitch Duo
Gail Israelievitch, Director
6166 Sheridan Road
Chicago, IL 60626
(312) 465-7859
Gail Israelievitch, harp; Jacques Israelievitch, violin. Flute and viola often included.
20th century chamber music, new and experimental music.

Lyric Chamber Players
Arthur Lewis, Director
Illinois State University
Normal, IL 61761
(309) 438-5536
Russell Bedford, bassoon; Aris Chavez, clarinet; Harold Gray, piano; Tong-Il Han, piano; Philip Hillstrom, French horn; Tim Hurtz, oboe; Ko Iwasaki, violoncello; Won-Mo Kim, violin; Arthur Lewis, viola; William Reeder, tenor voice; Max Schoenfeld, flute; David Shrader, percussion.
Chamber music.

Northwestern University Contemporary Music Ensemble
M. William Karlins, Steve Syverud, Directors
Northwestern University
School of Music
Evanston, IL 60201
(312) 492-7575
Variable number of student performers.
New and experimental music. Encourages students to learn and perform new music for Chicago area audiences.

University Of Illinois Contemporary Chamber Players
Paul Zonn, Conductor
University of Illinois
School of Music
Urbana, IL 61801
(217) 333-3635
Variable number of student and professional performers.
20th century chamber music, new and experimental music. Performs new multi-media works, chamber operas, live electronic works, and masterpieces from the early 20th century. Is available with or without the Ineluctable Modality of the University of Illinois, Urbana, for concerts, lecture-demonstrations, clinics, and residencies.

University of Illinois Percussion Ensemble
Thomas Siwe, Director
University of Illinois
School of Music
Urbana, IL 61801
(217) 333-2620
Variable number of student performers, ranging from 2 to 24.
Chamber music, new and experimental music. A course in percussion ensemble performance.

Vermeer Quartet
c/o Shmuel Ashkenasi
Northern Illinois University
Music Department
De Kalb, IL 60115
(815) 753-1000
Shmuel Ashkenasi, violin; Nabuko Ima, viola;
Marc Johnson, violoncello; Pierre Menard, violin.
Chamber music.
In residence at Northern Illinois University.
Alternate address:
Columbia Artists Management, Inc.
165 West 57th Street
New York, NY 10019
(212) 397-6900.

Indiana

Da Camera Brass Quintet
David Greenhoe, Director
Ball State University
School of Music
Muncie, IN 47306
(317) 285-4336
David Greenhoe, trumpet; Edward Malterer,
trombone; Larry McWilliams, trumpet; Bruce
Schmidt, French horn; J. Lesley Varner, tuba.
Chamber music. Exposes and promotes new brass
music.

DePauw Chamber Symphony
Orcenith Smith, Director
DePauw University
School of Music
Greencastle, IN 46135
(317) 653-9721 Ext. 224
26 student performers. Instrumentation: 2 flutes,
oboe, 2 clarinets, saxophone, 2 bassoons, 2 French
horns, 2 trumpets, 3 trombones, percussion,
keyboard, 4 violins, viola, 3 violoncellos, double
bass.
Chamber orchestra music. Performs works of all
eras. Commissions and premieres pieces to be
performed on tour and at the DePauw University
Annual Contemporary Music Festival.

Earlham Jazz Ensemble
Charles Brown, Director
Earlham College
Richmond, IN 47374
(317) 962-6561
18 student performers.
Jazz.

The Ensemble For New Music
Dr. Cleve L. Scott, Director
Ball State University
Muncie, IN 47306
(317) 285-7072
Variable number of student performers.
20th century chamber music, new and
experimental music. Promotes the performance
and appreciation of new music.

Gee-Tatlock Duo
Harry R. Gee, Director
419 South 32nd Street
Terre Haute, IN 47803
(812) 232-3875
Harry R. Gee, clarinet, bass clarinet, alto
saxophone, tenor saxophone; Stella V. Tatlock,
piano.
20th century chamber music, new and
experimental music. Presents many newly-
commissioned American works for clarinet and
saxophone with piano.

Indiana Chamber Orchestra
T. Briccetti, Director
927 South Harrison
Fort Wayne, IN 46802
(219) 742-1321
23 to 27 performers.
Chamber orchestra music, new and experimental
music. Performs works of all eras throughout the
Midwest. Commissions 2 to 3 works per season to
be performed in a subscription series and on tour.
Agent: R. Eisenstein
Fort Wayne Philharmonic Orchestra
927 South Harrison
Fort Wayne, IN 46802
(219) 742-1321.

**Indiana University Contemporary Chamber
Ensemble**
Keith Brown, Conductor
Indiana University
School of Music
Bloomington, IN 47401
(812) 337-1582
Variable number of student performers.
20th century chamber music.

The McLean Mix
Barton McLean, Director
58412 Locust Road
South Bend, IN 46614
(219) 287-7540
Barton McLean, electronics; Priscilla McLean, electronics.
New and experimental music. Performs works by Barton and Priscilla McLean on electronic equipment.

Multimedium
Bruce Hemingway, Director
736 South Eddy Street
South Bend, IN 46615
(219) 282-2261
Variable number of performers, with a maximum of 4. Instrumentation: video synthesizer, EMS synthi 100, mini-computer, synthi AKS.
New and experimental music, multi-media. Experiments with new technology in live performance.

Sounds Of Inner Peace
Rev. Kent E. Schneider, Director
320 North Street
West Lafayette, IN 47906
(317) 743-4821
Tim Beers, electric bass guitar; R. Breen, piano; Dick Daugherty, saxophone, flute; Rob Hockman, percussion; Dolores Layer, voice; James McBride, saxophone, flute; Kent Schneider, trumpet, flugelhorn.
Jazz. Performs liturgical jazz in workshops and concerts at colleges.

Iowa

Center For New Music
Richard Hervig, William Hibbard, Directors
University of Iowa
Iowa City, IA 52242
(319) 353-3346
Monte Asbury, double bass; James Avery, piano; Paul Bendzsa, clarinet, bass clarinet; Carolyn Berdahl, violoncello; Gerald Chenoweth, composer; Elaine Erickson, piano; William Hibbard, viola; Catherine Holtzman, harp; Karen Milne, violin; William Parsons, percussion; Jan Pompilo, flute; Chris Sheppard, composer; Kathleen Young, soprano voice; Richard Zimdars, piano.
20th century chamber music, new and experimental music. Functions as a laboratory and performance extension for the University's composers, and as a repertoire ensemble for new music.
In residence at the University of Iowa.

The De Greet Expedition
Peter Lewis, Director
University of Iowa
School of Music
Iowa City, IA 52240
(319) 353-4313
4 performers, 2 permanent. Peter Lewis, synthesizer; William Parsons, percussion.
New and experimental music. Explores the expressive potential of the interaction between live performers and electronic music systems.

Fajilawa
Gary T. Gray, Director
3635 Cornell
Des Moines, IA 50313
(515) 243-5835
Variable number of performers, ranging from 2 to 6. T. Davis, Ghanian talking drums, tenor saxophone; L. Dillon, Western and African flutes; Gary T. Gray, mbira, percussion; Scott Hayward, mbira; Bill Parsons, percussion.
New and experimental music. Combines African and Western instruments.

Iowa Brass Quintet
John Beer, Director
University of Iowa
School of Music
Iowa City, IA 52242
(319) 353-4070
Paul Anderson, French horn; John Beer, trumpet; John Hill, trombone; Paul Smoker, trumpet; Robert Yeats, tuba.
Chamber music. Performs brass quintets of all eras.
Agent: Frothingham Management
156 Cherry Brook Road
Weston, MA 02193
(617) 894-7571.

Manhattan String Quartet
Eric Lewis, Director
Grinnell College
Music Department
Grinnell, IA 50112
(515) 236-7071
Andrew Berdahl, viola; Mahlon Darlington,

violin; Judith Glyde, violoncello; Eric Lewis, violin.

Chamber music. Performs string quartets of all eras, including many 20th century works. Presents concerts, workshops, and lecture-demonstrations locally and on tour. Commissions new works. In residence at Grinnell College.

Agent: Jane Bleyer
Thea Dispeker Artists' Representative
40 Seneca Lane
Pleasantville, NY 10570
(914) 769-4162.

The Mirecourt Trio
c/o Terry King
Grinnell College
Grinnell, IA 50112
(515) 236-6181
Kenneth Goldsmith, violin; John Jensen, piano; Terry King, violoncello.

Chamber music. Performs duos and piano trios of all eras, emphasizing new works and neglected American works. Premieres works.

Agent: Elliot A. Siegel
Elliot A. Siegel Music Management, Inc.
4701 Connecticut Avenue N.W., Suite 304
Washington, D.C. 20008
(202) 966-0003.

Kansas

Emporia Kansas State College Jazz Workshop
See Jazz Workshop

Jaws
Michael Steinel, Director
937 Watson
Emporia, KS 66801
(316) 343-3464
John Rowland, bass; Michael Steinel, piano, flugelhorn; Michael Theis, trumpet, flugelhorn; Craig Wright, drums, percussion. Cookie Jordon, who reads poetry to the group's accompaniment, is often included.

Jazz. Performs works by Chick Corea, Miles Davis, Charlie Parker, and Michael Steinel.

Jazz Workshop
Tom Wright, Director
Emporia Kansas State College
Emporia, KS 66801
(316) 343-1200
19 student performers.

A course in jazz, new and experimental music performance.

Mid-America Woodwind Quintet
c/o James Fleisher
Emporia Kansas State College
Emporia, KS 66801
(316) 343-1200 Ext. 431
James Fleisher, clarinet; Howard Halgedahl, bassoon; Ronald Lemon, French horn; Lorraine Carlson Webb, flute; Jason Weintraub, oboe.

Chamber music.

University Of Kansas Percussion Ensemble
George Boberg, Director
University of Kansas
Murphy Hall
Lawrence, KS 66045
(913) 864-3600
Variable number of student performers.

Chamber music, new and experimental music. Performs percussion works of all eras, emphasizing the 20th century.

Kentucky

Collegium Musicum Winds
Dr. Frederick A. Mueller, Director
Morehead State University
Music Department
Morehead, KY 40351
(606) 783-2221
4 student performers. Instrumentation: flute, oboe, clarinet, bassoon.

Chamber music, new and experimental music. Performs chamber works of all eras.

Morehead State University Faculty Woodwind Quintet
c/o William Bigham
Morehead State University
Music Department
Morehead, KY 40351
(606) 783-3242
Mary Albers, oboe; William Bigham, clarinet; Frederick Mueller, bassoon; Robert Pritchard, flute; Robert Walshe, French horn. Piano often included.

Chamber music. Performs woodwind duos, trios, quartets, and quintets of all eras at campus and community concerts.

Morehead State University Jazz Ensemble III
Jay Flippin, Director
Morehead State University
Morehead, KY 40351
(606) 783-3340
20 student performers. Instrumentation: woodwinds, flugelhorn, trumpet, trombone, tuba, percussion, keyboard, guitar, double bass.
A course in jazz performance.

Wolfrom-Bennes 'Cello-Piano Duo
Gaye Bennes, Lyle Wolfrom, Directors
Eastern Kentucky University
Richmond, KY 40475
(606) 622-2141
Gaye Bennes, piano; Lyle Wolfrom, violoncello. Another instrument is often included to form a trio.
Chamber music. Performs works of all eras.

Louisiana

The Chamber Arts Brass Quintet
Dr. Douglas Baer, Business Manager
Northeast Louisiana University
School of Music
Monroe, LA 71201
(318) 342-4078
Douglas Baer, trombone; Robert Eidenier, trumpet; Paul Everett, trumpet; Peter Linn, tuba; Jerry Vance, French horn.
Chamber music.
In residence at Northeast Louisiana University.

The Contemporary Wind Quintet
Eugene W. Steinquest, Director
Northeast Louisiana University
Monroe, LA 71201
(318) 342-2120
David Gibson, bassoon; James Gillespie, clarinet; Lowry Riggins, oboe; Eugene Steinquest, flute; Jerry Vance, French horn.
Chamber music. Performs quintets of all eras. Presents concerts, clinics, and symposiums on the university level.
Members are on the faculty of Northeast Louisiana University.

Louisiana Festival Arts Trio
c/o Dinos Constantinides
Louisiana State University
School of Music
Baton Rouge, LA 70803
(504) 388-3261

Thaddeus Brys, violoncello; Dinos Constantinides, violin; Daniel Sher, piano.
Chamber music, new and experimental music. Performs piano trios of all eras.
In residence at Louisiana State University.

The New Music Ensemble
William Blackwell, Director
1447 Gwen Drive
Baton Rouge, LA 70815
(504) 272-1914
Dorothy Blackwell, bassoon; William Blackwell, French horn; Kenneth Kussman, clarinet; William Lewis, oboe. Flutist undetermined.
20th century chamber music. Encourages the composition of new music for woodwind quintet.

New Times Players
Dinos Constantinides, Director
Louisiana State University
School of Music
Baton Rouge, LA 70803
(504) 766-3487
Variable number of performers with a maximum of 10. James Atwood, percussion; Harold Aymé, clarinet; Thaddeus Brys, violoncello; Larry Campbell, trombone; Dinos Constantinides, violin; Paul Knowles, voice; Nancy Saxon, piano.
20th century chamber music, new and experimental music. Performs in concerts on campus, in the community, and throughout the state.
Performers are affiliated with Louisiana State University School of Music.

Nouveaux Arts Trio
Ron Nethercutt, Director
Southeaster Louisiana University
P.O. Box 803
Hammond, LA 70401
(504) 549-2323
Ron Nethercutt, trombone; Bob Priez, trombone. Bass trombonist undetermined.
Chamber music, new and experimental music, jazz. Performs trombone trios of all eras in concerts and recital-clinics.
In residence at Southeastern Louisiana University.

Timm Woodwind Quintet
Earnest E. Harrison, Director
Louisiana State University
School of Music
Baton Rouge, LA 70803
(504) 388-3261

Paul Dirksmeyer, clarinet; Earnest Harrison, oboe; Richard F. Norem, French horn; John Patterson, bassoon; Jeanne Timm, flute.
Chamber music. Performs works of all eras.
In residence at Louisiana State University.

Maine

Portland Symphony String Quartet
Millicent Vetterlein, Manager
30 Myrtle Street
Portland, ME 04111
(207) 773-8191
Stephen Kecskemethy, violin; Ronald Lantz, violin; Julia Moseley, viola; Paul Ross, violoncello.
Chamber music. Performs string quartets of all eras, in concerts and lecture-demonstrations.
Members are principals in string section of the Portland Symphony Orchestra.

Maryland

American Camerata For New Music
John Stephens, Director
P.O. Box 1502
Wheaton, MD 20902
Joel **Berman**, concertmaster; violins: Larry Crosley, Barbara Gholz, Jean Harmon, Sheryl Krohn, Nathan Lerner, Judy Shapiro, principal; violas: Pat Braunlich, Ellen Ferry, Peggy Motter, principal; violoncellos: Thea Cooper, Evelyn Elsing, principal, Susan Kelly, Douglas Wolters; string bass: Michael Singer; harp: Cecile Ceo-Sieben; flute, piccolo: Margaret Ink; English horn: Michelle Foley; clarinet: James Hill; bass clarinet: Michael Kelly; bassoon: Richard Seidler; French horns: William Cowart, Arthur LaBar, principal; trumpets: John Ensminger, principal, Paul Taylor; trombone: Roy Guenther; tuba: Danny Brown; percussion: Kenneth Krohn, Gene Sittenfeld.
20th century chamber orchestra music. Performs works of this century exclusively, including pieces by Pierre Boulez, Edgard Varese, Anton Webern, and Charles Wuorinen.

Annapolis Brass Quintet
David Cran, Director
951 Forest Drive
Arnold, MD 21012
(301) 974-0451
Tim Beck, trombone; David Cran, trumpet; Robert Posten, bass trombone; Calvin Smith, **French** horn; Robert Suggs, trumpet.
Chamber music. Performs works of all eras in over 200 annual concerts. Presents educational concerts in colleges and communities. Available for mini-residencies.
Agent: Jane Bleyer
Thea Dispeker Artists' Representative
40 Seneca Lane
Pleasantville, NY 10570
(914) 769-4162.

The Columbia Piano Trio
Paula Gorelkin, Director
c/o Recital Associates
P.O. Box 583
Laurel, MD 20810
(301) 953-9343
Thea Cooper, violoncello; Paula Gorelkin, piano; Melissa Graybeal, violin.
Chamber music. Performs piano trios of all eras.

Contemporary Music Forum
Dr. Stephen Bates, Director
2004 Rittenhouse Street
Hyattsville, MD 20782
(301) 422-1989
Stephen Bates, clarinet; Donald Bick, percussion; Barbro Dahlman, piano; Al Gifford, flute; Alf Grahn, electronics, composer.
20th century chamber music, new and experimental music. Performs works by living composers. Encourages communication between composers and performers. Attempts to combine music with other art forms.

Maryland Chamber Ensemble
Joel Berman, Director
University of Maryland
Department of Music
College Park, MD 20742
(301) 454-2501
Ronald Barnett, percussion; Yvonne Beaty, piano; Joel Berman, violin; David Bragunier, tuba, euphonium; H. Stevens Brewster, double bass; Thomas Dumm, viola; Evelyn Elsing, violoncello; George Ethridge, saxophone; Evelyn Garvey, piano; Robert Genovese, clarinet; Stewart Gordon, piano; Fred Gruenebaum, oboe; Emerson Head, trumpet; Norman Heim, clarinet; Gary Horton, voice; Richard Jarvis, piano; Roy Johnson, piano; Edward Kiehl, trombone; Robert Kraft, trombone; Charlton Meyer, piano; William Montgomery, flute; Orrin Olson, horn; Kenneth Pennington, voice; Thomas Schumacher, piano; Richard Seidler, bassoon; Phyllis Sutherland, voice; Nelita True, piano; Louise Urban, voice.

The New Music Group
Jon Bauman, Director
Frostburg State College
Department of Music
Frostburg, MD 21532
(301) 698-4381
Variable number of student and faculty performers.
20th century chamber music.

Richard Reiter And Fusion
Richard Reiter, Director
8206 17th Avenue
Adelphi, MD 20783
(301) 445-1343
Bob Hallahan, piano; Derwyn Holder, double bass; Richard Reiter, soprano saxophone, alto saxophone, tenor saxophone, flute, clarinet; Mike Shepherd, drums, percussion.
Jazz. Performs works by group members and other composers. Blends jazz with elements of rock and traditional music. Encourages audience involvement.

Towson State College Jazz Ensemble
Hank Levy, Director
Towson State College
York Road
Towson, MD 21204
(301) 823-7500
25 student performers.
A course in jazz, new and experimental music performance.

Towson State College Percussion Ensemble
Dale Rauschenberg, Director
Towson State College
York Road
Towson, MD 21204
(301) 823-7500
Variable number of student performers, ranging from 2 to 18.
Chamber music, new and experimental music, jazz. Performs percussion works of all eras on primitive, African, and Western instruments.

University Of Maryland Chamber Ensemble
See Maryland Chamber Ensemble

University Of Maryland Quartet
University of Maryland
Department of Music
College Park, MD 20742
(301) 454-2501
Joel Berman, violin; Thomas Dumm, viola; Evelyn Elsing, violoncello; Evelyn Garvey, piano.

University Of Maryland Trio
Joel Berman, Director
University of Maryland
Department of Music
College Park, MD 20742
(301) 454-2501
Joel Berman, violin; Evelyn Elsing, violoncello; Evelyn Garvey, piano.

University Of Maryland Woodwind Quintet
University of Maryland
Department of Music
College Park, MD 20742
(301) 454-2501
Robert Geneovese, clarinet; Fred Gruenebaum, oboe; William Montgomery, flute; Orrin Olson, French horn; Richard Seidler, bassoon.

Massachusetts

Annex Players
Lawrence Scripp, Director
c/o Creative Media, Inc.
P.O. Box 74
Nahant, MA 01908
(617) 354-1139 or 787-2512
Variable number of performers. 1 to 20 musicians, dancers, and actors perform single and multi-media programs. See also Annex String Quartet, Massachusetts; and Kinesis, Massachusetts.
New and experimental music, multi-media. Concerned with the interpenetration of the visual, dramatic, technical, choreographic, and musical arts. Dedicated to the performance of works by living creators of contemporary art forms.

Annex String Quartet
c/o Creative Media, Inc.
Christopher Yavelow, Director
P.O. Box 74
Nahant, MA 01908
(617) 354-1139 or 787-2512
Joseph Conte, violin; Frank Grimes, viola; Janet Packer, violin; Lawrence Scripp, clarinet; Deborah Thompson, violoncello.

Chamber music. Performs works of all eras. All members belong to Annex Players.

Boston Bach Ensemble
Lawrence Scripp, Director
c/o Creative Media, Inc.
P.O. Box 74
Nahant, MA 01908
(617) 354-1139 or 787-2512
23 performers. Instrumentation: 2 flutes, 2 oboes, 2 clarinets, 2 French horns, harpsichord or piano, 4 first violins, 4 second violins, 3 violas, 2 violoncellos, double bass.
Chamber orchestra music. Performs works of all eras.
Agent: Debby Luppold
Frothingham Management
156 Cherry Brook Road
Weston, MA 02193
(617) 894-7571.

Boston Musica Viva
Richard Pittman, Director
c/o Cultural Communications Association
64 Church Street
Somerville, MA 02143
(617) 666-9222
Dean Anderson, percussion; Elsa Charlson, soprano voice; Nancy Cirillo, violin; Jan Curtis, mezzo-soprano voice; John Heiss, flute; Robert Sullivan, guitar; Marcus Thompson, viola; Raymond Toubman, oboe; William Wrzesien, clarinet; Evelyn Zuckerman, piano.
20th century chamber music, new and experimental music. Performs standard 20th century repertoire, and commissions new works by young composers.

Boston Philharmonia Orchestra
James Paul, Principal Conductor
c/o Management in the Arts, Inc.
551 Tremont Street
Boston, MA 02116
(617) 426-2387
Robert Brink, concertmaster; first violins: Dorothy Alpert, Maynard Goldman, Peter Kent, Kay Knudsen, Tison Street, Sophia Vilker; second violins: Lillian Braden, Charlotte Marty, Dianne Pettipaw, Sheila Vitale, Hazel Weems, Aideen Zeitlin; violas: Mary Hadcock, Barbara Kroll, Louise Newell, Judith Stafford; violoncellos: Joan Esch, Corinne Flavin, George Seaman, Olivia Toubman; double basses: Anthony Beadle, Francis J. Gallagher; flutes: Nancy Jerome, Elinor

Preble; oboes: Ira Deutsch, Raymond Toubman, Alan Williams; clarinets: Andre Lizotte, William Wrzesien; bassoons: Donald Bravo, Frank Nizzari; French horns: David Allan, Edwin Goble, Michael Johns; trumpets: Peter Chapman, Charles Lewis, James Simpson; percussion: Everett Beale, Fred Buda; harpsichord: John Gibbons.
Chamber orchestra music. Performs music rarely presented by larger orchestras. 50% of the repertoire is by 20th century composers.

Boston Symphony Chamber Players
Daniel Gustin, Manager
Symphony Hall
Boston, MA 02115
(617) 266-1492
Doriot Anthony Dwyer, flute; Jules Eskin, violoncello; Burton Fine, viola; Everett Firth, percussion; Armando Ghitalla, trumpet; William Gibson, trombone; Ralph Gomberg, oboe; Charles Kavaloski, French horn; Henry Portnoi, double bass; Joseph Silverstein, violin; Sherman Walt, bassoon; Harold Wright, clarinet.
Chamber music, new and experimental music. Performs chamber works of all eras locally and on tour. Presents master classes and workshops.
Members are principals in the Boston Symphony Orchestra.
Agent: Michael Ries
Columbia Artists Management, Inc.
165 West 57th Street
New York, NY 10019
(212) 397-6900.

Bowforte Ensemble
c/o Joan Huntley
6 Cornell Road
Beverly, MA 01915
(617) 927-6636
Joan Brayton, violin, viola; Margaret Eaton, violin, viola; Joan Huntley, violin, viola; Fern Meyers, violoncello, arranger; Alicia Pocharski, piano, harpsichord.
Chamber music. Performs works of all eras in schools and the community. Specializes in children's miniature concerts in schools. Emphasizes American composers, particularly those from New England.

Collage - Contemporary Music Ensemble Of Boston
Frank Epstein, Director
186 Pleasant Street
Brookline, MA 02146
(617) 738-5259
Frank Epstein, percussion; Ronald Feldman, violoncello; Paul Fried, flute, alto flute, piccolo; Joan Heller, soprano voice; Christopher Kies, piano; Ronald Knudsen, violin, viola; Felix Viscuglia, clarinet, bass clarinet; Lawrence Wolfe, double bass.
20th century chamber music, new and experimental music. Performs 20th century chamber and solo works. Commissions works, and promotes Boston based composers.
Personnel mostly from the Boston Symphony Orchestra.
Agent: Sheldon Soffer Management, Inc.
130 West 56th Street
New York, NY 10019
(212) 757-8060.

Earth Music Ensemble
c/o William Patterson
82 Waltham Street, Apartment 3B
Boston, MA 02118
(617) 426-4032
René Arlain, strings; Butch Campbell, strings; Chris Henderson, trap drums, percussion; Keith Lawrence, reeds; William Patterson, strings; Sao, percussion; Soyé, trumpet, various brass. Voices and additional strings occasionally included.
New and experimental music.
Agent: Ima Henderson
North Village, Apartment D-12
Amherst, MA 01002
(413) 549-0318.

Eastern SoundSpace Arkestra
c/o René Arlain
46 Westland Avenue, Apartment 42
Boston, MA 02115
(617) 536-6120
Variable number of performers, ranging from 7 to 15. René Arlain, strings; C. Campbell, strings, percussion, voice; Chris Henderson, drums, percussion; Keith Lawrence, reeds; William Patterson, strings, percussion, voice; Sao, African percussion; Soyé, brass, percussion.
New and experimental music, jazz. Attempts to stimulate images through sound.
Agent: William Henderson
North Village, Apartment D-12

Amherst, MA 01002
(413) 549-0318.

Empire Brass Quintet
David Ohanian, Director
c/o Management in the Arts, Inc.
551 Tremont Street
Boston, MA 02116
(617) 426-2387
Raymond Cutler, trombone; Charles A. Lewis, Jr., trumpet; David Ohanian, French horn; Samuel Pilafian, tuba; Rolf Smedvig, trumpet.
Chamber music, new and experimental music, jazz. Revives difficult and obscure brass quintets, arranges and performs new ones.

Fara Chamber Players
c/o Ann Danis
80 Quarry Street
Fall River, MA 02723
Ann Danis, violin; Faust D. Fiore, flute. Anna Fiore-Smith, piano, harpsichord; Ruth E. Trexler, violoncello.
Chamber music.
Alternate address: Ann Danis
23-C Rolling Green Drive
Fall River, MA 02720
(617) 672-1049.

The Mark Harvey Group
Mark Harvey, Director
P.O. Box 8721 J.F.K. Station
Boston, MA 02114
(617) 262-0440
Peter Bloom, woodwinds, percussion; Craig Ellis, percussion; Mark Harvey, brass, percussion; Michael Standish, percussion.
New and experimental music. Explores areas of collective composition, compositional and improvisational synthesis, and conceptual music.

James Houlik & Friends
c/o The Frothingham Management
156 Cherry Brook Road
Weston, MA 02193
(617) 894-7571
Richard Foley, oboe; James Houlik, saxophone; Paul Tardif, piano; David Wright, clarinet.
Chamber music. Available for workshops in ensemble and solo playing.

Kinesis
Christopher Yavelow, Director
7 Potter Park
Cambridge, MA 02138
(617) 354-1139
Variable number of performers drawn from the Annex Players, Massachusetts. Instrumentation: flute, oboe, clarinet, bassoon, French horn, trumpet, trombone, percussion, 2 violins, viola, violoncello, double bass. Artists include mimes, dancers, lighting technician.
New and experimental music. Performs contemporary theater works, combining instrumental music with mime and dance.
Alternate address: Creative Media, Inc.
P.O. Box 74
Nahant, MA 01908
Agent: Frothingham Management
156 Cherry Brook Road
Weston, MA 02193
(617) 894-7571 or 894-7574.

Latimer-Lytle Jazz Combo
c/o The Frothingham Management
156 Cherry Brook Road
Weston, MA 02193
(617) 894-7571
Mitchell Covic, double bass; James Latimer, percussion; Cecil Lytle, piano.
Jazz.

Springfield Symphony Chamber Ensemble
Robert Gutter, Director
49 Chestnut Street
Springfield, MA 01103
(413) 739-4728
20th century chamber music, new and experimental music. Performs concerts in schools throughout Western Massachusetts.
Members belong to the Springfield Symphony Orchestra.

Unity Ensemble
Chris Henderson, Sulieman Hakim, Directors
25 Edgerly Road, No. 12
Boston, MA 02115
(617) 536-6120
Variable number of performers, ranging from 2 to 12. Permanent members: Sulieman Hakim, reeds, percussion; Chris Henderson, drums, African and European percussion. Instruments frequently included: oboe, clarinet, trumpet, piano, koto, tablas, guitar, double bass.
New and experimental music, jazz. Performs music combining African, American, and experimental sounds.
Manager: Professor Max Roach
University of Massachusetts
Amherst, MA 01002.

University Of Massachusetts Jazz Workshop
Frederick Tillis, Director
University of Massachusetts
Amherst, MA 01002
(413) 545-2227
18 student performers. Instrumentation: 4 trumpets, 4 trombones, 5 saxophones, percussion, piano, double bass, guitar.
Jazz.

The Anthony Zano Orchestra
Anthony Zano, Conductor
P.O. Box 195
Wilmington, MA 01887
(617) 664-4552 or (212) 582-8800
20 performers. Instrumentation: 5 woodwinds, 4 trumpets, 4 trombones, percussion, piano, double bass, guitar.
New and experimental music, jazz.
Agent: Ambrose Associates
P.O.Box 195
Wilmington, MA 01887
(617) 664-4552.

Michigan

American Artists Series
Joann Freeman Shwayder, Director
435 Goodhue Road
Bloomfield Hills, MI 48013
(313) 647-2230
Variable number of performers including operatic artists and Detroit Symphony members.
20th century chamber music, new and experimental music, chamber music for unusual instrumental combinations. Presents 5 annual concerts including modern, standard repertoire, and some rarely heard works. Bicentennial project: to commission 5 American composers to write chamber works to be performed and recorded in 1976.

Cold Mountain New Music Ensemble
James Dawson, Clifford Pfeil, Directors
Oakland University
Rochester, MI 48016
(313) 377-2030
Variable number of student and professional performers.
20th century chamber music, new and experimental music. Performs works by John Cage, Yannis Xenakis, and Japanese, European, and American composers.

Contemporary Arts Improvisation Ensemble
Dr. James J. Hartway, Director
20524 Shady Lane
St. Clair Shores, MI 48080
(313) 771-9359
Virginia Catanese, clarinet; Jim Hartway, piano; Joy Kellman, dancer; Don Lewandowski, bass; Marc McCulloch, actor; Joanne Peters, flute; Denise Szykula, dancer; Sam Tundo, percussion. Light and slide operators frequently added.
New and experimental music, multi-media. Performs conservative and experimental 20th century multi-media works, including improvisational pieces. Intends to increase audience appreciation of new music.
Agent: Marc L. McCulloch
5200 Woodward Avenue
Detroit, MI 48202
(313) 832-2731.

Contemporary Directions Ensemble
George Balch Wilson, Coordinator
University of Michigan
School of Music
Ann Arbor, MI 48105
(313) 764-5594 or 764-8509
Uri Mayer, Conductor
15 to 20 student performers. Instrumentation: 2 flutes, 2 clarinets, bass clarinet, bassoon, 1 to 2 trumpets, French horn, 2 trombones, percussion, piano, strings.
20th century chamber music, new and experimental music. Presents new music in Contemporary Directions Series, presents works by student composers in Composer's Forum Series. Studies the notational and instrumental techniques of contemporary music.

Kalamazoo College Jazz Workshop
Dr. Lawrence R. Smith, Director
Kalamazoo College
Kalamazoo, MI 49001
(616) 383-8400
Variable number of student performers.
A course in jazz performance.

Michigan State University Improvisation Ensemble
Charles H. Ruggiero, Director
Michigan State University
Department of Music
East Lansing, MI 48824
(517) 355-1810
Variable number of student and faculty performers, ranging from 4 to 6. Instrumentation: flute, bass flute, trombone, saxophone, percussion, vibraphone, piano, bass, electronic equipment.
Jazz. Performs jazz of all styles, including third stream, progressive, and hard bop. Presents several free concerts in the greater Lansing area.

New Music Ensemble
Ramon Zupko, Director
Western Michigan University
Department of Music
Kalamazoo, MI 49001
(616) 383-0907
20 to 30 student performers.
New and experimental music. Presents premieres of works by young composers in a concert series at Western Michigan University.

New Musical Arts Ensemble
Charles H. Ruggiero, Director
Michigan State University
Department of Music
East Lansing, MI 48824
(517) 355-1810
Variable number of student and faculty performers.
New and experimental music. Performs free concerts for the Lansing community.

The Richards Quintet
Edgar Kirk, Director
Michigan State University
Music Department
East Lansing, MI 48824
(517) 353-9134
Israel Borouchoff, flute; Douglas Campbell, French horn; Edgar Kirk, bassoon; Elsa Ludewig-Verdehr, clarinet; Daniel Stolper, oboe.

Chamber music. Performs quintets of all eras, emphasizing works of the 20th century.

In residence at Michigan State University.

Agent: Albert Kay

Albert Kay Associates

58 West 58th Street

New York, NY 10019

(212) 759-7329.

The Tribe

Marcus Belgrave, Wendell Harrison, Phil Ranelin, Directors

81 Chandler

Detriot, MI 48202

(313) 875-2024

Tony Austin, bass; Will Austin, bass; Marcus Belgrave, trumpet; Wendell Harrison, reeds; Harold McKinney, piano; Phil Ranelin, trombone; Bud Spangler, drums; Wayne Warlow, guitar.

New and experimental music, jazz. Presents original music which reflects today's social conditions.

University Jazz Lab Band

Robert M. Davidson, Director

Western Michigan University

Kalamazoo, MI 49001

(616) 383-0910 or 383-0797

19 student performers.

A course in jazz performance.

Verdehr Trio

Elsa Ludewig-Verdehr, Director

Michigan State University

Music Department

East Lansing, MI 48824

(517) 355-7646

Elsa-Ludewig-Verdehr, clarinet; Walter Verdehr, violin. Pianist varies.

Chamber music. Performs solos, duos, and trios of all eras for violin, clarinet, and piano.

Minnesota

Brescian Quartet

See Saint Paul Chamber Orchestra Brescian Quartet.

Carleton Contemporary Ensemble

William Wells, Director

Carleton College

Northfield, MN 55057

(507) 645-4431 Ext. 416

Variable number of student and professional performers.

20th century chamber music, new and experimental music. Performs 20th century classics and some new works.

The Milo Fine Free Jazz Ensemble

Milo Fine, Director

7700 Penn Avenue South, Apartment 2

Richfield, MN 55423

(612) 861-2964

Variable number of performers. Permanent performer: Milo Fine, clarinet, drums, piano. Jazz. Improvises atonal and arhythmic jazz.

Art Resnick Quartet

Art Resnick, Director

c/o SRO Productions

2910 Bloomington Avenue South

Minneapolis, MN 55407

(612) 724-3864

Jeff Johnson, electric bass, double bass; Paul Lagos, drums; Tim Lewis, trumpet; Dick Oatts, saxophone; Art Resnick, piano.

Jazz.

The Saint Paul Chamber Orchestra

Dennis Russell Davies, Conductor

305 Old Federal Courts Building

75 West 5th Street

St. Paul, MN 55102

(612) 291-1144

Sheila Higby, Marketing Director

Romuald Tecco, concertmaster; first violins: Bruce Allard, Juan Cuneo, Hanley Daws; second violins: Carolyn Daws, Kathy Judd, James Riccardo, Eugene Vuicich; violas: Betty Benthin, John Gaska, Salvatore Venittelli; violoncellos: Edouard Blitz, Felice Magendanz, Daryl Skobba; double bass: Susan Matthew-Allard; flute: Carol Wincenc; oboes: Richard Killmer, Thomas Tempel; clarinet: Ronald Dennis; bassoon: Matthew Shubin; French horns: Lawrence Barnhart, Priscilla McAfee; keyboard: Layton James.

Chamber orchestra music, new and experimental music. Performs works of all eras, strongly emphasizing contemporary pieces. One third of its repertoire is by American composers.

Commissions works. Tours extensively. The Perspective Series features contemporary works for small ensembles, with composer interviews and explanations. The Capital Series features contemporary works for chamber orchestra. Available for residencies, clinics, workshops as a chamber orchestra or in smaller ensembles. Each performer belongs to one of the following Saint Paul Chamber Orchestra Ensembles: Brescian Quartet, Chamber Arts Consort, Piano Trio, Wind Quintet. See further explanation below. Agent: Sheldon Soffer Management, Inc.
130 West 56th Street
New York, NY 10019
(212) 757-8060.

The Saint Paul Chamber Orchestra Brescian Quartet
c/o M. Janet McNeill, Director of Public Relations
305 Old Federal Courts Building
75 West 5th Street
St. Paul, MN 55102
(612) 291-1144
Carolyn Daws, second violin; Hanley Daws, first violin; John Gaska, viola; Daryl Skobba, violoncello.
Chamber music. Performs works of all eras.

The Saint Paul Chamber Orchestra Chamber Arts Consort
John DeMain, Conductor
305 Old Federal Courts Building
75 West 5th Street
St. Paul, MN 55102
(612) 291-1144
Bruce Allard, violin; Lawrence Barnhart, French horn; Betty Benthin, viola; Edouard Blitz, violoncello; Juan Cuneo, violin; Carolyn Daws, violin; Hanley Daws, violin; John Gaska, viola; Layton James, piano, harpsichord; Kathy Judd, violin; Susan Matthew-Allard; double bass; Marlene Mazzuca, bassoon; James Ricardo, violin; Daryl Skobba, violoncello; Thomas Tempel, oboe; Eugene Vuicich, violin.
Chamber music. Performs works of all eras, specializing in Baroque pieces.

The Saint Paul Chamber Orchestra Piano Quartet
c/o M. Janet McNeill, Director of Public Relations
305 Old Federal Courts Building
75 West 5th Street
St. Paul, MN 55102
(612) 291-1144
Betty Benthin, viola; Dennis Russell Davies, piano; Peter Howard, violoncello; Romuald Tecco, violin.
Chamber music. Performs piano quartets of all eras.

The Saint Paul Chamber Orchestra Wind Quintet
c/o M. Janet McNeill, Director of Public Relations
305 Old Federal Courts Building
75 West 5th Street
St. Paul, MN 55102
(612) 291-1144
Ronald Dennis, clarinet; Richard Killmer, oboe; Priscilla McAfee, French horn; Charles Ullery, bassoon; Carol Wincenc, flute.
Chamber music. Performs woodwind quintets of all eras.

University Of Minnesota-Duluth Jazz Ensemble I
John C. Smith, Director
University of Minnesota
Duluth, MN 55812
(218) 726-8215
20 student performers.
Jazz.

Whole Earth Rainbow Band
Steve Kimmel, Director
1426 South 5th Street
Minneapolis, MN 55404
(612) 333-1883
Steve Kimmel, vibraphone, drums, tabla, various percussion; Steve Lockwood, piano; Terry Tilley, bass, synthesizer; Bruce Wintervold, vibraphone, drums, tabla, various percussion.
New and experimental music, jazz. Performs improvisatory works influenced by jazz, *musique concrète*, and non-Western music.

Mississippi

Ole Mississippi Jazz Band
Dr. Robert Jordan, Director
University of Mississippi
University, MS 38677
(601) 232-7268
Variable number of student performers. Instrumentation: 5 trumpets, 5 trombones, 5

saxophones, percussion, traps, conga drum, piano, double bass, guitar, voice.
A course in jazz performance.

University Of Southern Mississippi Jazz Lab Band
Raoul F. Jerome, Director
University of Southern Mississippi
P.O. Box 458 Southern Station
Hattiesburg, MS 39401
(601) 266-7276
18 to 24 student performers. Instrumentation: 5 trumpets, 5 trombones, 5 saxophones, percussion. French horns often included.
A course in contemporary jazz performance. Presents concerts locally and on tour.

Missouri

Jazz Lab Band And Studio Band
Robert M. Gifford, Director
Central Missouri State University
Warrensburg, MO 64093
(816) 429-4909
Variable number of student performers.
A course in jazz performance. Presents works by student composers and arrangers.

St. Louis Jazz Quartet
Terry Kippenberger, Manager
7150 Princeton Avenue
St. Louis, MO 63130
(314) 726-5062 or 997-4990
Terry Kippenberger, double bass; Edward Nicholson, piano; Charles Payne, drums; Jeanne Trevor, voice. Willie Akins, saxophones, included when necessary.
Jazz. Presents concerts and workshops.
Agent: Torrence/Perrotta Management
1860 Broadway
New York, NY 10023
(212) 541-4620.

UMKC String Quartet
Tiberius Klausner, Director
4420 Warwick Boulevard
Kansas City, MO 64111
(816) 276-2731
Hugh Brown, viola; Tiberius Klausner, violin; Sebe Sarser Morgulis, violoncello; Merton Shatzkin, violin.
Chamber music. Performs works of all eras on tour and in 4 annual concerts in the University of Missouri Chamber Music Series.

In residence at the University of Missouri, Kansas City.

Montana

Gallatin Woodwind Quintet
c/o Larry Sowell
Montana State University
Music Department
Bozeman, MT 59715
(406) 994-3561
John Fisher, French horn; Alan Leech, bassoon; Karen Leech, flute; Lorna Nelson, oboe; Larry Sowell, clarinet.
20th century chamber music. Performs in Montana and neighboring states.
In residence at Montana State University.

Rocky Mountain College Jazz Ensemble
Dr. William L. Waggoner, Director
Rocky Mountain College
Poly Drive
Billings, MT 59102
(406) 245-6151 Ext. 258
Variable number of student performers. Instrumentation: French horn, 5 trumpets, 5 trombones, 2 alto saxophones, 2 tenor saxophones, baritone saxophone, flute, percussion.
A course in jazz, new and experimental music performance.

Nevada

Contemporary Guitar Quartet Of Las Vegas
Havard Smith, Director
6308 Dayton Avenue
Las Vegas, NV 89107
(702) 870-4433
Electric guitars: Sid Jacobs, Fred McDermott, Michael Petruso, Havard Smith. Bass and drums sometimes included. Ensemble members also play steel string, acoustic, and 12-string guitar, banjo, mandolin.
New and experimental music. Intends to stimulate composition for guitar quartet. Performs transcriptions.

Las Vegas Chamber Players
Virko Baley, Director
University of Nevada
Department of Music
Las Vegas, NV 89154
(702) 739-3332
20th century chamber music, new and

experimental music. Performs and commissions new music, and presents 20th century classics. Presents multi-media works and vocal, instrumental, and electronic music at the Las Vegas Contemporary Music Festival. Tours.

University Of Nevada, Las Vegas Collegium Musicum
Richard L. Soule, Director
University of Nevada
Department of Music
Las Vegas, NV 89154
(702) 739-3332
Variable number of student performers.
Chamber music, new and experimental music. A course in the discovery and performance of new and Renaissance music.

New Hampshire

Apple Hill Chamber Players
c/o Ruth Waterman
Apple Hill Farm
East Sullivan, NH 03445
(603) 847-9706
Frederic Cohen, oboe; Julie Feves, bassoon; Richard Hartshorne, bass; Betty Hauck, viola; Bonnie Insull, flute; Peggy James, violin; David Jolley, French horn; Robert Merfeld, piano; Freddy Ortiz, violin; Beth Pearson, violoncello; Ernestine Schor, violin; Eric Stumacher, piano; Ruth Waterman, violin.
Chamber music. Presents 50 to 60 annual concerts in New England.
Agent: Dan Savage
Chamber Artists Management
P.O. Box 100
East Sullivan, NH 03445
(603) 847-9706.

Concord String Quartet
Mark Sokol, Director
Dartmouth College
P.O. Box 746
Hanover, NH 03755
(603) 646-1110
Norman Fischer, violoncello; Andrew Jennings, second violin; John Kochanowski, viola; Mark Sokol, first violin.
Chamber music, new and experimental music. Performs works of all eras, commissions many pieces.
In residence at Dartmouth College.
Agent:

Sheldon Soffer Management, Inc.
130 West 56th Street
New York, NY 10019
(212) 757-8060.

The New Arts Ensemble
c/o Donald Pistolesi
P.O. Box 234
Laconia, NH 03246
(603) 524-7037(8)
Melissa Bohl, oboe; Daniel Maki, flute; Donald Pistolesi, violoncello, piano; Sara Bohl Pistolesi, violin, viola. Clarinet, bassoon, piano, and voice included when necessary.
20th century chamber music. Performs works representative of the numerous trends of this century.

New Music Ensemble
Malcolm Goldstein, Director
Dartmouth College
Music Department
Hanover, NH 03755
(603) 646-1110
Variable number of student performers.
20th century chamber music, new and experimental music. A workshop in contemporary music performance. Presents concerts to the college community.

New Jersey

Andrew Cyrille And Maono
Andrew Cyrille, Director
18 River Street Extension, Apartment 321
Little Ferry, NJ 07643
(212) 541-7600 or (201) 440-8958
Andrew Cyrille, percussion; Ted Daniel, trumpet; Stafford James, bass violin; Donald Smith, piano; David S. Ware, tenor saxophone.
New and experimental music, jazz. Presents concerts demonstrating the roots and new directions of jazz.

Douglass College Woodwind Quintet
James Scott, Director
Douglass College Music Department
Rutgers University
New Brunswick, NJ 08903
(201) 932-7020
Ruth Dahlke, oboe; Randy Haviland, bassoon; George Jones, clarinet; Vincent Schneider, French horn; James Scott, flute.

Chamber music. Performs works of all eras, emphasizing the standard repertoire.
In residence at Douglass College, Rutgers University.

Force Of Attraction
Keith Purpura, Director
175 North Pleasant Avenue
Ridgewood, NJ 07450
(201) 444-2389
Ed Alstrom, piano, organ, bass, bassoon, voice; Craig Purpura, tenor saxophone, flute, bass clarinet; Keith Purpura, guitar, bass, sitar, bassoon; David Van Tieghem, drums.
Jazz. Performs works by group members, and classics of the jazz repertoire by such composers as John Coltrane, Thelonious Monk, and Charlie Parker.

Hawthorne Trio
c/o David Shapiro
20 Hawthorne Terrace
Leonia, NJ 07605
(201) 944-6513
Barbara Mallow, Violoncello; Alvin Rogers, violin; David Shapiro, piano.
Chamber music.

Jazz Impact
Harold Lieberman, Director
428 Cambridge Road
Ridgewood, NJ 07450
(201) 445-8468
Ron Bedford, drums; Arnie Lawrence, saxophone; Jay Leonhart, bass; Harold Lieberman, trumpet, flugelhorn; Ron Prestià, guitar, banjo, voice; Sonny Russo, trombone; Derek Smith, piano.
Jazz. Presents lecture-demonstrations tracing the development of contemporary jazz from its beginnings.
Agent: Carol Bruckner
c/o Harry Walker
Empire State Building
New York, NY 10001
(212) 563-0700.

Leonia Chamber Players
c/o David Shapiro
20 Hawthorne Terrace
Leonia, NJ 07605
(201) 944-6513
Richard Dickler, viola; Paul Gershman, violin; Barbara Mallow, violoncello; Alvin Rogers, violin;

Peter Rosenfeld, violoncello; David Shapiro, piano.
Chamber music.

Manhattan Percussion Ensemble
Paul Price, Conductor
470 Kipp Street
Teaneck, NJ 07666
(201) 836-8207
Percussionists: Charles Anderson, Thomas Beyer, Gary Burke, Justin DiCioccio, Frank Pagano, James Peterscak, James Preiss, Alan Silverman. Elizabeth Marshall, piano.
Chamber music, new and experimental music. Performs percussion works of all eras.
Manager: Thomas Beyer
167 Serpentine Road
Tenafly, NJ 17676
(201) 567-2828.

Alfred Mayer Electronic Music Workshop
c/o Alfred Mayer
128 James Street
Morristown, NJ 07960
(201) 539-1040
Alfred Mayer, synthesizer, digionic music sequencer, ionicamera visual displayer; Scott Mayer, synthesizer, digionic music sequencer, ionicamera visual displayer.
New and experimental music, jazz. Gives live demonstrations of multi-voiced control of electronic music, utilizing new technologies and designs on synthesizer, music sequencer, and visual displayer. Uses digital programming. Lectures in schools.

The Millstone Trio
c/o Randolph Haviland
19 Cedar Avenue
Highland Park, NJ 08904
(201) 828-7320
Randolph Haviland, bassoon; Phyllis Lehrer, piano; Jayn Rosenfeld, flute.
Chamber music, new and experimental music. Performs trios of all eras, encouraging the composition of works for this instrumental combination.
Agent: Westminster Artists Management
Westminster Choir College
Princeton, NJ 08540
(609) 92!-7100.

Montclair Harp Quartet
Rosalie R. Pratt, Director
Montclair State College
Upper Montclair, NJ 07043
(201) 893-5231 or 744-7366
Harpists: Margaret Leskiw Pierce, Helen Podence, Rosalie R. Pratt, June Wachtler.
Chamber music, new and experimental music. Performs works of all eras, emphasizing contemporary pieces.
In residence at Montclair State College.

Phoenix Woodwind Quintet
Andrejs Jansons, Manager
73 Glenwood Avenue
Leonia, NJ 07605
(201) 944-1273
Stuart Butterfield, French horn; Randolph Haviland, bassoon; Andrejs Jansons, oboe; Margaret Schecter, flute; William Shadel, clarinet.
20th century chamber music, new and experimental music. Introduces American music to European audiences and unknown European music to American audiences. Presents educational concerts to students, encouraging audience participation.
Agent: Jane Bleyer
Thea Dispeker Artists' Representative
40 Seneca Lane
Pleasantville, NY 10570
(914) 769-4162.

Ramapo Faculty Ensemble
c/o Roger Johnson
Ramapo College
Contemporary Arts Building
Mahwah, NJ 07430
(201) 825-2800
Roger Johnson, cornetto, French horn, electronics; Arnold Jones, piano; Harold Lieberman, trumpets; David Welch, piano. Bassoon, trombone, harpsichord, strings often included.
Chamber music, new and experimental music. Performs works of all eras on the Ramapo College campus.

Rutgers Chamber Ensemble
Jefferson Connell, Conductor
Douglass College Music Department
Rutgers University
New Brunswick, NJ 08903
(201) 932-7020
Ruth Dahlke, oboe; Randolph Haviland, bassoon; George Jones, clarinet; Joseph Kovacs, violin;

Paul Kueter, piano; Robert Martin, violoncello; Vincent Schneider, French horn; Daniel Schuman, viola; James Scott, flute; John van der Weg, percussion.
20th century chamber music. Performs standard contemporary works and new compositions by Rutgers University composers.
In residence at Rutgers University.

Tower Brass Trio
Jersey City State College
Music Department
Jersey City, NJ 07305
(201) 547-6000
Edwin Black, French horn; Arnold Fromme, trombone; Richard Lowenthal, trumpet.
Chamber music. Performs works of all eras, emphasizing Renaissance and contemporary works. Presents concerts and lecture-recitals.
In residence at Jersey City State College.
Address mail to agent:
Eastman Boomer Management
157 West 57th Street, Suite 504
New York, NY 10019
(212) 582-9364(5).

Walden Trio
c/o Joan Stein
95 Palisade Avenue
Leonia, NJ 07605
(201) 947-1459
Gwyndolyn Mansfield, flute; Maxine Neuman, violoncello; Joan Stein, piano. Guest artists frequently included.
20th century chamber music, new and experimental music. Performs trios of all eras, emphasizing new works and rarely performed works of the past.

New Mexico

New Mexico State University Woodwind Ensemble
Charles West, Director
New Mexico State University
P.O. Box 3F
Las Cruces, NM 88003
(505) 646-3735 or 646-2421
20 to 30 student, amateur, and professional performers.
20th century chamber music.

New York State

Excluding New York City

Berta-Lafford Duo
Joseph M. Berta, Director
Hobart and William Smith Colleges
Department of Music
Geneva, NY 14456
(315) 789-5500 Ext. 421
Joseph M. Berta, clarinet; Lindsay Lafford, piano.
Chamber music. Available for concerts and workshops.

Brass Quintet Of The American Concert Band
Dr. Kirby Jolly, Director
29 21st Street
Jericho, NY 11753
(516) 822-2373
Carol Abbe, second trumpet; Eric Berman, tuba; Michael Canipe, trombone; Dr. Kirby Jolly, first trumpet; James Park, French horn.
20th century chamber music, new and experimental music, jazz.

The Brocken Brass
Peter Piacquadio, Hale Rood, Directors
44 South Mountain Road
New City, NY 10956
(914) 634-0184 or (212) 865-0131
Sarah Larson, French horn; Bob Miliken, trumpet, flügelhorn; Peter Piacquadio, trumpet, flugelhorn, piccolo trumpet; Joe Randazzu, bass trombone; Hale Rood, trombone. Alternate performers: Charles Camilieri, trumpet, flugelhorn; Julie Landsman, French horn; Steve Richmond, French horn.
20th century chamber music. Performs works for brass sextet by group members and others.

Buffalo Jazz Ensemble
Philip Di Re, Director
322 Bedford Avenue
Buffalo, NY 14216
(716) 876-8193
Variable number of performers, ranging from 5 to 10. Permanent members: Nasara Abadey, drums; Sabul Adeyola, bass; Philip Di Re, reeds, composer; Joe Ford, reeds; Lou Marino, drums. Instruments usually included: guitar, double bass, horn.
Jazz. Performs works by local composers.

Capricorn Chamber Players
Joseph Dechario, Director
19 North Street
Geneseo, NY 14454
(716) 243-1178
Leone Buyse, flute, piano; Ruth Cahn, percussion; Barbara Dechario, harp; Joseph Dechario, piano. Guest violinist frequently included.
20th century chamber music. Intends to make 20th century chamber music available and approachable to a wide variety of audiences.

Cazenovia String Quartet
See Syracuse Symphony Cazenovia String Quartet, New York State.

Center Of The Creative And Performing Arts
Creative Associates
Jan Williams, Music Director
State University of New York
102 Cooke Hall
Buffalo, NY 14222
(716) 831-4507
Renee Levine, Managing Director
Variable number of performers drawn from a group of 8. Eberhard Blum, flute; Linda Cummiskey, violin; Julius Eastman, piano, voice, choreographer; Ralph Jones, electronics, horn; Donald Knaack, percussion; Joseph Kubera, piano; Robert Moran, keyboard, composer; Nora Post, oboe. Guest performers frequently included.
New and experimental music. Performs over 300 works by contemporary composers of all stylistic persuasions as well as the classics of the early 20th century. Presents a series known as Evenings For New Music throughout the U.S.A. and Canada, in which many works are premiered, including multi-media pieces. Offers annual Creative Associate resident fellowships to young professionals in new music and the contemporary performing arts.

College Jazz Ensemble
Raymond Shiner, Director
State University of New York
Crane School of Music
Potsdam, NY 13676
(315) 268-2969
22 to 26 student performers. Instrumentation: 4 French horns, 5 trumpets, 4 trombones, tuba, 5 saxophones, percussion, piano, bass, guitar.
Jazz.

Crane Percussion Ensemble
James Petercsak, Director
State University of New York
Crane School of Music
Potsdam, NY 13676
(315) 268-2966
6 to 10 student percussionists.
20th century chamber music. Performs percussion works from the 20th century exclusively. Tours, presents clinics, performs on educational television.

Creative Associates
See Center Of The Creative And Performing Arts Creative Associates.

Eastman Jazz Ensemble
Rayburn Wright, Director
University of Rochester
Eastman School of Music
Rochester, NY 14604
(716) 275-3026
28 student performers. Instrumentation: 2 flutes, 4 French horns, 5 trumpets, 3 trombones, bass trombone, tuba, 5 saxophones, 2 keyboards, percussion.
Jazz.

The Eastman Musica Nova Ensemble
Sydney P. Hodkinson, Conductor
University of Rochester
Eastman School of Music
Rochester, NY 14604
(716) 275-3025
Variable number of student performers.
20th century chamber music, new and experimental music, jazz. A course in contemporary music performance. Presents community concerts of new music for soloists, chamber ensemble, and chamber orchestra. Guest composers often included.

The Eastman Quartet
c/o Frank Glazer
University of Rochester
Eastman School of Music
Rochester, NY 14604
(716) 275-3037
Frank Glazer, piano; Alan Harris, violoncello; Millard Taylor, violin; Francis Tursi, viola.
Chamber music, new and experimental music. Performs piano quartets of all eras in concerts, workshops, seminars, and master classes.

Members are on the faculty of Eastman School of Music.
Agent: Herbert Barrett Management
1860 Broadway
New York, NY 10023
(212) 245-3530.

The Entourage Music And Theatre Ensemble
Joe Clark, Director
P.O. Box 589
Millbrook, NY 12545
Variable number of performers, ranging from 3 to 15. Instrumentation: flute, piccolo, soprano saxophones, percussion, acoustic piano, electric keyboards, viola, acoustic guitar, electric guitar, double bass, electric bass, recorder, voice, synthesizer.
New and experimental music. Performs multimedia and experimental works, often by group members.

Feit And Moulton Duo
David Moulton, Director
c/o Dondisound Studios, Inc.
12 St. John Street
Red Hook, NY 12571
(914) 758-5167
Richard Feit, synthesizer; David Moulton, synthesizer.
New and experimental music.

Fredonia Chamber Ensemble
James East, Director
State University of New York
Fredonia, NY 14063
(716) 673-3151 or 673-3463
Sheila Marie Allen, soprano voice; James East, clarinet, bass clarinet; Phyllis East, piano; Mario Falcao, harp.
Chamber music, new and experimental music. Performs works of all eras, emphasizing contemporary pieces. Premieres works written for the ensemble.
In residence at State University of New York, Fredonia.

The Fredonia Saxophone Ensemble
Dr. Laurence Wyman, Director
State University of New York
Music Department
Fredonia, NY 14063
(716) 673-3151
Variable number of student performers. Instrumentation: soprano saxophone, 2 alto

saxophones, tenor saxophone, baritone saxophone, bass saxophone.

Chamber music. Performs contemporary music and transcriptions of works of all eras.

The Fredonia Woodwind Quintet

James East, Director
State University of New York
Music Department
Fredonia, NY 14063
(716) 673-3151

James East, clarinet; Robert Gehner, French horn; John Gillette, bassoon; Donald Hartman, flute; John Maier, oboe.

Chamber music. Performs works of all eras, emphasizing the 20th century. Presents concerts and workshops on campus and throughout New York State. Available for out-of-state appearances.

In residence at State University of New York, Fredonia.

Improvisation

Bud DeTar, Director
24 Fairview Drive
Brockport, NY 14420
(716) 637-3317

Ed DeMatteo, bass; Bud DeTar, piano; Bradley Paxton, percussion.

Jazz.

Jazz And Contemporary Ensemble

William A. Hawkins, Director
State University of New York
Plattsburgh, NY 12901
(518) 564-2056

20 student performers. Instrumentation: 5 trumpets, 5 trombones, 5 saxophones, piano, bass, 2 guitars, vibraphone.

A course in jazz performance.

The Kazoophony

Barbara Stewart, Manager
3485 Elmwood Avenue
Rochester, NY 14610
(716) 381-7163

A touring kazoo quartet from the imaginary country of Ludakravia performing satires on serious music.

Laurentian Chamber Players

Michael Rudiakov, Director
Sarah Lawrence College
Bronxville, NY 10708
(914) 337-0700

Gerardo Levy, flute; Ronald Roseman, oboe; Catherine Rowe, soprano voice; Michael Rudiakov, violoncello; Joel Spiegelman, harpsichord, electronic keyboard.

Chamber music, new and experimental music. Performs works of all eras in concerts, lectures, master classes, and workshops on university campuses.

In residence at Sarah Lawrence College.

Live/Electronic Ensemble For New Music

Ralph Wakefield, Director
State University of New York
Potsdam, NY 13676
(315) 268-2969

Variable number of student performers, ranging from 20 to 25. Instrumentation: synthesizers, electric violins, electric flutes, electric guitar, electric piano, strings, percussion, woodwinds.

20th century chamber music, new and experimental music, jazz, non-Western music. Presents various styles of 20th century works, using acoustic and electronic instruments.

The Long Island Chamber Ensemble Of New York

Lawrence Sobol, Director
190 North Linden Street
North Massapequa, NY 11758
(516) 541-7637

Peter Basquin, piano; Neal Boyar, percussion; Louise Schulman, viola; Lawrence Sobol, clarinet. Guest performers often included.

20th century chamber music, new and experimental music.

Agent: Harry Beall Management, Inc.
119 West 57th Street
New York, NY 10019
(212) 586-8135.

Long Island Composers' Alliance

Herbert A. Deutsch, Marga Richter, Directors
12 New Street
Huntington, NY 11743
(516) 421-5315 or 427-4050
Variable number of performers.

20th century chamber music, new and and experimental music, jazz, multi-media, electronic music. Performs and sponsors concerts of works by Long Island composers. Encourages student composers.

Mother Mallard's Portable Masterpiece Company
David Borden, Steve Drews, Directors
1191 East Shore Drive
Ithaca, NY 14850
(607) 273-2188 or 273-9355
David Borden, electric piano, synthesizers; Steve Drews, electric piano, synthesizers; Linda Fisher, electric piano, synthesizers, voice.
New and experimental music. Performs live electronic music characterized by repetitious rhythmic patterns, often called 'trance music.'
Agent: Jane Yockel
Performing Artservices
463 West Street
New York, NY 10014
(212) 989-4953.

The New Dixie Minstrels
Alan Schmidt, Director
191 Park Forest Drive
Amherst, NY 14221
(716) 633-7846
Charles Braungart, tenor banjo, guitar, mandolin; John Bruno, clarinet, tenor saxophone; William Champion, trombone, tuba, vibraphone, piano; Curtis Chase, trumpet, flugelhorn; Paul Jones, drums, voice; Alan Schmidt, piano, soprano saxophone.
Jazz. Performs Chicago-style Dixieland jazz primarily, and some ragtime, Latin American, and mainstream jazz.
Agent: Angela Faust
Entertainment Promotions Unlimited
1377 Main Street
Buffalo, NY 14209
(716) 883-1032.

The New Wing For Contemporary Music
Bruce Levine, Director
135 Clinton Street, Apartment 6U
Hempstead, NY 11550
(516) 292-9398
Variable number of performers.
20th century chamber music, new and experimental music. Performs rarely heard works.

New York Festival Brass
Douglas Hedwig, Director
2 Keenan Place
Garden City, NY 11530
(516) 746-1633
Allan Freilich, trumpet; Douglas Hedwig, trumpet; Sean Mahony, trombone; Barbara Oldham, French horn; Jesse Rosen, bass trombone.
Chamber music. Performs brass duets, trios, quartets, and quintets of all eras.

New York Philomusica
A. Robert Johnson, Director
174 Oak Tree Road
Tappan, NY 10983
(914) 359-6092
Seymour Bernstein, piano; Alvin Brehm, double bass; Isidore Cohen, violin; Timothy Eddy, violoncello; Felix Galimir, violin; John Graham, viola; Nobuko Imai, viola; A. Robert Johnson, French horn; Richard B. Johnson, double bass; Robert Levin, piano; Joseph Rabbai, clarinet; Ronald Roseman, oboe; John Wummer, flute.
Chamber music, new music. Performs works of all eras. Commissions works. Active in Bicentennial activities.

Nexus
c/o Bob Becker
107 Council Rock
Rochester, NY 14610
(716) 244-0550
Percussionists: Bob Becker, William Cahn, Michael Craden, Robin Engelman, Russell Hartenberger. Guest soloists and composers often included.
20th century chamber music, new and experimental music, jazz, non-Western music. Performs works composed, improvised, arranged, or discovered by group members. Presents concerts and workshops in improvisation, Western and non-Western percussion music.

Pentaphonic Winds
c/o Dorothy Belford
14 Vernon Parkway
Mount Vernon, NY 10552
(914) 668-4017
Dorothy Belford, clarinet; Lynn Cushman, flute; Don McGeen, bassoon; Paul Rosenblum, French horn; Brenda Schuman, oboe.
Chamber music. Performs works of all eras,

emphasizing the 20th century. Wants to perform new works.

The C. W. Post College Music Faculty In Concert

Daniel Shulman, Conductor
C. W. Post College
Northern Boulevard
Greenvale, NY 11548
(516) 299-2474

Judith Allen, soprano voice; Joan Barrdea, flute; Frederic Belec, trumpet; Anne Chamberlain, piano; Genevieve Chinn, piano; Erich Graf, flute; Lewis Kaplan, violin; Josef Marx, oboe; Laurel Miller, soprano voice; Paul Sperry, tenor. Guest artists often included.

Chamber music. Performs works for various instrumental and vocal combinations.

Agent: Ann O'Donnell
New York Recital Associates
353 West 57th Street
New York, NY 10019
(212) 581-1429.

Sea Cliff Chamber Players

Herbert Sucoff, Director
P.O. Box 311
Sea Cliff, NY 11579
(516) 671-6263

Chris Finckel, violoncello; Hamao Fujiwara, violin; Jacob Glick, viola; Marsha Heller, oboe; Susan Jolles, harp; Sue Ann Kahn, flute; Barbara Speer, piano; Herbert Sucoff, clarinet.

Chamber music. Performs works of all eras.

S.E.M. Ensemble

Petr Kotik, Director
P.O. Box 482
Buffalo, NY 14240
.(716) 883-6669

Variable number of performers. Group includes: Julius Eastman, voice, keyboard; Petr Kotik, flute; Garrett List, trombone; Nora Post, oboe; Jan Williams, percussion.

New and experimental music. Performs works by group members and other composers, including John Cage, Marcel Duchamp, Frederic Rzewski, and La Monte Young.

Solid State

Hugh G. Burritt, Director
State University of New York
Music Department
Oswego, NY 13126
(315) 341-2130 or 341-4265

25 student performers. Instrumentation: 5 trumpets, 5 trombones, 6 saxophones, 2 pianos, percussion, 2 basses, 2 guitars.

A course in the performance, composition, and arrangement of big band jazz.

Sonora

Judith Martin, Director
225 Bird Avenue
Buffalo, NY 14213
(716) 881-2585

Linda Anderson, voice; Judith Martin, synket, electronics; Sandra Reher, photography; Margaret Wolfson, film, dance. Frequent guest performers: Bruce Anderson, electric guitar; Bertram Turetzky, contrabass.

New and experimental music, multi-media. Performs electronic music, microtonal music, concrete sound poetry, and multi-media works combining theater, dance, photography, and film. Frequently uses electronic instruments, including electric guitar, electric violin, and a mini-moog.

Alternate address: Judith Martin
State University of New York
Music Department
Buffalo, NY 14214.

Syracuse Symphony Brass Ensemble

Sandor Kallai, General Manager
113 East Onondaga Street
Syracuse, NY 13202
(315) 472-5293

George Coble, trumpet; William Harris, trombone; Stephen Lawlis, French horn; Thomas Lindemann, tuba; Peter Voisin, trumpet.

Chamber music. Performs works of all eras.

Members belong to the Syracuse Symphony Orchestra.

Syracuse Symphony Cazenovia String Quartet

Sandor Kallai, General Manager
113 East Onondaga Street
Syracuse, NY 13202
(315) 472-5293

Eugene Altschuler, violin; Irving Becker, viola; Michael Gelfand, violoncello; Rose MacArthur, violin.

Chamber music. Performs works of all eras.

Members belong to the Syracuse Symphony Orchestra.

Syracuse Symphony Percussion Ensemble
c/o Herbert Flower
113 East Onondago Street
Syracuse, NY 13202
(315) 472-5293
Percussionists: Henry L. Carey, Herbert Flower, Douglas Igelsrud, Ernest Muzquiz.
New and experimental music. Members perform on more than 100 percussion instruments, in concerts, lecture-demonstrations, and clinics.
Members belong to the Syracuse Symphony Orchestra.

Syracuse Symphony Rock Ensemble
Calvin Custer, Director
113 East Onondaga Street
Syracuse, NY 13202
(315) 472-5293
Henry L. Carey, Jr., percussion; George Coble, trumpet, piccolo trumpet; Calvin Custer, guitar, recorder, alto cornet; Herbert Flower, percussion; Robert Hagreen, French horn; William Harris, trombone; Eric Kurzdorfer, electric piano; Philip MacArthur, oboe; Daniel Sapochetti, trumpet; Angel Sicam, electric bass.
Chamber music, new music. Performs works by Calvin Custer and his arrangements of works by such composers as J. S. Bach, Gabriel Faure, and Sergei Prokofiev.
Members belong to the Syracuse Symphony Orchestra.

Syracuse Symphony String Quartet
Sandor Kallai, General Manager
113 East Onondaga Street
Syracuse, NY 13202
(315) 472-5293
C. Gay Custer, viola; A. Lindsay Groves, violoncello; Susan Jacobs, violin; Fred Klemperer, violin.
Chamber music. Performs string quartets of all eras in lecture-demonstrations, concerts, and school programs.
Members belong to the Syracuse Symphony Orchestra.

Syracuse Symphony Wind Quintet
Sandor Kallai, General Manager
113 East Onondaga Street
Syracuse, NY 13202
(315) 472-5293
Anthony De Angelis, bassoon; Robert Hagreen, French horn; Philip MacArthur, oboe; John Oberbrunner, flute; Gerald Zampino, clarinet.
Chamber music. Performs woodwind quintets of all eras.
Members belong to the Syracuse Symphony Orchestra.

Syracuse University Jazz Ensemble
Stephen Marcone, Director
Syracuse University
200 Crouse College
Syracuse, NY 13210
(315) 423-2191
Variable number of student performers, with a core group of 20 to 23. Instrumentation: 5 trumpets, 4 trombones, 5 saxophones, piano, bass, percussion.
A course in big band jazz performance.

Timpani In Solo And Ensemble
Jesse Kregal, Director
681 Auburn
Buffalo, NY 14222
(716) 881-2736
John Burgess, flute; Lynn Harbold, percussion; Jim Kennedy, violoncello; Jesse Kregal, timpani; Marilyn Kregal, violin; John Landis, piano.
Chamber music, new and experimental music. Performs chamber works of all eras, featuring the timpani.
Agent: Mr. Rubin
Bernard and Rubin Management
255 West End Avenue
New York, NY 10023
(212) 877-3735.

Together
c/o Joel Chadabe
State University of New York
Music Department
Albany, NY 12222
(518) 457-2147
Variable number of performers including Joel Chadabe, composer, electronics; David Gibson, violoncello; Jan Williams, percussion.
New and experimental music. Performs works by John Cage, Joel Chadabe, David Gibson, and

David Tudor, involving interaction between people, machines, and visual processes.

The U. B. Jazz Orchestra
Milton Marsh, Director
State University of New York
Baird Music Hall
Buffalo, NY 14214
(716) 831-3411 or 831-3312
21 student performers. Guest artists often included.
Rehearses and performs works by major jazz composers.

New York City

Bronx

Bronx Arts Ensemble
William Scribner, Director
3636 Fieldston Road
Bronx, NY 10463
(212) 549-1899
Variable number of performers. Permanent members: Martin Burnbaum, trumpet; Zeda Carrol, piano; John Moses, clarinet; Setsuko Nagata, violin; Dorothy Pixly, violin; Al Redney, flute; Michael Rudiakov, violoncello; Robert Rudie, violin; Vincent Schneider, French horn; Louise Schulman, viola; Louise Scribner, oboe; William Scribner, bassoon; Johannes Somary, conductor.
Chamber music. Performs works of all eras in a concert series at Riverdale-Yonkers Society for Ethical Culture, Bronx, New York. Premieres works.
Members belong to the Bronx Arts Ensemble Orchestra.

Gramercy String Quartet
c/o Allan Schiller
Herbert H. Lehman College
Bronx, NY 10468
(212) 960-8881
William Barbini, violin; Eugene Becker, viola; Paul Clement, violoncello; Allan Schiller, violin.
Chamber music.

Jimmy Lyons Ensemble
Jimmy Lyons, Director
1834 Andrews Avenue
Bronx, NY 10453
(212) 872 4695
Karen Borca, bassoon; Hayes Burnett, double bass; Andrew Cyrille, percussion; Jimmy Lyons, alto saxophone; Raphe Malik, trumpet.
Jazz. Performs works derived from the tradition of black music.

Riverdale Quartet
Robert Rudie, Director
Riverdale School of Music
253rd Street and Post Road
Bronx, NY 10471
(212) 549-8034
Richard Locker, violoncello; Setsuko Nagata, violin; Robert Rudie, violin; Louise Schulman, viola.
Chamber music. Performs works of all eras.

Telphy's Sound Ensemble
Barry Telphy, Director
120-20 Alcott Place
Bronx, NY 10475
(212) 671-6772
Phil Bingham, piano; Eddie Martin, tenor saxophone; Jimmy Siever, alto saxophone; Barry Telphy, trumpet; George Wheeler, drums; Richard Williams, bass.
Jazz. Performs all styles of jazz, including be-bop, contemporary, and experimental.

Tycho
Peter Leonard, Director
2400 Johnson Avenue, Apartment 11K
Bronx, NY 10463
(212) 796-2927
Joseph Anderer, French horn; Bruce Bonivissuto, trombone; Andree Briere, double bass; Andrew Cordle, bassoon; Rolla Durham, trumpet; Rosemary Glyde, viola; Trudy Kane Hartman, flute; George Hirner, clarinet; Barry Jekowsky, percussion; Myron McPherson, piano; Lionel Party, harpsichord; Linda Quan, violin; Mark Shuman, violoncello; Steve Taylor, oboe. Performers included when necessary: John Aler, tenor voice; Joy Blackett, mezzo-soprano voice; Dorothy Setian, soprano voice; Robert Shiesley, baritone voice. Also sometimes included: dancer, actress.
Chamber music. Presents programs combining works of all eras in order to demonstrate the relationship of new music with works from the past. Emphasizes 20th century pieces and Baroque stage works. Attempts to unify the arts by combining music, dance, and drama.

Brooklyn

Brooklyn College Percussion Ensemble
Morris Lang, Director
Brooklyn College
Music Department
Brooklyn, NY 11210
(212) 780-5286
Variable number of student performers.
20th century chamber music, new and experimental music.

Contemporary Gospel Ensemble
David S. Butler, Director
361 Livonia Avenue, Apartment 10B
Brooklyn, NY 11212
(212) 385-2150 or 498-2104
Roma V. Simmons, Assistant Director
(212) 566-1858
Jacuba Abiona, conga drum; Jean Antley, soprano voice; David S. Butler, piano; Sheila McCurtis, soprano voice, piano; Paul Ramsey, double bass; Barbara Snell, alto voice, organ; Kasya Wakweli, saxophone, horn, flute; George Wheeler, drums; Shirley Williams, soprano voice; Denver Wright, organ.
20th century choral chamber music. Performs contemporary arrangements of gospels in community concerts at schools, prisons, hospitals, and churches. Presents workshops, open rehearsals, and lecture-demonstrations.
Agent: Byrl Zitch
The Contemporary Forum
2528A West Jerome Street
Chicago, IL 60645
(312) 764-4383.

Footnotes
c/o Martha Siegel
135 Eastern Parkway, Apartment 15C
Brooklyn, NY 11238
(212) 636-6026
Michelle Berne, dancer; Jordan Engel, clarinet, flute, saxophone; Ann Garvey, flute, drum, voice; Susan Griss, dancer; Alain LeRazer, dancer; Myrna Packer, dancer; Keith Purpura, guitar, sitar; Martha Siegel, violoncello, voice; David Van Tieghem, percussion, voice.
New and experimental music, improvisational music and dance. Experiments with improvisation, group composition, choreography, and the relationship of sound and human movement. Explores individual and collective creativity.

IND String Quartet
c/o Martha Siegel
135 Eastern Parkway, Apartment 15C
Brooklyn, NY 11238
(212) 636-6026
Emily Karr Andres, violin; Linda Blanche, viola; Olga Gussow, violin; Martha Siegel, violoncello.
Chamber music. Performs string quartets of all eras.

The New York Bass Violin Choir
Bill Lee, Director
165 Washington Park
Brooklyn, NY 11205
(212) 858-6848
Lisle Atkinson, double bass; Ron Carter, double bass; Richard Davis, double bass; Michael Fleming, double bass; Billy Higgins, percussion; Milt Hinton, double bass; Bill Lee, double bass; A. Grace Lee Mims, soprano voice; Consuela Lee Morehead, piano. Additional percussionist occasionally included.
Jazz. Performs excerpts of folk operas composed or arranged by Bill Lee in a blues style.
Agent: Alex Howard
Lee-Fam Enterprises
16303 Stockbridge Avenue
Cleveland, OH 44128
(216) 991-2693.

New York Lyric Arts Trio
Gena Raps, Director
359 Parkside Avenue
Brooklyn, NY 11226
(212) 284-1897
Mary Freeman Blankstein, violin; Wendy Brennan, violoncello; Gena Raps, piano.
Chamber music. Performs works of all eras, emphasizing rarely heard works.

Jack Reilly Jazz Ensemble
Jack Reilly, Director
125 Prospect Park West
Brooklyn, NY 11215
(212) 768-4053
Joe Cocuzzo, drums; Jack Reilly, piano; Jack Six, bass. Dan Lincoln, baritone voice often included. Chorus, string quintet, and soloists included when necessary.
Jazz. Performs works by Jack Reilly. These works combine Western European, Eastern, and American musical influences. Liturgical pieces based on Eastern philosophy are also performed.
Agent: Norman Currie

Maximus
39 West 56th Street
New York, NY 10019
(212) 581-4144.

Sounds Out Of Silent Spaces
Philip Corner, Director
109 8th Avenue, Apartment 3R
Brooklyn, NY 11215
(212) 636-1651
Philip Corner, bass trombone, voice, rattles,
Daniel Goode, clarinet; Alison Knowles,
silkscreen, voice; Ana Lockwood, voice; Charlie
Morrow, trumpet, voice; Carole Weber, alto flute,
voice, rattles; Julie Winter, voice, meditation.
New and experimental music, multi-media.
Performs music, rituals, and meditations based on
minimalist concepts, such as pulse and single
tones. Performs works by group members.

A Touch Of Class
Steven Kroon, Director
149 East 43rd Street
Brooklyn, NY 11203
(212) 693-1193
Harry Constance, piano; Jimmy Heywood,
saxophone; Blake Hines, bass; Steven Kroon,
percussion; Sargent Sepio, guitar; Tyrone Walker,
drums. Vocalist occasionally included.
Jazz.

Manhattan

Aeolian Chamber Players
Lewis Kaplan, Director
c/o Harry Beall Management
119 West 57th Street
New York, NY 10019
(212) 587-8135
Edmond Battersby, piano; Erich Graf, flute;
Thomas Hill, clarinet; Lewis Kaplan, violin;
Ronald Thomas, violoncello.
Chamber music. Performs works of all eras.

The Rashied Ali Quartet/Quintet
Rashied Ali, Director
77 Greene Street
New York, NY 10012
(212) 966-6740
Rashied Ali, drums, traps, conga drums; James
Vass, soprano saxophone, alto saxophone, flute;
Benny Wilson, bass. Pianist varies; guitar
occasionally substituted for piano; trombone or
trumpet occasionally included.
Jazz. Brings black music to the public.

Agent: Jack Whittemore
80 Park Avenue
New York, NY 10016
(212) 986-6854.

The American Brass Quintet
c/o Edward Birdwell
1860 Broadway, Suite 401
New York, NY 10023
(212) 581-2196
Robert Biddlecome, bass trombone; Edward
Birdwell, French horn; Raymond Mase, trumpet;
Louis Ranger, trumpet; Herbert Rankin, tenor
trombone
Chamber music. Performs works of the
Renaissance, and 19th and 20th centuries. Intends
to increase the appreciation of brass chamber
music by American and international audiences.
Agent: Melvin Kaplan, Inc.
85 Riverside Drive
New York, NY 10024
(212) 877-6310.

American Chamber Trio
Esta Ehrmann, Publicity Director
American Chamber Concerts, Inc.
890 West End Avenue
New York, NY 10025
(212) 662-5849
Peter Basquin, piano; June DeForest, violin;
Daniel Morganstern, violoncello.
Chamber music. Performs works of all eras in
concerts, lecture-recitals, and master classes.

Anagnoson-Kinton Duo-Pianists
James Anagnoson, Director
320 West 83rd Street
New York, NY 10024
(212) 874-2622
Pianists: James Anagnoson, Leslie Kinton.
Chamber music, new and experimental music.
Performs duo-piano works of all eras.

Arcadia Nova Chamber Ensemble
Gena Rangel, Director
207 West 107th Street
New York, NY 10025
(212) 865-6808
Marilyn DuBow, violin; Judith Martin,
violoncello; Gena Rangel, soprano voice; Frances
Smith, flute; Ellen Wright, harpsichord.
Chamber music.

The Arioso Woodwind Quintet
Gary McGee, Director
P.O. Box 1125 Ansonia Station
New York, NY 10023
(212) 595-5536
Sheryl Henze, flute, piccolo, alto flute, bass flute;
Anne Leek, oboe, English horn; Gary McGee,
clarinet; David Wakefield, French horn; Daniel
Worley, bassoon.
Chamber music. Performs woodwind quintets of
all eras, and encourages composition of new
quintets.

Baumel-Booth-Smith Trio
Herbert Baumel, Director
c/o Eastman Boomer Management
157 West 57th Street, Suite 504
New York, NY 10019
(212) 582-9364(5)
Herbert Baumel, violin; Allan Booth, piano;
Patrick Smith, violoncello.
Chamber music. Performs works of all eras.
Commissions works.

The Bloomingdale Ensemble
c/o Richard Wasley
Bloomingdale House of Music
323 West 108th Street
New York, NY 10025
(212) 663-6021
Carol Buck, violoncello; Larry Fader, viola;
Marsha Heller, oboe; Susan Minkoff, flute; Lucy
Shelton, soprano voice; Richard Wasley, clarinet.
Guest pianist sometimes included.
Chamber music.

The Boehm Quintette
Don Stewart, Director
P.O. Box 660
New York, NY 10023
(212) 362-6100 Ext. 43 or 245-3500
Joseph Anderer, French horn; Phyllis Bohl, oboes;
Don Stewart, clarinets; Susan Stewart, flutes;
Richard Vrotney, bassoon, recorders.
20th century chamber music and earlier neglected
chamber works, new and experimental music.
Performs many contemporary American works.
Commissions and transcribes works.
Agent: Monty Byers
Herbert Barrett Management
1860 Broadway
New York, NY 10023
(212) 245-3500.

The Ruby Braff/Georges Barnes Quartet
Ruby Braff, George Barnes, Directors
c/o Louis P. Randell, Esq.
1501 Broadway, Suite 2900
New York, NY 10036
(212) 279-8800
George Barnes, guitar; Ruby Braff, cornet; Vinnie
Corrao, guitar; Michael Moore, double bass.
Performs traditional jazz.

Cantilena Chamber Players
Edna Michell, Director
1 West 85th Street
New York, NY 10024
Frank Glazer, piano; Edna Michell, violin; Paul
Olefsky, violoncello; Harry Zaratgian, viola.
Chamber music.

The C.B.A. Ensemble (Collective Black Artists)
Stanley Cowell, Frank Foster, Jimmy Owens,
Musical Directors
P.O. Box 94 Times Square Station
New York, NY 10036
(212) 255-4814
Sinclair Acey, trumpet; Roland Alexander, tenor
saxophone; Al Bryant, trumpet; Stanley Cowell,
piano; Frank Foster, tenor saxophone; Dick
Griffin, trombone; Jimmy Owens, trumpet;
William 'Buddy' Pearson, alto saxophone; Charli
Persop, drums; Kenny Rogers, baritone
saxophone; Charles Stephens, trombone; Bob
Stewart, tuba; Bob Torrence, alto saxophone; Joe
Lee Wilson, voice; Reggie Workman, bass; Kiane
Zawadi, trombone.
Jazz. Performs many forms of black music,
including contemporary, traditional, rhythm and
blues, calypso, gospel, and avant-garde music.
Also performs arrangements by John Coltrane,
Tadd Dameron, Kenny Dorham, Benny Golson,
J. J. Johnson, and James Spaulding.

Chamber Music Society Of Lincoln Center
Charles Wadsworth, Director
c/o Columbia Artists Management, Inc.
165 West 57th Street
New York, NY 10019
(212) 397-6900
Leonard Arner, oboe; Gervase De Peyer, clarinet;
Loren Glickman, bassoon; Richard Goode, piano;
Jaime Laredo, violin; Leslie Parnas, violoncello;
Paula Robison, flute; Walter Trampler, viola;
Barry Tuckwell, French horn; Charles
Wadsworth, piano, harpsichord. Guest artists and
ensembles frequently included.

20th century chamber music. Performs works of all eras in an annual series at Alice Tully Hall, Manhattan. Premieres and commissions works.

Chamber Society Of Washington Square

Nancy Uscher, Director
17 West 70th Street
New York, NY 10023
(212) 595-6596

Jack Kreiselman, clarinet; Nora Post, oboe; William Scribner, bassoon; Nancy Uscher, viola. Additional instruments included when necessary.

20th century chamber music. Performs in public facilities and charitable institutions, such as hospitals, schools, and senior citizens centers.

Chelsea Composers Cooperative

Warren Cytron, Matthew Greenbaum, Directors
433 West 22nd Street
New York, NY 10011
(212) 924-2720 or 243-1179

Anne Chamberlain, piano; Cynthia Chamberlain, piano; Josef Marx, oboe; David Miller, bassoon; Maxine Neuman, violoncello; Linda Quan, violin; Patricia Spencer, flute; Mary Washburn, soprano voice.

20th century chamber music, new and experimental music. Performs works by Stefan Wolpe and his followers. Provides performing space for composers not affiliated with universities.

Suzanne Ciani

43 East 10th Street
New York, NY 10003
(212) 673-9518

Suzanne Ciani, Buchla synthesizer; William Hearn, technician.

New and experimental music, electronic music, multi-media. Performs spontaneous compositions by Suzanne Ciani. Works are performed live on the Buchla synthesizer in concerts, lecture-demonstrations, and workshops. Available to work with other ensembles and dancers.

Agent: Bill Perrotta
Torrence/Perrota Management
1860 Broadway
New York, NY 10023
(212) 541-4620.

Clarion Music Society, Inc.

John L. Hurley, Jr., Executive Director
415 Lexington Avenue, Room 1110
New York, NY 10017
(212) 697-3862

Chamber music. Performs works of all eras, emphasizing master works of the 17th and 18th centuries. Performs one contemporary work per season, often commissioning the work performed.

George Coleman Octet

c/o MsManagement
463 West Street, Suite 419
New York, NY 10014
(212) 691-0481

Lisle Atkinson, double bass; George Coleman, tenor saxophone, arranger, composer; Harold Maybern, piano; Danny Moore, trumpet; Eddie Moore, drums; Mario Revera, baritone saxophone; Frank Strocier, alto saxophone; Harold Vick, tenor saxophone.

Jazz. Performs original compositions and arrangements. Available for seminars and workshops, and tours throughout the U.S.A. and abroad.

The Composers Ensemble

Joe Spivack, Director
201 West 89th Street, Apartment 8ff
New York, NY 10024
(212) 362-7493

10 composer-performers. Stephen Dydo, guitar; Ken Hosley, percussion; Peter Lieberson, conductor, piano; Erik Lundborg, conductor, piano; Alison Nowak, violin; David Olan, clarinet; Martha Siegel, violoncello; Joe Spivack, flute, piccolo; Joyce Suskind, soprano voice; Bruce Taub, bassoon.

New music. Performs works by members of the ensemble and other composers associated with the group.

Composers Festival Orchestra

John Watts, Director
Composers Theatre
25 West 19th Street
New York, NY 10011
(212) 989-2230

Variable number of performers. Musicians performing regularly with the orchestra in 1975: Samuel Baron, flute; Stephen Bell, guitar; Alvin Brehm, conductor; Jerome Bunke, clarinet; Allan Dean, trumpet; Jan DeGaetani, mezzo-soprano voice; Raymond DesRoches, percussion; Richard

Fitz, percussion; Jeanne Benjamin Ingraham, violin; Paul Ingraham, French horn; Susan Jolles, harp; Gilbert Kalish, piano; Caroline Levine, viola; Julius Levine, double bass; Donald MacCourt, bassoon; Ronald Roseman, oboe, English horn; Catherine Rowe, soprano voice; Michael Rudiakov, violoncello; Charles Russo, clarinet; Jay Shanman, trombone; Gerald Tarack, violin; Philip West, oboe, English horn.
New and experimental music. Performs contemporary American works in an annual May Festival of Contemporary American Music.

Composers String Quartet
c/o Anahid Ajemian
285 Central Park West
New York, NY 10024
(212) 787-7778
Anahid Ajemian, violin; Jean Dane, viola; Matthew Raimondi, violin; Michael Rudiakov, violoncello.
Chamber music. Performs works of all eras.
Agent: Melvin Kaplan, Inc.
85 Riverside Drive
New York, NY 10024
(212) 877-6310.

Concord String Quartet
Mark Sokol, Director
c/o Sheldon Soffer Management, Inc.
130 West 56th Street
New York, NY 10019
(212) 757-8060
Norman Fischer, violoncello; Andrew Jennings, second violin; John Kochanowski, viola; Mark Sokol, first violin.
Chamber music, new and experimental music. Performs works of all eras, commissions many pieces.
In residence at Dartmouth College, New Hampshire.

Contemporary Chamber Ensemble
Arthur Weisberg, Director
c/o Melvin Kaplan, Inc.
85 Riverside Drive
New York, NY 10024
(212) 877-6310
Allen Blustine, clarinet; Allan Dean, trumpet; Raymond DesRoches, percussion; Paul Dunkel, flute; Jacob Glick, viola; Georges Haas, oboe; Jeanne Benjamin Ingraham, violin; Paul Ingraham, French horn; Gilbert Kalish, piano; Donald MacCourt, bassoon; Donald Palma,

double bass; Fred Sherry, violoncello; John Swallow, trombone.
20th century chamber music, new and experimental music. Performs new works and classics of the 20th century, commissions works.

The Contemporary Ensemble Of The Manhattan School Of Music
Harvey Sollberger, Director
Manhattan School of Music
120 Claremont Avenue
New York, NY 10027
(212) 749-2802
Variable number of student performers, ranging from 1 to 25.
20th century chamber music. Performs major works of this century in 3 annual concerts. Composers and professional conductors rehearse with the ensemble.

Jack Cross Jazz Ensemble
Jack Cross, Director
P.O. Box 848 Peter Stuyvesant Station
New York, NY 10009
(212) 473-4616
Variable number of performers. Permanent members: Lokbin Abdullah II, bongo drums; Duke Clements, bass, arranger; Jack Cross, trumpet, flugelhorn, arranger; Al Drears, drums, percussion; Chuck Fowler, acoustic and electric pianos.
New and experimental music, jazz. Presents concerts, workshops, and seminars at universities, concert halls, and private clubs.
Agent: Pamela H. Cross
Melaja, Creative Arts Association
P.O. Box 848 Peter Stuyvesant Station
New York, NY 10009
(212) 473-4616.

Da Capo Chamber Players
c/o Helen Harbison
545 West 111th Street
New York, NY 10025
(212) 662-3606
Allen Blustine, clarinet; Helen Harbison, violoncello; Joel Lester, violin; Patricia Spencer, flute; Joan Tower, piano.
20th century chamber music exclusively. *Da Capo* refers to the ensemble's practice of repeating a new work or playing two pieces by the same composer in a single concert, in order to increase understanding of the music. Repertoire of 50 works covering the entire 20th century.

Agent: Judith Liegner
1860 Broadway, Suite 1610
New York, NY 10023
(212) 582-5795.

Dalcroze Faculty Ensemble

Dr. Hilda M. Schuster, Director
161 East 73rd Street
New York, NY 10021
(212) 879-0316
Ardyth Alton, violoncello; Arcadie Birkenholz, violin; Claire Coci, organ; Eugenie L. Dengel, viola; William Gephart, baritone voice; David Glazer, clarinet; Edward Gold, piano; Antonio Iervolino, French horn; Andrew Lolya, flute; Patricia Ann Lutness, piano; Homer R. Mensch, double bass; Milton Moskowitz, clarinet; Martin Ormandy, violoncello; Karl Ulrich Schnabel, piano; Hilda M. Schuster, piano; Ralph Silverman, violin; Emanuel Tivin, oboe; Michele Wilt, piano; Manuel J. Zegler, bassoon.
20th century chamber music.
Members are on the faculty of Dalcroze School of Music.

Dal Segno Ensemble

Stanley Hoffman, Director
110 Riverside Drive, Apartment 2E
New York, NY 10024
(212) 724-2807
Variable number of performers, with a maximum of 9. Permanent members: Eleanor Amlen, voice; Stanley Hoffman, first violin; Louise Moed, second violin.
Chamber music, vocal music, new music. Performs works of all eras. Commissions and premieres new pieces. Performs neglected works of earlier centuries.
Agent: Norman J. Seaman
1697 Broadway
New York, NY 10019
(212) 245-9250.

Dorian Wind Quintet

c/o Edith Ann Hall, Manager
Lyra Management, Inc.
16 West 61st Street
New York, NY 10023
(212) 582-5300
Barry Benjamin, French horn; Jerry Kirkbride, clarinet; Karl F. Kraber, flute; Charles Kuskin, oboe; Jane Taylor, bassoon.
Chamber music, new and experimental music. Presents works of all eras, emphasizing contemporary American pieces. Intends to commission American works and expose audiences to new sounds.

Earthforms

c/o MsManagement
463 West Street, Suite 419
New York, NY 10014
(212) 691-0481
Jack Gregg, double bass; Gunter Hampel, flute, vibraphone, composer; Jeanne Lee, voice, poetry, choreography; Steve McCall, drums; Perry Robinson, clarinet.
New music, jazz. Combines poetry, music, and dance rituals. Tours the U.S.A. and abroad.

Eastern Brass

c/o Torrence/Perrotta Management
1860 Broadway
New York, NY 10023
(212) 541-4620
Charles Baxter, French horn; Robert Fanning, trombone; Richard Green, trumpet; Tucker Jolly, tuba; William Wich, trumpet.
Chamber music. Performs brass quintets of all eras.

The Ensemble

Dennis Russell Davies, Conductor
c/o Sheldon Soffer Management, Inc.
130 West 56th Street
New York, NY 10019
(212) 757-8060
George Cochran, Promotion Director
John Beal, double bass; Allen Blustine, clarinet; Julie Feves, bassoon; Gordon Gottlieb, percussion; Barry Jekowsky, percussion; David Jolley, French horn; Betsy Kane, harp; Max Lifschitz, piano; Garrett List, trombone; Linda Moss, viola; Susan Palma, flute; Linda Quan, violin; James Stubbs, trumpet; Joel Timm, oboe; Eric Wilson, violoncello.
20th century chamber music, new and experimental music. Specializes in new music with instrumentation that includes a woodwind quartet, brass trio, and string quartet. Presents the New and Newer Music Series at Alice Tully Hall, Manhattan.

45

Exit
Rick Cutler, Director
36 West 38th Street
New York, NY 10018
(212) 354-0673
Rich Boukas, guitar; Rick Cutler, keyboards; Lawrence Feldman, reeds; Dave Katzenberg, bass; Howie Levy, percussion; Billy Mintz, drums. Jazz, rock music. Performs works by group members who wish to communicate their dreams through music to their audience.

Festival Winds
c/o Melvin Kaplan, Inc.
85 Riverside Drive
New York, NY 10024
(212) 877-6310
Allen Blustine, clarinet; Lester Cantor, bassoon; Ralph Froelich, French horn; Melvin Kaplan, oboe; John Solum, flute; Arthur Weisberg, bassoon.
Chamber music. Performs works of all eras.

Fine Arts Quartet
c/o Melvin Kaplan, Inc.
85 Riverside Drive
New York, NY 10024
(212) 877-6310
Abram Loft, violin; George Sopkin, violoncello; Leonard Sorkin, violin; Bernard Zaslav, viola.
Chamber music. Performs works of all eras.

Four Rivers
Michael Moss, Director
Sunrise Studios
122 2nd Avenue
New York, NY 10003
(212) 533-4030
Greg Kogan, piano; Mike Mahaffay, drums; Michael Moss, clarinets, saxophones, flutes; Badal Roy, tabla; John Shea, bass.
20th century chamber music, new and experimental music, jazz, ethnic music. Blends Western, Indian, Oriental, and Middle Eastern music.

Free Energy
Michael Moss, Director
Sunrise Studios
122 2nd Avenue
New York, NY 10003
(212) 533-4030
Laurence Cook, percussion; Wyldon King, violin; Greg Kogan, piano; Sarah Larson, violin, French

horn; Michael Moss, clarinets, saxophones, flutes; John Shea, bass; Martha Siegel, violoncello; Mark Whitecage, alto saxophone, alto clarinet, flutes; John Wolf, trombone.
20th century chamber music, new and experimental music, jazz, ethnic music. Combines Western, Oriental, Middle Eastern, Indian, African, and Latin music with Tibetan chanting.

Free Life Communications
Michael Moss, President
Sunrise Studios
122 2nd Avenue
New York, NY 10003
(212) 533-4030
Mike Mahaffay, Vice President
Richie Beirach, piano; Laurence Cook, drums; John Fischer, piano; Armen Halburian, percussion; Nancy Janoson, tenor saxophone, reeds; Wyldon King, voice; Dave Liebman, tenor saxophone, reeds; James Madison, drums; Mike Mahaffay, drums; Michael Moss, reeds; Bill O'Connell, piano; Michael Rod, reeds; Badal Roy, tabla; Roberta Rutkin, voice; John Shea, bass; Gloria Tropp, voice; Steve Tropp, poetry; Frank Tusa, bass; Jeff Williams, drums.
Jazz. A cooperative of musicians who combine free jazz with poetry and song.

Galimir Quartet
Felix Galimir, Director
225 East 74th Street
New York, NY 10021
(212) 744-0169
Felix Galimir, first violin; John Graham, viola; Fred Sherry, violoncello; Chiroko Yajima, second violin.
Chamber music. Performs works of all eras, emphasizing the 19th century. Presents 5 annual East Coast concerts, which include American works.

The Jimmy Giuffre 3
Jimmy Giuffre, Director
25 West 15th Street
New York, NY 10011
(212) 924-2863
Jimmy Giuffre, flute, alto flute, bass flute, clarinet, tenor saxophone; Randy Kaye, percussion; Kiyoshi Tokunaga, double bass.
New and experimental music, jazz. Performs works by Jimmy Giuffre.

Philip Glass Ensemble
Philip Glass, Director
c/o Performing Artservices
463 West Street
New York, NY 10014
(212) 989-4953
Jon Gibson, amplified woodwinds; Philip Glass, electric piano, composer; Joan La Barbara, voice, keyboard; Richard Landry, amplified woodwinds; Kurt Munkacsi, audio engineer; Richard Peck, saxophone, flute; Michael Riseman, electric piano.
New and experimental music. Performs amplified music, based on repetitive structure and sustained tones.

The Gotham Trio
William Harry, Director
817 West End Avenue, Apartment 8D
New York, NY 10025
(212) 865-8167
William Harry, violoncello; Leonard Klein, piano; Nannette Levi, violin. Guest artists occasionally included.
Chamber music, new and experimental music. Performs works of all eras, including at least one contemporary work per concert. Presents concerts and clinics in universities.
Agent: Albert Kay Associates, Inc.
58 West 58th Street
New York, NY 10019
(212) 759-7329.

The Group For Contemporary Music
Daniel Shulman, Harvey Sollberger, Charles Wuorinen, Conductors
Manhattan School of Music
120 Claremont Avenue
New York, NY 10027
(212) 749-2802
Variable number of performers. Ronald Anderson, trumpet; Barry Benjamin, French horn; Judith Bettina, voice; Robert Biddlecome, trombone; Virgil Blackwell, clarinet; Allen Blustine, clarinet; Alvin Brehm, double bass; Richard Frisch, voice; Jacob Glick, viola; John Graham, viola; Claire Heldrich, percussion; Susan Jolles, harp; David Jolley, French horn; Jack Kreiselman, clarinet; Donald MacCourt, bassoon; Robert Miller, piano; Ursula Oppens, piano; Donald Palma, double bass; Joe Passaro, percussion; Nora Post, oboe; Linda Quan, violin; Daniel Reed, violin; Gerard Schwartz, trumpet; Fred Sherry, violoncello; Harvey Sollberger, flute; Patricia Spencer, flute;

Stephen Taylor, oboe; Howard Van Hyning, percussion; Charles Wuorinen, piano.
20th century chamber music, new and experimental music. Emphasizes contemporary works by American composers, including electronic and chamber orchestra pieces. Encourages composer involvement in performances. Rehearses extensively when necessary.
Agent: Ruth Uebel
205 East 63rd Street
New York, NY 10021
(212) 753-9527.

Guarneri String Quartet
c/o Harry Beall Management, Inc.
119 West 57th Street
New York, NY 10019
(212) 586-8135
John Dalley, second violin; David Soyer, violoncello; Arnold Steinhardt, first violin; Michael Tree, viola.
Chamber music. Performs works of all eras. Presents concerts, workshops, and master classes. Tours nationally and internationally. Available for residencies.

Interface
John Fischer, Director
83 Leonard Street
New York, NY 10013
(212) 431-5786
John Fischer, piano, voice; Armen Halburian, percussion; Rick Kilburn, bass; Perry Robinson, clarinet; Mark Whitecage, alto saxophone.
New and experimental music, jazz. Performs collective improvisations and works by group members. Encourages audience participation.
Agent: John Stewart
66 West 83rd Street
New York, NY 10024.

International Festivals
Thruston Johnson, Director
c/o Harvey Publications
15 Columbus Circle, 2nd Floor
New York, NY 10023
(212) 582-2244
David Garvey, piano; Thruston Johnson, violin.
Chamber music, new and experimental music. Performs neglected works of the past, and premieres new works. Presents annual International Festival Series.

47

International Percussion
Michael Mahaffay, Director
Sunrise Studios
122 2nd Avenue
New York, NY 10003
(212) 533-4030
Armen Halburian, Armenian percussion; Teiji Ito, Japanese and Haitian percussion; Michael Mahaffay, Western percussion; Badal Roy, tabla.
New and experimental music, jazz.

Istomin, Stern, Rose Trio
c/o Hurok Concerts, Inc.
1370 Avenue of the Americas
New York, NY 10019
(212) 245-0500
Eugene Istomin, piano; Leonard Rose, violoncello; Isaac Stern, violin.
Chamber music. Performs works of all eras. Tours internationally.

Izenzon
David Izenzon, Director
316 East 3rd Street
New York, NY 10009
(212) 254-1777
Variable number of performers with a maximum of 7. Instrumentation: strings, woodwinds, brass, percussion.
Jazz.

Jankry Chamber Ensemble
Larry Karush, Director
7 Lispenard Street
New York, NY 10013
(212) 966-6013
Variable number of performers. Permanent members: Frank Clayton, bass, drums; Jay Clayton, voice, composer; Larry Karush, piano, tabla, composer; Glen Moore, bass.
New and experimental music, jazz. Performs improvisatory music.

Jazz Composer's Orchestra
Michael Mantler, Director
6 West 95th Street
New York, NY 10025
(212) 749-6265
Variable number of performers, ranging from 15 to 25 selected from a pool of 60.
New and experimental music, jazz. Performs and records new jazz compositions. Presents free workshops to rehearse and perform the works of

such composers as Karl Berger, Gunter Hampel, David Izenzon, and Frederic Rzewski.

Jazzmobile, Inc.
S. David Bailey, Executive Director
361 West 125th Street
New York, NY 10027
(212) 866-4900
Jazz. A traveling jazz organization that presents prominent jazz ensembles in free public concerts in the streets of New York City. Gives public school programs that discuss the history of jazz as a unique American art form. Offers instruction in harmony, sight reading, instrumental technique, and ensemble work.

Juilliard Quartet
Robert Mann, Director
c/o Colbert Artists Management, Inc.
111 West 57th Street
New York, NY 10019
(212) 757-0782
Earl Carlyss, violin; Joel Krosnick, violoncello; Robert Mann, violin; Samuel Rhodes, viola.
Chamber music. Performs works of all eras. Premieres major new works.

Joan La Barbara - Voice Is The Original Instrument
Joan La Barbara, Director
127 Greene Street
New York, NY 10012
(212) 533-2022
Bruce Ditmas, percussion; Joan La Barbara, voice, composer.
New and experimental music. Explores the potentialities of the human voice as one of the first sources of music.
Agent: Mimi Johnson
Artservices, Inc.
463 West Street
New York, NY 10014
(212) 989-4953.

Peter La Barbera Quartet
Peter La Barbera, Director
11 West 18th Street
New York, NY 10011
(212) 989-2509
Calvin Hill, bass; Ryo Kawasaki, guitar; Peter La Barbera, vibraharp; Eddy Moore, drums.
Jazz. Performs works by contemporary composers including Chick Corea, Miles Davis, and Freddy Hubbard.

The LaSalle Quartet
c/o Columbia Artists Management, Inc.
165 West 57th Street
New York, NY 10019
(212) 247-6900
Peter Kamnitzer, viola; Jack Kirstein, violoncello;
Walter Levin, violin; Henry Meyer, violin.
Chamber music. Performs works of all eras,
emphasizing the 20th century. Commissions many
works, and tours extensively.
In residence at University of Cincinnati, College-
Conservatory of Music, Ohio.

Hugh Lawson Trio
c/o MsManagement
463 West Street, Suite 419
New York, NY 10014
(212) 691-0481
Louis Hayes, drums; Stafford James, bass; Hugh
Lawson, piano.
Jazz. Performs improvisations and composed
works. Tours the U.S.A. and abroad.

Lenox Quartet
c/o Herbert Barrett Management
1860 Broadway
New York, NY 10023
(212) 245-3530
Toby Appel, viola; Peter Marsh, violin; Donald
McCall, violoncello; Delmar Petty, violin.
Chamber music. Performs works of all eras.
Premieres and commissions works. Tours
internationally.

Light Fantastic Players
Daniel Shulman, Director
340 Riverside Drive
New York, NY 10025
(212) 865-6793
Nancy Allen, harp; Susan Barrett, English horn;
Ken Bell, bass voice; Judith Bettina, soprano
voice; Virgil Blackwell, bass clarinet; Andree
Briere, double bass; Paul Cohen, saxophone;
Rolla Durham, trumpet; Claire Heldrich,
percussion; David Holzman, piano; Steve Johns,
tuba; Glenn Kenwreigh, trombone; Scott Kuney,
guitar; Julie Landsman, French horn; Curtis
Macomber, violin; Lois Martin, viola; Michael
Parloff, flute; Joe Passaro, percussion; Linda
Quan, violin; Laura Rayes-Otalora, clarinet;
Daniel Reed, violin, viola, mandolin; Fred Sherry,
violoncello; Mark Shuman, violoncello; Patricia
Spencer, flute; Steve Taylor, oboe.
20th century chamber orchestra music. Performs
works by European and American composers.
Commissions works.

Lookout Farm
Dave Liebman, Director
Sunrise Studios
122 2nd Avenue
New York, NY 10003
(212) 533-4030
Richard Berrach, piano; Dave Liebman,
saxophones, flutes; Badal Roy, tabla; Frank Tusa,
bass; Jeff Williams, drums.
Jazz, rock, ethnic music. Performs in Boston, New
York and Europe.

Manhattan Saxophone Quartet
Michael Rod, Director
Sunrise Studios
122 2nd Avenue
New York, NY 10003
(212) 533-4030
Ken Berger, baritone saxophone; Thom Gambino,
alto saxophone; Don Palmer, tenor saxophone;
Michael Rod, soprano saxophone.
20th century chamber music, new and
experimental music, jazz. Explores every avenue
open to the saxophone.

Marlboro Trio
c/o Harry Beall Management
119 West 57th Street
New York, NY 10019
(212) 586-8135
Mitchell Andrews, piano; Charles McCracken,
violoncello; Gerald Tarack, violin.
Chamber music.

The Josef Marx Ensemble
Josef Marx, Director
201 West 86th Street, Apartment 706
New York, NY 10024
(212) 799-5214
Susan Barrett, oboe family; Josef Marx, oboe
family; David Miller, bassoon; Ilonna Pederson,
oboe family. Piano and percussion often included.
Chamber music, new and experimental music.
Performs works of all eras. Premieres pieces
written for the ensemble.

49

Metropolitan Opera Studio Ensemble
William Nix, Manager
c/o Sheldon Soffer Management, Inc.
130 West 56th Street
New York, NY 10019
(212) 757-8060
Repertory company of 50 performers, who tour in groups of 5 throughout the U.S.A.
Vocal music of all eras.

Music From Marlboro
c/o Columbia Artists Management, Inc.
165 West 57th Street
New York, NY 10019
(212) 397-6900
A touring ensemble of 3 to 9 musicians who participate in the annual Marlboro Music Festival in Vermont.
Chamber music.

National Chorale
Martin Josman, Director
250 West 57th Street
New York, NY 10019
(212) 582-0870
Variable number of singers, ranging from 4 to 35.
Choral music. Performs exclusively American works, from the Revolutionary Era to contemporary works.

National Jazz Ensemble
Chuck Israels, Director
463 West Street
New York, NY 10014
(212) 989-4665
Variable number of performers, with 17 permanent members. Dennis Anderson, alto saxophone; Benny Aronov, piano; Lisle Atkinson, double bass; David Berger, trumpet; Ken Berger, baritone saxophone; Steve Brown, guitar; Lawrence Feldman, tenor saxophone; Bill Goodwin, drums; Tom Harrell, trumpet; Danny Hayes, trumpet; Greg Herbert; alto saxophone; Chuck Israels, bass; Jimmy Knepper, tuba; Rod Levitt, tuba; Jim Maxwell, trumpet; Sal Nistico, tenor saxophone; Joe Randazzo, bass trombone.
Performs classics of the jazz repertoire, and commissions new works.

Natural Sound
Kirk Nurock, Director
143 West 21st Street
New York, NY 10111
(212) 691-0198 or 532-1100
Variable number of performers, ranging from 4 to 24. Rhythm instruments sometimes included.
New and experimental music, jazz. Explores the sonic range of the human voice and body, based on Kirk Nurock's belief that all human beings are musicians naturally. Nurock states that 'each of us can develop an amazing variety of personal sounds which can be organized and performed as contemporary music.' The ensemble sometimes encourages audience participation.

Max Neuhaus
210 Fifth Avenue
New York, NY 10010
(212) 683-9222
New and experimental music, environmental electronics. Presents electronic music in public spaces, such as subway stations and underground tunnels. This includes permanent sound installations generated by computers from environmental noises. The Metropolitan Transportation Building in New York has such a permanent sound installation.

New American Trio
c/o M. Bichurin Concert Corporation
Carnegie Hall, Suite 609
154 West 57th Street
New York, NY 10019
(212) 586-2349
Thomas Hrynkiv, piano; Esther Evangeline Lamneck, clarinet; Michael McCraw, bassoon.
Chamber music. Performs works of all eras, including solos, clarinet-bassoon duos, clarinet or bassoon-piano duos, and trios.

New Hungarian Quartet
Denes Koromzay, Director
c/o Colbert Artists Management, Inc.
111 West 57th Street
New York, NY 10019
(212) 757-0782
Denes Koromzay, viola; Andor Toth, first violin; Andor Toth, Jr., violoncello; Richard Young, second violin.
Chamber music.

The New Music Consort

Keith Romano, Conductor
251 West 102nd Street
New York, NY 10025
(212) 865-0296

Susan Barrett, oboe; Susan Deaver, flute; Nancy Elan, violin; Claire Heldrich, percussion; Madeline Shapiro, violoncello.

20th century chamber music, new and experimental music. Performs classics of the 20th century, and seldom heard contemporary works. Premieres pieces.

New Structures Ensemble

Matthias Kriesberg, Director
300 Riverside Drive
New York, NY 10025
(212) 663-7621

Johana Arnold, mezzo-soprano voice; Susan Deaver, flute; Nancy Elan, violin; Claire Heldrich, percussion; Mitchell Kriegler, clarinet; Matthias Kriesberg, piano; Nora Post, oboe; Keith Romano, conductor; Madelaine Shapiro, violoncello; Mara Waldman, piano.

20th century chamber music. Intends to advance the standard of contemporary music performance through extensive rehearsals and numerous performances of a repertoire combining works by unknown Americans and more prominent composers.

New Wilderness Events

Charlie Morrow, Director
365 West End Avenue, Apartment 8C
New York, NY 10024
(212) 799-0636

Greg Borst, bells, rattles, flutes, drums, native American flute; Phillip Corner, trombone, percussion, piano, voice; Anna Lockwood, chanting, percussion, recorder, ecologist; Charlie Morrow, bugles, trumpets, rattles, bells; Carol Weber, various flutes and pipes, percussion. Guests frequently included.

Cross-cultural music. Combines music and other aural arts, such as poetry and sound sculpture with natural and animal sounds. Performs American Indian music, Tibetan, Gregorian, and Hebrew Chant; Sacred Harp hymns; and New Guinian Music. Involves the audiences in rituals of healing, laying on hands, and trance states.

The New York Camerata

c/o Glenn Jacobson
135 West 79th Street
New York, NY 10024
(212) 799-6626

Charles Forbes, violoncello; Paula Hatcher, flute, recorder; Glenn Jacobson, piano, harpsichord. Tabla, ethnic flutes, and electric bass occasionally included.

Chamber music. Performs works of all eras. Commissions works. Participates in community residency programs and children's concerts.
Agent: Cone-Sussman Agents
14 East 60th Street
New York, NY 10024
(212) 688-0895.

New York Chamber Soloists

c/o Melvin Kaplan, Inc.
85 Riverside Drive
New York, NY 10024
(212) 877-6310

Fortunato Arico, violoncello; Charles Bressler, tenor voice; Eugene Drucker, violin; Melvin Kaplan, oboe; Karl Kraber, flute; Helen Kwalwasser, violin; Julius Levine, double bass; Ynez Lynch, viola; Harriet Wingreen, piano, harpsichord.

Chamber music. Performs works of all eras.

New York Harp Ensemble

Aristid von Wurtzler, Director
c/o M. Bichurin Concerts Corporation
Carnegie Hall, Suite 609
154 West 57th Street
New York, NY 10019
(212) 586-2349

Harpists: Monika Jarecka, Eva Maria Jaslar Oddo, Dagmar Platilova, Aristid von Wurtzler, Barbara Zofia von Wurtzler.

Chamber music. Performs harp music of all eras, including works by Aristid von Wurtzler. Tours internationally.

New York Jazz Quartet

c/o Raymond Weiss Artist Management, Inc.
300 West 35th Street
New York, NY 10019
(212) 581-8478

Ron Carter, bass; Roland Hanna, piano; Ben Riley, drums; Frank Weiss, flute, saxophone.
Jazz.

51

The New York Kammermusiker
Ilonna Pederson, Director
736 West End Avenue, Apartment 9B
New York, NY 10025
(212) 564-3250 or 749-2207
Chamber music, new and experimental music, jazz. Performs works of all eras for various instrumental combinations. Performs compositions by group members and works that they have commissioned.
Alternate address: Ilonna Pederson
Rural Route 2
Rolette, ND 58366.

New York Masterplayers
Mary Louise Boehm, Director
210 Riverside Drive, Apartment 8G
New York, NY 10025
Arthur Bloom, clarinet; Mary Louise Boehm, piano; Avron Coleman, violoncello; Paul Doktor, viola; Paul Kantor, second violin; Kees Kooper, first violin; Humbert Lucarelli, oboe; John Wion, flute.
Chamber music. Specializes in early romantic and contemporary American works. Tours extensively in the Northeast.
Agent: M. Bichurin Concerts Corporation
Carnegie Hall, Suite 609
154 West 57th Street
New York, NY 10019
(212) 586-2349.

New York Philharmonic Chamber Quintet
c/o Vincent Attractions, Inc.
119 West 57th Street
New York, NY 10019
(212) 765-3047
Lorin Bernsohn, violoncello; Stanley Drucker, clarinet; Kenneth Gordon, violin; David Kates, viola; Newton Mansfield, violin.
Chamber music. Performs works of all eras.
Members belong to the New York Philharmonic Orchestra.

New York Saxophone Quartet, Ltd.
c/o Melvin Kaplan, Inc.
85 Riverside Drive
New York, NY 10024
(212) 877-6310
Ray Beckenstein, soprano saxophone; Walter Kane, baritone saxophone; Al Regni, alto saxophone; David Tofani, tenor saxophone.
20th century chamber music. Performs contemporary saxophone quartets.

New York Woodwind Quintet
Ronald Roseman, Director
c/o Sheldon Soffer Management, Inc.
130 West 56th Street
New York, NY 10019
(212) 757-8060
David Glazer, clarinet; Donald MacCourt, bassoon; Thomas Nyfenger, flute; William Purvis, French horn; Ronald Roseman, oboe.
Chamber music, new and experimental music. Performs works of all eras. Performs and premieres works written for the ensemble.

Notes From Underground
c/o Alyssa Hess
276 Riverside Drive, Apartment 4B
New York, NY 10025
(212) 663-4651
Peter Leonard, Andrew Thomas, Conductors
Nadine Asin, flute; Barbara Bogatin, violoncello; Rolla Durham, trumpet; Alyssa Hess, harp; Barry Jekowski, percussion; Curtis Macomber, violin; Gary McGee, clarinet; Andrew Violette, piano.
20th century chamber music, new music. Performs chamber works by living composers, especially those young or not established. Offers seminars in new music techiques and performance problems.

Open Sky Trio
Dave Liebman, Director
Sunrise Studios
122 2nd Avenue
New York, NY 10003
(212) 533-4030
Dave Liebman, tenor saxophone, soprano saxophone; Bob Moses, drums; Frank Tusa, bass.
New and experimental music, jazz. The trio describes itself as a metaphysical jazz experiment. The music is improvised based upon the following symbolic instrumentation: the drums and bass represent the earth and moving water; the saxophone represents trees, birds, and skyward growth.

Orpheus
Julian Fifer, Director
808 West End Avenue
New York, NY 10025
(212) 850-2220
Violins: Ronnie Bauch, Sin tung Chiu, William Henry, Joanna Jenner, Susan Lang, Eriko Sato, Philip Setzer, Naoko Tanaka; violas: Dan Avshalomov, Guillermo Figueroa, Masao Kawasaki; violoncellos: Julian Fifer, Sharon

Robinson; double bass: Donald Palma; flute: Rebecca Troxler; oboe: Gerard Reuter; clarinet: Jane Hamborsky; bassoons: Michael McCraw, Peter Simmons; French horns: David Jolley, Dennis Lawless.

Chamber orchestra music. Performs works of all eras without conductor.

Agent: Charles Strickland

Torrence/Perrotta Management

1860 Broadway

New York, NY 10023

(212) 541-4620.

Orpheus Trio

Michael Ries, Director

Columbia Artists Management, Inc.

165 West 57th Street

New York, NY 10019

(212) 247-6900

Heidi Lehwalder, harp; Scott Nickrenz, viola; Paula Robison, flute.

Chamber music.

Parnassus

c/o Florence Moed

504 A Grand Street

New York, NY 10002

(212) 254-4342

Lori Berkowitz, violin, viola; Katharine Flanders, flute; Florence Moed, piano; Meryl Sacks, clarinet; Jane Ziff, mezzo-soprano voice.

20th century chamber music, new music. Performs vocal and instrumental pieces, devoting extensive rehearsals to new works.

The Barberi Paull Musical Theatre, Inc.

Barberi Paull, Director

345 West 58th Street

New York, NY 10019

(212) 586-7051

Richard Averre, choral music coordinator; Eddie Fay, percussion; John Glasel, trumpet; Gordon Gottlieb, percussion; Paul Keuter, piano; Loraine Persson, dancer; Judith Valentine, actress.

20th century chamber music, new and experimental music, jazz, musical theater. Performs multi-media works, combining theater, music, and electronics. Many works are by group members.

The Performers' Committee For Twentieth-Century Music

Joel Sachs, Cheryl Seltzer, Directors

333 West End Avenue, Apartment 16C

New York, NY 10023

Variable number of performers.

20th century chamber music. Presents the annual Composer's Retrospective Series in Manhattan, featuring the works of one 20th century composer per concert. Presents concerts, master classes, and dicussion groups in colleges outside New York.

Perigee

John Shea, Director

Sunrise Studios

122 2nd Avenue

New York, NY 10003

(212) 533-4030

Ramsay Ameen, violin; Laurence Cook, drums; John Shea, bass; Mark Whitecage, reeds.

20th century chamber music, new and experimental music, jazz, ethnic music. Improvises music based on Eastern and Middle Eastern forms, emphasizing a cross-cultural stylistic blend.

Poum!

John Fischer, Director

83 Leonard Street

New York, NY 10013

(212) 431-5786

Laurence Cook, percussion; John Fischer, piano, voice; Armen Halburian, percussion; Rick Kilburn, bass; Mike Mahaffay, percussion; Michael Moss, reeds; Perry Robinson, clarinet; John Shea, bass; Mark Whitecage, saxophone.

New and experimental music, jazz. Performs new music and experimental jazz written by group members.

Quad Delay Performers

Richard Landry, Director

10 Chatham Square

New York, NY 10038

(212) 962-6048

Richard Landry, flute, saxophone, guitar, bamboo flutes; Kurt Munkasci, mixers, amplifiers, speakers, tape recorders.

New and experimental music. Experiments with quadrophonic sound, using modern and primitive instruments. Performs experimental saxophone works.

Jude Quintiere And Musicians
Jude Quintiere, Director
47 Greene Street
New York, NY 10013
(212) 226-7837
Sin Cha Hong, dancer; Dave Chamberlain, flute; Frank Clayton, bass, percussion; Jay Clayton, voice; Joan La Barbara, voice; Bob Mover, alto saxophone; Barbara Oldham, French horn; Jude Quintiere, synthesizer; Judy Sherman, voice.
New and experimental music. Performs works by Jude Quintiere and other group members.

Reality Unit Concept
William J. Hooker, Director
444 West 52nd Street
New York, NY 10019
(212) 581-6470
Variable number of performers. Instrumentation: brass, double bass, percussion.
New music.

Steve Reich And Musicians
Steve Reich, Director
16 Warren Street
New York, NY 10007
(212) 925-1107
Robert Becker, percussion, keyboard; Steve Chambers, keyboard, percussion; Jay Clayton, voice; Pamela Fraley, voice; Ben Harms, percussion, viola da gamba; Russell Hartenberger, percussion, keyboard; Janice Jarrett, voice; James Preiss, percussion, keyboard; Steve Reich, percussion, keyboard, composer; Leslie Scott, piccolo, bass clarinet; Glen Velez, percussion, keyboard.
New and experimental music. Performs music by Steve Reich exclusively.

Revolutionary Ensemble
c/o Leroy Jenkins
P.O. Box 838 Peter Stuyvesant Station
New York, NY 10009
(212) 255-9145
Jerome Cooper, percussion, piano; Leroy Jenkins, violin, viola; Sirone, double bass, trombone.
New and experimental music, jazz. Performs contemporary black American concert music.

Marco Rizo Latin-Jazz Percussion Ensemble
Marco Rizo, Director
310 Lexington Avenue
New York, NY 10016
(212) 867-5521
Instrumentation: flute, saxophone, drums, conga drums, piano, electric piano, bass, voice.
Jazz. Performs contemporary Latin American jazz, attempting to demonstrate its influence on North American jazz.

Romeros Quartet
Herbert O. Fox, Charles K. Jones, Directors
Columbia Artists Management, Inc.
165 West 57th Street
New York, NY 10019
(212) 247-6900
Guitars: Angel Romero, Celedonio Romero, Celin Romero, Pepe Romero.
Chamber music. Performs guitar solos, duos, trios, and quartets of all eras. Commissions works. Tours extensively.

St. Luke's Chamber Ensemble
Michael Feldman, Conductor
487 Hudson Street
New York, NY 10014
(212) 924-5960
Joseph Anderer, French horn; David Hopkins, clarinet; Jack Kalowick, bass; Louise Schulman, viola; Stephen Taylor, oboe; Rebecca Troxler, flute; Richard Vrotny, bassoon.
Chamber music, new music. Performs works of all eras, including rarely heard chamber operas performed with St. Luke's Chapel Choir. Commissions and premieres American works.

Shirley Scott Trio
c/o MsManagement
463 West Street, Suite 419
New York, NY 10014
(212) 691-0481
Eddie Gladden, drums; Shirley Scott, organ; Harold Vick, tenor saxophone.
Jazz. Offers concerts and workshops in the U.S.A. and abroad.

The Gregg Smith Singers
Gregg Smith, Director
171 West 71st Street
New York, NY 10023
(212) 877-7817
16 to 20 performers. Soprano voices: Catherine Aks, Mary Barnidge, Elizabeth Farr, Sharon

Powers, Patricia Price, Rosalind Rees; alto voices: Linda Eckard, Fay Kittleson, Priscilla Magdoma, Suzanne Maslanka; tenor voices: Thomas Bogdan, William Carey; Jeffrey Meyer, Paul Parker; bass voices: Albert de Ruiter, Lin Garber, Patrick Mason, James Pfafflin, Jan Opalach.

20th century choral chamber music. Performs works of all eras, emphasizing the 20th century and American works.

Agent: Walter Gould
Century Artists, Inc.
866 Third Avenue
New York, NY 10022
(212) 752-3921.

Soho Ensemble

Gerard Schwarz, Director
131 Prince Street
New York, NY 10012
(212) 982-7855 or 533-6027

John Deak, double bass; Natasha Ghent, viola; Sherman Goldscheid, violin; Jerry Grossman, violoncello; Leonard Hindell, bassoon; Bert Lucarelli, oboe; John Moses, clarinet; Al Regni, flute; Gerard Schwarz, trumpet; Don Whyte, violin.

Chamber music. Performs works of all eras.

Sonic Arts Union

Mary Elizabeth Johnson, Administrator
c/o Performing Artservices, Inc.
463 West Street
New York, NY 10014
(212) 989-4953

4 composer-performers: Robert Ashley, David Behrman, Alvin Lucier, and Gordon Mumma.

New and experimental music, electronic music. Robert Ashley writes theatrical works concerned with social conditions. David Behrman and Gordon Mumma design their own systems of electronic components for sound production and control. Alvin Lucier is concerned with natural systems, such as brainwaves, bat and dolphin sonar, and resonant frequencies of rooms.

Speculum Musicae

c/o Ursula Oppens
777 West End Avenue, Apartment 5B
New York, NY 10025
(212) 865-9593
Fred Sherry, President

Virgil Blackwell, clarinet; Paul Dunkel, flute; Richard Fitz, percussion; John Graham, viola; Karen Lindquist, harp; Ursula Oppens, piano;

Don Palma, double bass; Joe Passaro, percussion; Daniel Reed, violin; Rolf Schulte, violin; Gerard Schwarz, trumpet; Fred Sherry, violoncello; Steven Taylor, oboe. Guest artists often included.

20th century chamber music, new and experimental music. Performs works of this century exclusively, including new pieces and classics. Seeks to establish important new works within the standard repertoire of the 20th century through repeated performances.

Agent: Susan Wadsworth
Young Concert Artists
75 East 55th Street
New York, NY 10022
(212) 759-2541.

The Heiner Stadler Quartet

Heiner Stadler, Director
106 Haven Avenue
New York, NY 10032
(212) 568-3455

Musicians vary, but have included: Heiner Stadler, piano; Tyrone Washington, tenor saxophone, flute; Lenny White, drums; Reggie Workman, bass.

Jazz. Performs works by Heiner Stadler.

The Heiner Stadler Sextet

Heiner Stadler, Director
106 Haven Avenue
New York, NY 10032
(212) 568-3455

Musicians vary, but have included: Garnett Brown, trombone; Joe Chambers, drums; Joe Farrell, tenor saxophone; Don Friedman, piano; Jimmy Owens, trumpet; Barre Phillips, bass.

Jazz. Performs works by Heiner Stadler.

Tarack Chamber Ensemble

Gerald Tarack, Director
133 West 94th Street
New York, NY 10025
(212) 865-8464

Alvin Brehm, double bass; Kenneth Cooper, harpsichord; William Draper, clarinet; Jeanne Benjamin Ingraham, violin; Harold Jones, flute; Caroline Levine, viola; Charles McCracken, violoncello; Henry Schuman, oboe; Gerald Tarack, violin.

Chamber music. Performs works of all eras without conductor.

Tashi
Peter Serkin, Director
c/o Frank Salomon Associates
201 West 54th Street, Apartment 4C
New York, NY 10019
(212) 581-5197
Ida Kavafian, violin; Peter Serkin, piano; Fred
Sherry, violoncello; Richard Stoltzman, clarinet.
Chamber music. Performs works of all eras. Tours
internationally.

The Telephone
c/o Judith Otten
Perzanowski Management
155 West 81st Street
New York, NY 10024
(212) 787-0517
Edgar Dittemore, baritone voice; Judith Otten,
soprano voice. Pianist varies.
20th century operatic music. Performs Gian Carlo
Menotti's *The Telephone*, and other vocal works.

Todays Percussion Quartet
c/o Robert Gardiner, Manager
170 West 73rd Street
New York, NY 10023
(212) 873-5666
Percussionists: Paul Dowling, Norman Freeman,
Richard Kravetz, Scott Stevens.
Chamber music, new and experimental music.
Performs percussion works of all eras,
emphasizing contemporary pieces. Commissions
and premieres works. Presents master classes,
symposia, and concerts in community residencies.

Uni-Trio
Perry Robinson, Director
519 Broome Street
New York, NY 10013
(212) 226-1189
David Izenzon, bass; Randy Kaye, percussion;
Perry Robinson, clarinet.
Jazz. Performs original works.

Unity
J. Byron Morris, Director
c/o Eraa Productions, Inc.
G.P.O. Box 2301
New York, NY 10001
Frank Clayton, percussion, bass; Jay Clayton,
voice; Charles Ewbanks, piano, electric piano;
Lenny Martin, bass; Vince McEwan, trumpet,
flugelhorn; Byron Morris, alto saxophone, soprano
saxophone; Tyrone Walker, drums.

New and experimental music, jazz.
Alternate address:
J. Bryan Morris
P.O. Box 1723
Wheaton, MD 20902
(301) 598-5561.

Vermeer Quartet
c/o Michael Ries
Columbia Artists Management, Inc.
165 West 57th Street
New York, NY 10019
(212) 397-6900
Shmuel Ashkenasi, violin; Nabuko Imai, viola;
Marc Johnson, violoncello; Pierre Menard, violin.
Chamber music.
In residence at Northern Illinois University, De
Kalb.

Vieuxtemps String Quartet
c/o Masako Yanagita
435 West 57th Street, Suite 5P
New York, NY 10019
(212) 663-4198
Marnie Hall, second violin; Linda Lawrence,
viola; Evalyn Steinbock, violoncello; Masako
Yanagita, first violin.
Chamber music, new and experimental music.
Performs string quartets of all eras.

Voices For The 20th Century
Laurel Miller, Director
945 West End Avenue, Apartment 9C
New York, NY 10025
(212) 865-4056
Soprano voices: Gwendolyn DeLuca, Anna
Jeffrey, Gena Rangel, Mary Washburn.
20th century vocal ensemble music. Performs solo
and ensemble pieces for voice, including stage
works. Works closely with composers.

The Western Wind
Steven Urkowitz, Dramatic Advisor
c/o Colbert Artists Management, Inc.
111 West 57th Street
New York, NY 10019
(212) 757-0782
Lawrence Bennett, tenor voice; William Lyon Lee,
tenor voice; Elliot Levine, baritone voice; Janet
Steele, soprano voice; Janet Sullivan, soprano
voice; William Zukof, countertenor voice.
Vocal chamber music. Performs vocal sextets of all
eras, emphasizing works from the Middle Ages

through the Baroque period, and early American works. Commissions new works.

West Side Madrigalists
Judith Otten, Director
c/o Perzanowski Management
155 West 81st Street, Suite 5H
New York, NY 10024
(212) 787-0517
Albert de Ruiter, bass voice; Darrell Lauer, tenor voice; Judith Otten, soprano voice; Jacqueline Pierce, mezzo-soprano voice.
Vocal chamber music. Performs works of all eras, presenting special programs concerning Americana, Christmas, and the Renaissance.

The Whirlwinds
Kenneth Adams, Director
c/o G. Wagner
262 West 107th Street, Apartment 3B
New York, NY 10025
(212) 681-3447 or 666-8318
Kenneth Adams, clarinet; Hal Archer, flute; Edward Dieck, French horn; David Miller, bassoon; Geraldine Wagner, oboe.
Chamber music. Performs woodwind quintets of all eras, emphasizing works of this century. Premieres works.

Queens

Jungle Telegraph
Aiye Niwaju, Director
187-37 Tioga Drive
St. Albans, NY 11412
(212) 527-1582
Variable number of performers and instruments. Aiye Niwaju, flugelhorn; Yomi, African percussion. Instruments used by other performers: vibraphone, marimba, horn, drums, double bass.
Ethnic music. Performs African-American, African-Caribbean, and improvisational music in order to blend contemporary jazz with its African roots. Is dedicated to the perpetuation of African-American culture.

Musica Oggi
Marc-Antonio Consoli, Director
95-27 239th Street
Bellerose, NY 11426
(212) 347-8190
Variable number of performers, ranging from 3 to 6. Marc-Antonio Consoli, conductor; Elizabeth Szlek-Consoli, flute.

Staten Island

The Staten Island Chamber Music Players
Georgiana DiMauro, General Manager
27 Storer Avenue
Staten Island, NY 10309
(212) 356-2094
Variable number of performers, ranging from 1 to 16. Permanent members: Mary Barto, flute; Barry Bilowitz, clarinet; Daniel Bremer, bassoon; Victor DeRenzi, conductor; Caesar DiMauro, oboe; Georgiana DiMauro, French horn; Edward Greenstein, trombone; Robert Gresh, French horn.
Chamber music, chamber orchestra music. Performs works of all eras, including contemporary American pieces and works by local composers.

York Electric Ensemble
David Ernst, Director
2198 Richmond Road
Staten Island, NY 10306
(212) 979-0498
Jeffrey Berman, percussion; David Ernst, electronics; Grant Harders, electric bass; Lon Ivey, percussion; Raymond Reid, trombone.
New and experimental music, jazz. Performs free improvisations combined with live electronic sounds.
In residence at York College, City University of New York.

North Carolina

Clarion Wind Quintet
Mark Popkin, Director
North Carolina School of the Arts
P.O. Box 4657
Winston-Salem, NC 27104
(919) 784-7170
Frederick Bergstone, French horn; Philip Dunigan, flute; Robert Listokin, clarinet; Mark Popkin, bassoon; Joseph Robinson, oboe.
Chamber music.

Duke Jazz Ensemble
Jerry Coker, Director
Duke University
Music Department
Durham, NC 27708
(919) 684-3426
17 student performers.
A course in modern jazz performance.

New and experimental music. Performs music by young composers.

The Purple Why
Steven Tintweiss, Director
P.O. Box 509 Middle Village
Flushing, NY 11379
(212) 894-7231
Laurence Cook, drums; James DuBoise, trumpet; Charles Gerardi, percussion; Randy Kaye, percussion; Steven Tintweiss, double bass, voice; Mark Whitecage, alto saxophone, flute.
Jazz. Performs collective improvisations, and compositions by group members.
Agent: Harvey Michelman
Michelman and Michelman
250 West 57th Street, Suite 701
New York, NY 10019
(212) 586-1410.

Riverside Woodwind Quintet
Kent Eanes, Director
41-34 Frame Place
Flushing, NY 11355
(212) 939-5132
Kent Eanes, flute; Paul Harris, bassoon; David Niethamer, clarinet; Barbara Oldham, French horn; Patricia Wurst, oboe.
Chamber music, new music. Performs works of all eras, emphasizing 20th century music.

Steven Inkwhite Tintweiss Group
Steven Tintweiss, Director
P.O. Box 509 Middle Village
Flushing, NY 11379
(212) 894-7231
Charles Brackeen, tenor saxophone, soprano saxophone; Pat Dursi, piano, electric piano; Rosalie Harman, voice; Michael Keith, trombone; Billy Mintz, percussion; Judy Stuart, voice, guitar; Steven Tintweiss, double bass, melodica, Buchla synthesizer, voice.
New and experimental music, multi-media, jazz. Performs works by group members, often combining electronic music, singing, dancing, poetry, and visual art.
Alternate address:
Steven Tintweiss
41-15 46th Street, Apartment 5N
Flushing, NY 11379.

East Carolina University Faculty Woodwind Quintet
John Heard, Director
East Carolina University
School of Music
Greenville, NC 27834
(919) 758-6851
Marie Davis, flute; John Heard, oboe; George Knight, clarinet; James Parnell, French horn; Vincent Pitt, bassoon.
Chamber music. Performs works of all eras. Provides East Carolina University music students with a standard of performance.

Experimental Music Project
Dr. David W. Maves, Director
Duke University Music Department
P.O. Box 6695 College Station
Durham, NC 27708
(919) 684-2534
Variable number of performers and instruments.
New and experimental music. Intends to encourage and expand the imaginations of local composers and performers, and increase the public awareness of contemporary music activities. Includes film makers, sculptors, painters, dancers, and audiences in performances.

New Music Ensemble
Dr. Roger Hannay, Director
University of North Carolina
Chapel Hill, NC 27514
(919) 933-2276
Variable number of student performers, ranging from 1 to 24.
20th century chamber music, new and experimental music. Performs works by students and established composers.

Piedmont Chamber Orchestra
Nicholas Harsanyi, Conductor
P.O. Box 4657
Winston-Salem, NC 27107
(919) 784-7170
25 performers. Instrumentation: woodwinds, brass, percussion, strings.
Chamber orchestra music. Performs works of all eras.
Many members are on the faculty of North Carolina School of the Arts.
Agent: Herbert Barrett Management
1860 Broadway
New York, NY 10023
(212) 245-3530.

Razoumovsky String Quartet
Emile Simonel, Director
410 Keating Drive
Winston-Salem, NC 27104
(919) 768-0710
Marion Davies, violoncello; David Moskovitz, violin; Elaine Richey, violin; Emile Simonel, viola. Frequently included: oboe, flute, clarinet.
Chamber music, new and experimental music. Performs works of all eras.
Agent: Raymond Weiss Artist Management, Inc.
300 West 55th Street
New York, NY 10019
(212) 581-8478.

University Of North Carolina Jazz Laboratory Band
John R. Harding, Director
University of North Carolina
Room 110, Hill Hall
Chapel Hill, NC 27514
(919) 933-3915
20 student performers. Instrumentation: 5 trumpets, 4 trombones, tuba, 5 saxophones, percussion, piano, guitar, bass.
A course in jazz performance, presenting 12 annual concerts at University functions, night clubs, festivals, and on television.

Ohio

Ashland College Jazz Ensemble
Curt Wilson, Director
Ashland College
Ashland, OH 44805
(419) 289-5151
18 to 21 student performers. Instrumentation: 5 to 6 trumpets, 5 trombones, tuba, 5 to 6 saxophones, percussion, drums, piano, bass.
Jazz. Rehearses and performs contemporary and traditional jazz.

Bowling Green Woodwind Quintet
David Melle, Director
Bowling Green State University
College of Musical Arts
Bowling Green, OH 43402
(419) 372-2181
John Bentley, oboe; Edward Marks, clarinet; David Melle, flute; Robert Moore, bassoon; Herbert Spencer, French horn. Guest artists occasionally included.
20th century chamber music. Performs works of all eras at campus concerts and on tour. Presents clinics and lecture-demonstrations.
In residence at Bowling Green State University.

The Brass Company
c/o Alex Howard, Manager
Lee-Fam Enterprises
16303 Stockbridge Avenue
Cleveland, OH 44128
(216) 991-2693
Harry Hall, trumpet; Bill Hardman, trumpet; Billy Higgins, drums; Lonnie Hilliard, trumpet; A. Clifton Lee, flugelhorn; Bill Lee, double bass; Eddie Preston, trumpet; Charles Stevens, trombone; Bob Steward, tuba; Kiane Zawadi, euphonium.
Jazz.

The Cleveland Brass Quintet
Harry B. Herforth, Director
2940 Coleridge Road
Cleveland Heights, OH 44118
(216) 932-6668
Richard Barth, tuba; Robert Dolwick, second trumpet; Harry B. Herforth, first trumpet; James Taylor, trombone; Charles Ward, French horn.
Chamber music. Performs works of all eras at concerts, lecture-recitals, and clinics. Performs in the greater Cleveland area school system.

The Descendants Of Mike And Phoebe
c/o Alex Howard, Manager
Lee-Fam Enterprises
16303 Stockbridge Avenue
Cleveland, OH 44128
(216) 991-2693
Billy Higgins, percussion; A. Clifton Lee, flugelhorn, trumpet; Bill Lee, double bass; A. Grace Lee Mims, soprano voice; Consuela Lee Moorehead, piano.
Jazz. Performs African-American music, using elements of blues, spirituals, and folk music. Members compose and arrange most of the music performed.

Ensemble For New Music.
David Cope, Director
Miami University
Music Department
Oxford, OH 45056
(513) 523-8820
David Bell, trumpet; David Cope, violoncello, piano, bass; Winford Cummings, conductor; David Felder, synthesizer; Sam Pellman, piano,

synthesizer; Steven Scherff, percussion. Guests included: James Powers, tenor voice; Colleen Roberts, piano.
20th century chamber music, new and experimental music. Performs contemporary works, emphasizing experimental compositions written since 1950.

The Heidelberg Trio
c/o John Rinehart
Heidelberg College
Tiffin, OH 44883
(419) 448-2505
Jean Moore, violoncello; Ronald Pepper, violin; John Rinehart, piano.
Chamber music, new and experimental music. Performs works of all eras at Ohio college campuses and performing arts centers.
In residence at Heidelberg College.

Clifford Jordan Quartet I
c/o Alex Howard, Manager
Lee-Fam Enterprises
16303 Stockbridge Avenue
Cleveland, OH 44128
(216) 991-2693
Stanley Cowell, piano; Billy Higgins, drums; Clifford Jordan, tenor saxophone; Bill Lee, double bass.
Jazz.

Clifford Jordan Quartet II
Alex Howard, Manager
Lee-Fam Enterprises
16303 Stockbridge Avenue
Cleveland, OH 44128
(216) 991-2693
Billy Higgins, drums; Sam Jones, double bass; Clifford Jordan, tenor saxophone; Cedar Walton, piano.
Jazz.

Kent State University Faculty Brass Quintet
c/o Paul Wallace
Kent State University
Kent, OH 44242
(216) 672-2172
Christine Dolce, trumpet; Samuel Gindin, French horn; Harry Herforth, trumpet; Richard Jacoby, tuba; Paul Wallace, trombone.
Chamber music. Performs contemporary and early works in concerts and clinics on campus and throughout Northeastern Ohio.
In residence at Kent State University.

The La Salle Quartet
University of Cincinnati
College-Conservatory of Music
Cincinnati, OH 45221
(513) 475-2883
Peter Kamnitzer, viola; Jack Kirstein, violoncello; Walter Levin, violin; Henry Meyer, violin.
Chamber music. Performs works of all eras, emphasizing the 20th century. Commissions many works, and tours extensively.
In residence at University of Cincinnati, College-Conservatory of Music.
Agent: Columbia Artists Management, Inc.
165 West 57th Street
New York, NY 10019
(212) 247-6900.

New Music Ensemble And New Music Singers
Dr. Kenley Inglefield, Director
Bowling Green State University
College of Musical Arts
Bowling Green, OH 43403
(419) 372-2181
Variable number of student performers. 16 voice choir; instrumentation for any size ensemble up to a chamber orchestra.
20th century chamber music, new and experimental music.

Plum Creek Chamber Ensemble
Lawrence McDonald, Director
Oberlin Conservatory of Music
Oberlin, OH 44074
(216) 774-1221 Ext. 3182
Sanford Margolis, piano; Lawrence McDonald, clarinet; Marilyn McDonald, violin; Marlene Ralis Rosen, soprano voice; Michael Rosen percussion. Violoncello, flute, and synthesizer occasionally included.
Chamber music, new and experimental music. Performs works of all eras. Performers are on faculties of the Oberlin Conservatory of Music and the Cleveland Institute of Music.

Wittenberg String Ensemble
Marcia Leigh Ferritto, Director
Wittenberg School of Music
Springfield, OH 45501
(513) 327-7211
19 student performers. Instrumentation: 10 violins, 4 violas, 3 violoncellos, double bass, harpsichord. Winds and voice included when necessary.
String and chamber orchestra music.

Oklahoma

Living Arts Chamber Ensemble
Virginia Myers, Director
1436 South Oswego
Tulsa, OK 74112
(918) 936-6772
Dwight Dailey, clarinet; Jan Dailey, flute; Jean Douglass, violoncello; Robert McNally, violin; Virginia Myers, piano; Melvyn Raimon, percussion; James Reeves, double bass; Kay Ross, organ, harpsichord; Suzanne Tipps, soprano voice.
20th century chamber music, new and experimental music, multi-media. Performs new works for college and community audiences. Encourages community participation in program planning.

Oregon

The University Of Oregon Brass Choir
Ira D. Lee, Director
University of Oregon
School of Music
Eugene, OR 97403
(503) 686-3774 or 344-4151
26 student performers.
Chamber Music. A course in brass ensemble performance.

Pennsylvania

The Alard Quartet
c/o Joanne Zagst
Pennsylvania State University
105 Music Building
University Park, PA 16802
(814) 865-0431
Leonard Feldman, violoncello; Donald Hopkins, second violin; Raymond Page, viola; Joanne Zagst, first violin.
Chamber music. Performs string quartets of all eras, premiering many American works. Presents concerts at many schools, lecture-demonstrations, workshops, and clinics. Tours extensively.
In residence at Pennsylvania State University.
Agent: Raymond Weiss
Raymond Weiss Artists Management
300 West 55th Street
New York, NY 10019
(212) 581-8478.

Artists-In-Residence Quartet
Ivan Romanenko, Conductor
Thiel College
Department of Music
Greenville, PA 16125
(412) 588-7700
Herbert Neurath, viola; Lilly Neurath, violoncello; Carmen Romanenko, second violin; Ivan Romanenko, first violin.
Chamber music, new and experimental music.
In residence at Thiel College.

Carnegie-Mellon University Contemporary Music Ensemble
Leonardo Balada, Director
Carnegie-Mellon University
Department of Music
Pittsburgh, PA 15213
(412) 621-2600
Variable number of student performers.
20th century chamber music, new and experimental music. Presents contemporary works, including some theater pieces in collaboration with the University Drama Department.

Contemporary Players And Singers
Clifford Taylor, Director
Temple University
College of Music
Philadelphia, PA 19122
(215) 787-8313
Variable number of student performers.
20th century chamber music, new and experimental music. Performs music of the 20th century exclusively. Concerned with learning the performance techniques of the contemporary repertoire, paying particular attention to rhythm, tuning, and interpretation. Presents concerts, and rehearses regularly.

The Count Downs
J. Kenneth Delmar, Director
Drexel University
Philadelphia, PA 19104
(215) 895-2452
18 student performers. Instrumentation: 4 to 5 trumpets, 4 trombones, 5 saxophones, percussion.
A course in jazz performance.

Curtis String Quartet
Max Aronoff, Director
301 South 21st Street
Philadelphia, PA 19103
(215) 732-3966
Max Aronoff, viola; Jascha Brodsky, violin;
Orlando Cole, violoncello; Yomi Ninomiya, violin.
Chamber music. Performs works of all eras,
locally and on tour.
In residence at the New School of Music,
Philadelphia.

The Davidsbund Trio
Charles Parker, Director
148 Decatur Road
Havertown, PA 19083
(215) 446-3717
Pianists: Richard Amoroso, Sandra Carlock,
Charles Parker.
20th century chamber music, new music. Performs
contemporary pieces for 3 pianos, working closely
with composers.

De Pasquale String Quartet
c/o William de Pasquale
532 General Lafayette Road
Merion Park, PA 19066
(215) 667-5449
Joseph de Pasquale, viola; Robert de Pasquale,
second violin; William de Pasquale, first violin;
William Stokking, violoncello. Sylvia Glickman,
piano, is often included.
Chamber music. Performs works of all eras at
campus and community concerts.
In residence at Haverford College, Pennsylvania.

Derry Brass Quintet
Richard B. Hiler, Director
324 Leearden Road
Hershey, PA 17033
(717) 534-1587
Samuel Basehore, tuba; Harry Folmer, French
horn; William Grove, trombone; Richard Hiler,
trumpet; Edward Lewis, trumpet.
Chamber music. Performs in many concerts for
students, emphasizing 20th century music.

Johnstown Jazz Workshop
John E. Morris, Director
601 Somerset Street
Johnstown, PA 15901
(814) 539-3512
Trumpets: Ben Arellano, Craig Faulkner, Dick
Gardenhour, Nick Jacobs, Larry Shaffer;

trombones: Fred Fornwalt, Jim Holtzman, Bill
Scileny, Paul Walker; tuba: Kevin Wilson;
saxophones: Mike Stefanik, Lou Stinich, Bob
Tilley, George Voight; drums: Mike Bodolosky;
percussion: Jim Ballow, Mark Spenger; piano:
John Morris; bass: Oliver Haselrig.
Performs traditional and contemporary big band
jazz, including works by John E. Morris, Director.

Eric Kloss Quartet
Eric Kloss, Director
c/o Thomas G. Dreibelbis
115 Lenor Drive
State College, PA 16801
(814) 234-0762
Vince Guarico, piano, keyboards; Eric Kloss, alto
saxophone, tenor saxophone, soprano saxophone;
Dave LaRoca, bass; Spider Rondenilli, drums,
percussion.
Jazz. Performs improvisatory works.

Lafayette College Jazz Band
Leonard S. Geissel, Jr., Director
203 Lafayette College
203 Jenks Hall
Easton, PA 18042
(215) 253-6281 Ext. 329
22 member student ensemble. Instrumentation: 5
trumpets or flugelhorns, 3 tenor trombones, 2 bass
trombones, tuba, 2 alto saxophones, 2 tenor
saxophones, baritone saxophone, drums, piano, 2
guitars, electric bass.
Jazz. An extra-curricular musical activity, which
provides jazz performing experience.

Mozan's Dream
Kenny Gehret, Director
Rural Delivery 3
Wernersville, PA 19565
(215) 678-6272
Tim Baum, oboe, English horn, recorder, tenor
saxophone, flute, voice, percussion, vibraphone,
piano; Kenny Gehret, guitar, organ, piano, violin,
voice, percussion, Skip Moyer, double bass,
electric bass, voice, percussion; L. J. Palmer,
drums, percussion, voice, piano; Tom Smith,
soprano saxophone, alto saxophone, tenor
saxophone.
New and experimental music, jazz. Performs
works by group members for 2 to 5 performers on
acoustic and electric instruments.

Musica Orbis
c/o Susan Gelletly
302 Avondale Road
Wallingford, PA 19086
(215) 565-3207
Kitty Brazelton, voice, flute; David Clark, bass, percussion, keyboards, voice; Caille Colburn, harp, keyboards, voice; Susan Gelletly, keyboards, percussion, voice; Tom Stephenson, percussion, violoncello, synthesizer, voice.
New and experimental music. Performs original works exclusively, ranging from improvisatory to fully composed pieces. Incorporates jazz, folk, rock, medieval, and Eastern musical influences. Functions as a full time professional musical cooperative.
Alternate address:
P.O. Box 77
Walnut Hill Farms
Chester Heights, PA 19017.

New Art String Quartet
Peter Kucirko, Director
240 South Hutchinson Street
Philadelphia, PA 19107
(215) 627-5898
Maria Adamo, viola; Peter Kucirko, violoncello; Margaret Ma, violin; Michael Ma, violin.
Chamber music. Performs works of all eras.
Agent: Robert Arrow
Robert Arrow Music Enterprises
130 South 18th Street
Philadelphia, PA 19103
(215) 561-3838.

Panorphic Duo
c/o Claire Polin
374 Bairo Road
Merion, PA 19066
(215) 664-1923
Jude Mollenhauer, harp; Claire Polin, flute. Guest artists frequently included.
Chamber music, new and experimental music. Performs flute-harp duets of all eras, avoiding transcriptions. Premieres works in international performances.

Penn Contemporary Players
Richard Wernick, Director
University of Pennsylvania
518 Annenberg Center Court
Philadelphia, PA 19174
(215) 243-6244
Variable number of student and professional performers. Permanent members: Lance Elbeck, violin; Elin Frazier, trumpet; Dorothy Freeman, oboe; James Freeman, double bass; Barbara Haffner, violoncello; Allison Herz, clarinet; Jeffrey Langford, French horn; Anthony Orlando, percussion; Glenn Steele, percussion.
20th century chamber music, new music. Performs works for combinations of voices and instruments, including string quartets and cantatas, in a concert series at Harold Prince Theatre, Annenberg Center, University of Pennsylvania.
Alternate address:
University of Pennsylvania
Department of Music
201 South 34th Street, D8
Philadelphia, PA 19174.

Philadelphia Composers' Forum
Joel Thome, Director
H-305 Garden Court
4631 Pine Street
Philadelphia, PA 19143
(215) 747-2883
Chris Finckel, violoncello, guitar, sitar; Romulus Franceschini, electronics; Sue Kahn, flute; Jack Kulowitch, double bass; Arthur Maddox, piano; Eric Rosenblith, violin, viola; Michael Sirotta, percussion; Joel Thome, conductor; Richard Wasley, clarinet; Lawrence Weller, voice; Christopher Wolfe, clarinet; David Woodhull, percussion.
20th century chamber music, new and experimental music. Performs new works, commissioning 6 compositions annually. Performs the works of over 250 composers. Tours internationally.

Philadelphia New Music Group
Theodore Antoniou, Director
Philadelphia Musical Academy
313 South Broad Street
Philadelphia, PA 19107
(215) 735-9635
Variable number of performers, with a maximum of 20.
20th century chamber music.

The Philadelphia Trio
c/o Deborah Reeder
201 Cheswold Lane
Haverford, PA 19041
(215) 642-1361
Elizabeth Keller, piano; Deborah Reeder, violoncello; Barbara Sonies, violin.

Chamber music.

Pitt Composers Forum
Frank L. McCarty, Director
University of Pittsburgh
Music Department
Pittsburgh, PA 15260
(412) 624-4126
Variable number of graduate student composer-performers.
20th century chamber music, new and experimental music. Performs works by the faculty and students of the University of Pittsburgh.

Plus Orbis
Tom Stephenson, Director
302 Avondale Road
Wallingford, PA 19086
(215) 566-4029
Kitty Brazelton, voice, flute; David Clark, bass, percussion, voice; Caille Colburn, harp; Susan Gelletly, keyboards; Tom Stephenson, vibraphone, percussion.
20th century chamber music, new and experimental music. Attempts to demonstrate the basic unity that the musical experience offers amidst a diversity of style and form.

Satori Woodwind Quintet
Charles Holdeman, Director
P.O. Box 144
New London, PA 19360
(215) 869-9572
Charles Holdeman, bassoon, recorders; Patricia Valley Holdeman, flute, alto flute, piccolo, recorder; Robert Kendel, oboe, English horn; Timothy Maloney, clarinets, soprano saxophone, alto saxophone; Scott Temple, French horn.
Chamber music. Performs works of all eras, emphasizing the 20th century, in concerts, clinics, and workshops.
In residence at the University of Delaware.

Scranton Theatre Libre
Rory Giovanucci, Executive Director
Brooks Building, Suite 514
Scranton, PA 18503
(717) 344-4553
New and experimental music. A theater group which features some original contemporary music in musical and non-musical plays.

Temple University Trio
c/o Joanne Rile Management
119 North 18th Street
Philadelphia, PA 19103
(215) 569-4500
Alexander Fiorillo, piano; Michael Haran, violoncello; Helen Kwalwasser, violin.
Chamber music. Performs piano trios of all eras throughout the U.S.A.
In residence at Temple University, Pennsylvania.

The Thalia Trio
Robert Baisley, Director
Pennsylvania State University
Music Department
University Park, PA 16802
(814) 865-0431
Robert Baisley, piano; Leonard Feldman, violoncello; Joanne Zagst, violin.
Chamber music, new and experimental music. Performs piano trios of all eras.
In residence at Pennsylvania State University.

West Chester State College Jazz Ensemble
James Sullivan, Director
West Chester State College
West Chester, PA 19380
(215) 436-2678
15 to 20 student performers. Instrumentation: 5 trumpets, 5 trombones, 5 saxophones, percussion.
Contemporary jazz.

West Chester State College New Music Ensemble
Larry Nelson, Director
West Chester State College
School of Music
West Chester, PA 19380
(215) 436-2937
Variable number of student performers. Permanent members: Martin Beech, violin, viola; Jan Coward, clarinet; Cynthia Folio, flute; Robert Hoch, clarinet; Connie Middleton, violoncello; Albert Moretti, trumpet; Willis Rapp, percussion; Tom Stephenson, percussion.
20th century chamber music, new and experimental music.

Rhode Island

New Music Ensemble Of Providence
George Goneconto, Conductor
17-Keene Street
Providence, RI 02906
(401) 421-7038

Janet Chapple, violoncello; Linda Ellison, piano; George Goneconto, conductor, percussion; Thomas Greene, guitar, mandolin; Delight Immonen, oboe; Frank Marinaccio, clarinet; Barbara Poalarikas, violin; Margot Schevill, mezzo-soprano voice; Gerald Shapiro, synthesizer.

Performs 20th century chamber music, new and experimental music exclusively. Performs post-World War II chamber works and unknown pieces of the earlier 20th century in schools, community centers, and universities.

Manager: June Massey
65 Prospect
Providence, RI 02906
(401) 751-0053.

South Carolina

Galliard Woodwind Quintet
Robert Chesebro, Director
308 Covington Road
Greenville, SC 29609
(803) 246-5301

Gayle Chesebro, French horn; Robert Chesebro, oboe; Martha Hamilton, flute; Richard Manson, bassoon; Edmund Winston, clarinet.

Chamber music. Performs woodwind quintets of all eras.

South Dakota

Augustana Trio
Tyrone Greive, Director
Augustana College
Sioux Falls, SD 57102
(605) 336-5459

Janet Greive, violoncello; Tyrone Greive, violin; Mary Helen Schmidt, piano.

Chamber music.

Tennessee

Jazz Collegians
Aaron Schmidt, Director
Austin Peay State University
Clarksville, TN 37040
(615) 648-7818

22 to 25 student performers. Instrumentation: 5 trumpets, 5 trombones, 5 saxophones, percussion. A course in big band jazz.

Middle Tennessee State University Jazz Ensemble
Dr. John R. Duke, Director
Middle Tennessee State University
Murfreesboro, TN 37130
(615) 898-2490

Variable number of student performers. Instrumentation: 5 trumpets, 4 trombones, 5 saxophones, percussion, piano, guitar. A course in jazz performance.

The Nashville Baroque And Classical Society, Inc.
Patrick McGuffey, Conductor
835 J. C. Bradford Building
Nashville, TN 37219
(615) 255-1163

Concertmasters: Carl Gorodetzky, Sheldon Kurland; first violins: George Binkley, John Kelingos, Steven Smith, Mary Curtis Taylor, Stephenie Woolf; second violins: Virginia Christensen, Jo Ann Cruthirds, Lawrence Herzberg, Lillian Hunt, Marilyn Smith, Carol Walker; violas: David Becker, Marvin Chantry, Ovid Collins, Gary Van Osdale; violoncellos: Jean Bills, Roy Christensen, Martha Shipman, Peter Spurbeck; double basses: Ann Migliore, Ernest Szugyi; flutes: Jane Kirchner, Norma Rogers; clarinets: Dan Hearn, Stephen Sefsik; oboes: Laura Baker, Sharon Kane, Robert Taylor; bassoons: Cynthia Estill, Jon Sullivan; French horns: Jay Dawson, David Elliott, Eberhard Ramm; trumpets: George Cunningham, Kirby Lawson; timpani: William Wiggins; harpsichord: Peter Fyfe.

Chamber orchestra music. Performs works of all eras, emphasizing new music. Plans to become a recording orchestra, with a short concert season of free performances.

New Music Ensemble
Stephen E. Young, Director
University of Tennessee
Music Department
Knoxville, TN 37916
(615) 974-5164
Variable number of student performers, ranging
from 10 to 14. Instrumentation: flute, oboe,
clarinet, bassoon, French horn, trumpet,
trombone, percussion, keyboard, violin, viola,
violoncello, double bass.
20th century chamber music, new and
experimental music.

Tennessee Tech Troubadours
Wayne Pegram, Director
Tennessee Tech University
P.O. Box 5045
Cookeville, TN 38501
(615) 528-3165
16 to 22 student performers. Instrumentation: 5
woodwinds, 2 French horns, 5 trumpets, 5
trombones, tuba, percussion, piano, double bass.
A course in jazz performance.

University Of Tennessee Faculty Brass Quintet
c/o Ed Niedens
University of Tennessee
Music Department
Knoxville, TN 37916
(615) 974-3241
Bill Bommelje, French horn; Don Hough,
trombone; Sande MacMorran, tuba; Ed Niedens,
trumpet; Steve Squires, trumpet.
Chamber music, new and experimental music.
Performs brass trios, quartets, and quintets of all
eras, on campus and throughout Tennessee.
Presents concerts, clinics, and workshops in
communities.
In residence at the University of Tennessee.

Texas

Andraud Woodwind Quintet
Lee Gibson, Director
North Texas State University
School of Music
Denton, TX 76203
(817) 788-2545
Lee Gibson, clarinet; Clyde Miller, French horn;
George Morey, flute; Melvin Solomon, bassoon;
Charles Veazey, oboe.
Chamber music. Performs woodwind works for 3
to 5 players.

Beaux Eaux Brass Quintet
See Les Beaux Eaux Brass Quintet.

The Chamber Arts Ensemble
Arthur Ephross, Business Manager
9203 Regal Road
San Antonio, TX 78216
(512) 226-8167 or 342-8007
Clarence Bading, French horn; James Dickie,
bassoon; Arthur Ephross, flute; M. Fallis, piano,
organ, harpsichord; David Herbert, oboe; Jean
White, piano, organ, harpsichord; Ronald White,
clarinet; Flicka Wilmore, voice. Guest violoncellist
and harpist often included.
Chamber music. Performs works of all eras. Asks
composers to write for the ensemble.

Hespa!
Mark Holden, Director
5251 Grape Street
Houston, TX 77035
(713) 667-1696
Student ensemble of approximately 27 performers.
Instrumentation: woodwinds, brass, percussion,
keyboard, strings, vocal quartet.
Jazz.

Les Beaux Eaux Brass Quintet
Sterling Procter, Director
1308 Myrtle Street
Denton, TX 76201
(817) 387-7628
David Dorrough, tuba; Mike Funderburk,
trumpet; Sterling Procter, French horn; Dwight
Robinett, trombone; Ray Sasaki, trumpet.
Chamber music, new and experimental music.
Performs brass quintets of all eras, including
transcriptions of early works. Premieres and
commissions works. Members are affiliated with
North Texas State University, Denton, Texas.

Live Band
Freddy McLain, Director
8958 West 41st Street
Houston, TX 77018
(713) 681-3760
David Carey, double bass, electric bass; Keith
Karnaky, drums; Freddy McLain, acoustic guitar,
electric guitar; Lindy Pollard, flute, clarinet,
percussion.
Jazz.

Protean Woodwind Quartet

Noah A. Knepper, Director
3408 Westcliff Road South
Ft. Worth, TX 76109
(817) 927-0321
Gilbert Hills, flute, clarinet, baritone saxophone; Noah A. Knepper, flute, oboe, clarinet, alto saxophone; James Mahoney, flute, clarinet, soprano saxophone; Wallace Roberts, alto flute, clarinet, tenor saxophone, bassoon.
Chamber music, jazz. Performs works of all eras for flute quartet, clarinet quartet, saxophone quartet, or mixed woodwinds (flute, oboe, clarinet, bassoon).

Texas A & I Jazz Workshop

Dr. Joseph L. Bellamah, Director
Texas A & I University
Kingsville, TX 78363
(512) 595-2805
22 student performers. Instrumentation: 5 trumpets, 5 trombones, 5 saxophones, percussion.
A course in jazz performance.

University Of Texas Experimental Jazz Ensemble

Glen Daum, Director
University of Texas
Department of Music
Austin, TX 78712
(512) 471-2491
Variable number of student performers, ranging from 16 to 21.
Instrumentation: 5 woodwinds, 5 trumpets, 4 trombones, tuba, percussion, piano, guitar, double bass.
A course in jazz performance.

The University Of Texas Percussion Ensemble

George Frock, Director
University of Texas
Department of Music
Austin, TX 78712
(512) 471-2491
Variable number of student performers, ranging from 8 to 15.
20th century chamber music. Performs contemporary percussion and mallet ensemble works.

Utah

University Of Utah Jazz Ensembles

Loel T. Hepworth, Director
University of Utah
Salt Lake City, UT 84112
(801) 581-6762
18 to 24 student performers, often divided into small ensembles.
A course in jazz performance.

Utah Brass Ensemble

Stephen B. Ivey, Director
University of Utah
Music Hall
Salt Lake City, UT 84112
(801) 581-6762
Edward Allen, French horn; Charles Eckenrode, tuba; Stephen B. Ivey, trombone; Forrest Stoll, trumpet; William Sullivan, trumpet; Henry Wolking, trombone.
Chamber music. Performs brass works of all eras in campus and community concerts.
In residence at the University of Utah.

Vermont

The Jazzman's Bag

Richard Cutts, Director
7 Shaw Circle
Northfield, VT 05663
(802) 485-7250
Robert S. Bourdon, cornet; Richard Cutts, tenor saxophone; William Kinzie, drums; Edward Ledwith, bass; Sheldon Truax, guitar.
Jazz. Performs lecture-demonstrations for student and community audiences.

Northern Lights Ensemble

Melissa Brown, Director
P.O. Box 39 RFD
Lyndonville, VT 05851
(802) 626-5807 or 626-3335
Ray Anderson, violin, viola; Tom Asher, trumpet; Neil Boyer, oboe; Melissa Brown, violoncello, harpsichord; Peter Brown, violoncello, double bass; Anne Dorsam, piano; Alvin Shulman, violin; Don Stewart, clarinet, saxophone; Susan Stewart, flute, piccolo; Brian Taylor, classical guitar.
Chamber music, new and experimental music. Performs works of all eras throughout New England.

Trio Di Monti
c/o John Koch
P.O. Box 330
Norwich, VT 05055
(802) 295-5343
Elizabeth Clendenning, violin; John Koch, piano;
Bettina Roulier, violoncello.
Chamber music. Performs piano trios of all eras.

Virginia

Norfolk Chamber Consort
Allen Shaffer, Director
624 Redgate Avenue
Norfolk, VA 23507
(804) 622-4542
Laszlo Aranyi, second violin; Sandra Barnes,
French horn; William Bartdotta, trumpet; Mary
Ann Coe, flute; F. Gerard Errante, clarinet;
Patrick Gainer, oboe; Marian Harding, harp; H.
Burton Kester, bassoon; Janet Kriner, violoncello;
John Lindberg, percussion; John McCormick,
viola; Harold Protsman, piano; Clifford Rice,
trombone; Allen Shaffer, keyboard; Peter Zaret,
first violin.
20th century chamber music. Performs mainly
20th century music. Performs some works from
the 17th, 18th, and 19th centuries.
Many members are principals in the Norfolk
Symphony Orchestra.

Richmond Sinfonia
Jacques Houtmann, Conductor
112 East Franklin Street
Richmond, VA 23219
(804) 648-4461
Concertmaster: Jonathan Mott; first violins: Denis
Brown, Helen Coulson, Mark Lamprey, Celia
Moulyn; second violins: Mildred Boyer, Jane
Kapeller, Robert Land, Sharon Mitchell, Martha
Mott; violas: Ruth Erb, Leslie Mann, Raymond
Montoni, Carol Sasson; violoncellos: Todd
Hemmenway, June LeGrand, Frantisek Smetana;
double bass: Peter Bahler; flute: Judith Eastman
Britton; oboe: John O'Bannon; clarinet: Robert
Barker; bassoon: Jonathan Friedman; French
horn: Christian Wilhjelm.
Chamber orchestra music. Performs works of all
eras. Commissions and premieres works. Tours
extensively in Virginia.

Washington

American Sampler
Robert Suderburg, Director
c/o Olympic Artists Management
P.O. Box 15302 Wedgewood Station
Seattle, WA 98115
(206) 523-1554
Stuart Dempster, trombone, euphonium; Victor
Steinhardt, piano; Elizabeth Suderburg, soprano
voice; Robert Suderburg, piano.
Chamber music. Performs American works of the
19th and 20th century exclusively.

Cappa Trio
c/o Olympic Artists Management
P.O. Box 15302 Wedgewood Station
Seattle, WA 98115
(206) 523-1554
Charles Brennand, violoncello; Irwin Eisenberg,
violin; Helen Tazeriniti, piano.
Chamber music. Performs works of all eras,
particularly contemporary music. Available for
tours.

**The Contemporary Group At The University Of
Washington**
William Bergsma, William O. Smith, Directors
University of Washington
School of Music, DN 10
Seattle, WA 98195
(206) 543-1178
Variable number of student and professional
performers.
20th century chamber music, new and
experimental music. Performs exclusively works of
the 20th century, including solo and chamber
orchestra works. Repertoire includes conservative
and experimental pieces. Premieres and
commissions works.
In residence at the University of Washington.

**Eastern Washington State College New Music
Ensemble**
Roxann Ekstedt, Dennis Michel, Directors
Eastern Washington State College
Music Department
Cheney, WA 99004
(509) 359-2521
Variable number of student and professional
performers. Permanent members: Roxann
Ekstedt, viola; Dennis Michel, bassoon. Faculty
and guest artists included.
20th century chamber music, new and

experimental music. A course in contemporary chamber music performance.

The Jazz Workshop
Dr. Ralph D. Mutchler, Director
Olympic College
Music Department
Bremerton, WA 98310
(206) 478-4537
20 student performers. Instrumentation: 5 woodwinds, 5 trumpets, 5 trombones, percussion. New and experimental music, jazz.

Kronos String Quartet
David Harrington, Director
10724 Fremont Avenue North
Seattle, WA 98133
(206) 632-7923 or 364-4531
Walter Gray, violoncello; David Harrington, first violin; Tim Kilian, viola; James Shallenberger, second violin. Vocalist and dancer sometimes included.
Chamber music, new and experimental music. Performs works of all eras, emphasizing contemporary compositions. Premieres many works. Presents a minimum of 60 concerts per year. Plans to tour internationally in the future.

Music and Light
William O. Smith, Director
c/o Olympic Artists Management
P.O. Box 15302 Wedgewood Station
Seattle, WA 98115
(206) 523-1554
David Shrader, percussion; William O. Smith, clarinet.
20th century chamber music, new and experimental music, multi-media, jazz. Performs clarinet and percussion works of the 20th century. Tours extensively.

Philadelphia String Quartet
c/o Irwin Eisenberg
University of Washington
Music Department
Seattle, WA 98105
(206) 543-1200 or 543-6698
Charles Brennand, violoncello; Irwin Eisenberg, violin; Alan Iglitzin, viola; Veda Reynolds, violin.
Chamber music. Performs works of all eras. Commissions one new American work annually. Presents concerts, seminars, and coaching sessions on campus and on tour.
In residence at the University of Washington.

Soni Ventorum Wind Quintet
Felix Skowronek, Director
c/o Olympic Artists Management
P.O. Box 15302 Wedgewood Station
Seattle, WA 98115
(206) 523-1554
Arthur Grossman, bassoon; Christopher Leuba, French horn; William McColl, clarinet; Felix Skowronek, flute; Laila Storch, oboe.
Chamber music. Performs wind quintets of all eras. Tours extensively.
In residence at the University of Washington, Seattle.

West Virginia

Percussion '70
Phil Faini, Director
West Virginia University
Creative Arts Center
Morgantown, WV 26506
(304) 293-4501
Percussionists: Reed Bigham, Mark Cappellini, Tom Cunningham, Jeff Everett, Will Gilliam, Fred Griffen, John Grisso, Steve Lizotte, Barry Maughan, James Miltenberger, Frank Perry, Bob Ryczek, Randy Smith, Al Wrublesky.
20th century chamber music, African music, jazz. Performs percussion works at colleges and universities throughout the Eastern U.S.A.
Agent: James Benner
421 Richwood Avenue
Morgantown, WV 26505
(304) 292-6774.

Wisconsin

Fine Arts Quartet
Leonard Sorkin, Director
University of Wisconsin
School of Music
Milwaukee, WI 53211
(414) 272-0817
Abram Loft, violin; George Sopkin, violoncello; Leonard Sorkin, violin; Bernard Zaslav, viola.
Chamber music. Performs works of all eras.
Agent: Melvin Kaplan, Inc.
85 Riverside Drive
New York, NY 10024
(212) 877-6310.

The Geary Larrick Quartet
Geary Larrick, Director
University of Wisconsin
Department of Music
Stevens Point, WI 54481
(715) 346-3107
Tom Dehlinger, guitar; Geary Larrick, vibraphone; Jim Tucker, drums; Dennis Wayerski, bass.
New music, jazz. Performs improvisatory and notated experimental music.

Music From Almost Yesterday Ensemble
Yehuda Yannay, Director
University of Wisconsin
Department of Music
Milwaukee, WI 53201
(414) 228-4507
Variable number of performers, with a maximum of 14.
20th century chamber music, new and experimental music, multi-media. Presents a broad range of contemporary music, including pieces for live electronics, and theater. Emphasizes American composers.

New Music Ensemble
Conrad De Jong, Director
University of Wisconsin
Music Department
River Falls, WI 54022
(715) 425-3183
Variable number of student performers.
New and experimental music. A course in contemporary music performance. The class studies and performs many compositional and notational styles.

New Music Ensemble
Vincent McDermott, Sigmund Snopek, Directors
Wisconsin College-Conservatory
1584 North Prospect Avenue
Milwaukee, WI 53211
(414) 276-4350
Variable number of student performers.
A course in new and experimental music performance.

Pro Musica Nova
Tele Lesbines, Vincent McDermott, Directors
Wisconsin College-Conservatory
1584 North Prospect Avenue
Milwaukee, WI 53211
(414) 276-4350

Variable number of performers. Pavel Burda, percussion; Stephen Colburn, conductor, oboe; Russel Dagon, clarinet; Lee Dougherty, soprano voice; Margaret Hawkins, conductor of chamber choir; Danis Kelly, harp; Tele Lesbines, percussion; Vincent McDermott, electronics; Janet Millard, flute; Dennis Najoom, trumpet; Janet Ruggeri, viola; Roger Ruggeri, double bass; Marlee Sabo, soprano voice; Kenneth Schermerhorn, conductor; Donald St. Pierre, keyboard; James Yoghourtjian, guitar.
20th century chamber music. Performs all styles of 20th century chamber music.
Some members are on the faculty of Wisconsin College-Conservatory; some are in the Milwaukee Symphony Orchestra.

What On Earth
Mitchell Covic, Director
1716 North 38th Street
Milwaukee, WI 53208
(414) 342-6670
Mitchell Covic, double bass; L. Cowen, piano; J. Grassell, guitar; A. LoDuca, percussion; William Schaefgen, trombone.
Jazz. Performs works by group members.

Wisconsin Brass Quintet
Donald R. Whitaker, Director
University of Wisconsin
School of Music
Madison, WI 53706
(608) 263-1930
Nancy Becknell, French horn; Barry Hopper, trumpet; Fritz Kaenzig, tuba; William Richardson, trombone; Donald R. Whitaker, trumpet.
Chamber music. Performs works of all eras.
In residence at the University of Wisconsin.

Wisconsin Contemporary Music Forum
John Downey, Director
University of Wisconsin
School of Fine Arts-Music
Milwaukee, WI 53201
(414) 964-8158
New and experimental music. Performs works by composers born or educated in Wisconsin. A rotating group of professional performers from Wisconsin universities dedicated to performing contemporary music.

Wyoming

Western Arts Trio
David Tomatz, Director
University of Wyoming
Department of Music
Laramie, WY 82071
(307) 766-5242
Brian Hanly, violin; Werner Rose, piano; David Tomatz, violoncello. Instruments and artists included as required: viola, clarinet, oboe, violin, vocalist.
Chamber music, new and experimental music. Performs piano trios of all eras, emphasizing contemporary works. Commissions and premieres works in concerts at the Western Arts Summer Festival, and in Europe.
In residence at the University of Wyoming.

Agent: Pietro Menci
International Artists Agency
1564 18th Avenue
San Francisco, CA 94122
(415) 661-1962.

The Wyoming Woodwind Quintet
Charles Seltenrich, Director
University of Wyoming
Laramie, WY 82070
(307) 766-4181
Maryellen Delp, flute; Theodore Lapina, bassoon; Charles Seltenrich, oboe; William Stacy, French horn; Ralph Strouf, clarinet. Pianist sometimes included.
Chamber music, new and experimental music. Performs quintets of all eras in concerts and workshops throughout Wyoming.
In residence at the University of Wyoming.

Sponsoring Organizations

The sponsoring organizations listed here support music performance in the following ways:
1. They fund performing ensembles directly with grants, residencies, or competition awards
2. They fund agencies which sponsor performances or ensembles
3. They provide supportive services, such as publicity, administration, and booking
4. They donate facilities
5. They present or produce concerts and musical events

Some organizations listed must be asked precisely what kind of contemporary music activities they will support. They have only expressed a general interest in music. Others have indicated an interest in contemporary music, but have only noted projects supported in general areas such as chamber, orchestral, or operatic music.

Since budgets change rapidly and fiscal years vary, the budgetary information given here is only a general guide to the reader. Organizations submitted their budgets to us from November 1974 through April 1975.

Sponsor names followed by an asterisk were obtained from secondary sources. Contact these organizations directly for further information.

Fund Raising

Prepare to approach a potential sponsor in the following manner:
1. Know as much as possible about the sponsor, including his pattern of giving.
2. Be able to defend your project or organization, explain how you conform to the sponsor's pattern of giving, and what special needs you are able to meet.
3. Send him the following documents:
   A. A concise cover letter explaining:
   1. Who you are
   2. What your project is
   3. What needs it will fulfill
   4. Why you are approaching this particular sponsor
   5. What the full amount required is
   6. What amount you hope to obtain from this sponsor
   7. What other sources of funding you are seeking
   Conclude your letter by requesting an appointment.
   B. A concise proposal stating:
   1. The name of the project
   2. The person responsible
   3. The problem with which this project deals
      a. History of the problem
      b. Solution provided by this project
   4. Future plans, after receipt of funding, for becoming self-sustaining
   C. An exact budget which should include:
   1. Salaries of project personnel, including fringe benefits and payroll taxes
   2. Operating costs of project, including office rental, telephone, postage, stationery
   D. Proof of tax exempt status
   E. Financial statement, if available, or total budget of organization
   F. Appropriate supportive literature, such as brochures, 2 or 3 objective reviews, resumés of personnel, sample programs, photographs
4. The appointment. Be prompt, alert, and able to defend clearly the need for your organization or services.

5. Follow-up letter. Thank the potential sponsor for his interest and invite him to a performance, exhibit, or to observe your office operations.

6. If the grant is received, promptly send a letter thanking the sponsor.

For further information concerning foundations, consult:

The Foundation Center
888 Seventh Avenue
New York, NY 10019

The Foundation Center
1001 Connecticut Avenue, N.W.
Washington, D.C. 20036

Donor's Forum
208 South La Salle Street
Chicago, IL 60604

For further information concerning corporate support of music, consult:

Business Committee for the Arts, Inc.
1700 Broadway
New York, NY 10019

For further information concerning community arts agencies, consult:

Associated Councils of the Arts
1564 Broadway
New York, NY 10036

Sponsoring Organizations

Alabama

State Arts Agency:

Alabama State Council On The Arts And Humanities
M. J. Zakrzewski, Executive Director
322 Alabama Street
Montgomery, AL 36104
(205) 832-6758
Supports 20th century chamber music, jazz.
Provides technical and financial assistance to local organizations in sponsoring activities of quality in the various arts disciplines and the humanities.
Music Budget: $50,000-$99,000; 10%-20% for 20th century music.

Allied Arts Council Of Metropolitan Mobile*
Charles Manchester, Executive Director
401 Auditorium Drive
Mobile, AL 36602
(205) 432-9796
Supports chamber music.

Arts And Humanities Council Of Tuscaloosa County*
Doris Leapard, President
P.O. Box 2056
Tuscaloosa, AL 35401
(205) 345-4459
Supports chamber music, jazz, symphonic music, popular music.

Brewton Council Of The Arts*
Bob Maple, President
P.O. Box 432
Brewton, AL 36426
(205) 867-4832 or 867-7568
Supports symphonic music, operatic music, folk music.

Cherokee County Arts Council, Inc.*
Mary George Waite, Executive Director
P.O. Box 366
Centre, AL 35960
(205) 927-5189
Supports symphonic music, folk music.

Chilton County Fine Arts Guild*
Mary McKae, President
P.O. Box 776
Clanton, AL 35045
(205) 755-0722 or 755-0155
Supports chamber music.

Choctaw County Arts Council, Inc.
Judy Donellan, Executive Director
P.O. Box 188
Butler, AL 36904
(205) 459-2816
A county agency.
Supports 20th century chamber music, new and experimental music, jazz.
Provides performing facilities. Sponsors performances in public schools and universities. Encourages low-cost community performances.
Music Budget: $1,000.00-$4,999.00; 31%-40% for 20th century music.

Crenshaw Arts Council*
Dr. Warren Williams, President
P.O. Box 388
Luverne, AL 36049
(205) 355-5174 or 355-3585
Supports ethnic music.

Dale County Council Of Arts And Humanities*
Mrs. John Vowvalidis, President
P.O. Box 971
Ozark, AL 36360
(205) 774-9552
Supports chamber music.

DeKalb County Arts Council*
Edward L. Nelson, Chairman
East District Attorney's Office
DeKalb County Courthouse
Ft. Payne, AL 35967
(205) 845-1124
Supports chamber music, symphonic music, ethnic music.

Enterprise Music Club
Mrs. Fred W. Smith, Executive Director
1511 41st Street
Birmingham, AL 35208
(205) 822-3804
A private foundation serving Southern Alabama.

75

Supports vocal music, religious music.
Provides performing facilities, publicity. Promotes creative and performing arts in Southern Alabama.
Music Budget: $100.00-$499.00; 21%-30% for 20th century music.

Greater Birmingham Arts Alliance
J. R. Horlacher, Executive Director
P.O. Box 3325
Birmingham, AL 35205
(205) 251-1228
A non-profit organization.
Coordinates local arts activities.

Houston Arts And Humanities Council*
Mrs. William Nomberg, Chairman
P.O. Box 1369
Dolthan, AL 36301
(205) 792-3164
Supports chamber music.

Huntsville Chamber Music Guild
Kathleen Shuck, Executive Director
2112 Cecille Drive S.W.
Huntsville, AL 35803
(205) 881-9210
A non-profit organization.
Supports chamber music.
Provides financial support, performing facilities, advertising, and accommodations. Sponsors a concert series, Huntsville Chamber Music Guild Student Chamber Ensemble Festival, and workshops.
Music Budget: $100.00-$499.00; 21%-30% for 20th century music.

Jefferson County Committee For Economic Opportunity
G. David Singleton, Executive Director
1728 Third Avenue North
Birmingham, AL 35203
(205) 328-1545
Serves Jefferson County.
Supports African-American music.
Provides financial support. Exposes and educates in the arts economically disadvantaged youth. Provides Community Theatre for concerts.
Music Budget: $25,000.00-$49,000.00; 31%-40% for 20th century music.

Marion City Commission On Arts And Humanities*
James L. Scruggs, Jr., Chairman
City Hall
Marion, AL 36756
(205) 368-8135 or 683-2701
Supports jazz, symphonic music, popular music.

McCraney Arts Council*
James L. Bush, President
P.O. Box 607
Tallassee, AL 36078
Supports chamber music, folk music.

Mountain-Valley Council On The Arts
A. W. Laser, Jr., Executive Director
P.O. Box 177
Albertville, AL 35950
(205) 878-2136
Edwin C. Price, President
A non-profit organization serving Marshall County.
Supports 20th century chamber music, jazz.
Provides financial support. Sponsors jazz clinics and concerts and promotes music appreciation. Provides educational services and encourages community involvement in the arts.
Music Budget: $1,000.00-$4,999.00; 61%-70% for 20th century music.

Seminar Council Of Montgomery*
Mrs. Jen Mooney, Chairman
P.O. Box 511
Montgomery, AL 36101
(205) 262-5711 Ext. 200
Supports chamber music, operatic music, folk music.

Sylacauga Music Study Club
P.O. Box 803
Sylacauga, AL 35150
A private music club.
Brings music programs to its members and the community.
Music Budget: Under $100.00; 10%-20% for 20th century music.

Lurleen B. Wallace Community Arts Council
Toni Fountain Sikes, Executive Director
Lurleen B. Wallace State Junior College
Andalusia, AL 36420
(205) 222-6591
A regional agency serving Crenshaw, Choctaw, and Covington Counties.

Supports 20th century chamber music, new and experimental music, jazz, musical theater, popular music.

Promotes the arts in the community by encouraging local artists to perform and create.

Music Budget: $5,000.00-$9,999.00; Under 10% for 20th century music.

Alaska

State Arts Agency:

Alaska State Council On The Arts
Roy Helms, Executive Director
360 K Street, Suite 240
Anchorage, AK 99501
(907) 272-5342
Supports 20th century chamber music, new and experimental music, jazz, popular music.
Organizes tours to communities for 10 ensembles or soloists annually. Provides Alaskan audiences with programs not commercially feasible.
Music Budget: Over $100,000.00.

Alaska Association For The Arts*
Mrs. Wilbur B. Walker, President
P.O. Box 2786
Fairbanks, AK 99707
(907) 456-6769
Supports chamber music, jazz, symphonic music, popular music.

Anchorage Arts Council, Inc.
Carol Derfner, Executive Director
419 West 7th Avenue
Anchorage, AK 99501
(907) 274-7324
A community arts council serving Anchorage.
Supports 20th century chamber music, new and experimental music, jazz.
Provides financial support, performing facilities, administrative support. Coordinates musical activities in the community by arranging concert series, booking concerts and tours, and promoting contemporary music appreciation.

Anchorage Community College
Arts Affiliates and Special Programs
Mary Hale, Coordinator
2533 Providence Avenue
Anchorage, AK 99504
(907) 279-6622 Ext. 310
Supports campus jazz performances.
Provides performing facilities.

Bethel Council On The Arts*
Donna Dinsmore, Executive Director
P.O. Box 264
Bethel, AK 99559
(907) 543-2098
Supports chamber music, jazz, operatic music, symphonic music.

Cordova Arts And Pageants
Mazie Van Den Brock, Executive Director
P.O. Box 71
Cordova, AK 99574
(907) 424-3486
A non-profit concert association serving Cordova.
Supports new and experimental music, jazz.
Sponsors concerts, art shows, and workshops. Solicits out-of-state ensembles for performances.
Music Budget: $1,000.00-$4,999.00; 71%-80% for 20th century music.

Glenallen Committee On The Arts*
Nancy Davidson, President
P.O. Box 254
Glenallen, AK 99588
(907) 822-3360
Supports chamber music, jazz, operatic music, ethnic music, popular music.

Greater Juneau Arts And Humanities Council*
Joseph A. Sonneman, Chairman
P.O. Box 562
Juneau, AK 99801
(907) 789-7492
Supports chamber music, jazz, symphonic music, popular music.

Ketchikan Arts Council
Marjorie Cloudy, President
P.O. Box 621
Ketchikan, AK 99901
(907) 225-4548
A city agency serving Ketchikan.
Serves as a liason between state and local arts councils in seeking funding, coordinating cultural activities, promoting the arts and artists, and helping develop arts facilities.

Kivalina Arts Committee
Brian Paust, Executive Director
Kivalina School
Kivalina, AK 99750
A non-profit organization serving Kivalina.
Supports various types of music.
Provides financial support and performing

facilities. Supports local development of the arts by exposing the community to a wide variety of performers and performances.
Music Budget: $1,000.00-$4,999.00; 91%-100% for 20th century music.

Kodiak-Baranof Productions, Inc.*
Margaret Childs, President
P.O. Box 1792
Kodiak, AK 99615
(907) 486-5355
Supports symphonic music.

Nome Arts Council*
Mary Francis, Chairman
P.O. Box 233
Nome, AK 99762
(907) 443-2964
Supports chamber music, jazz, symphonic music, operatic music, ethnic music, popular music.

Southeast Alaska Regional Arts Council*
Jan Craddick, President
P.O. Box 678
Sitka, AK 99835
(907) 747-8581
Supports chamber music, symphonic music.

Tri-Valley Cultural Arts Association*
Doris Dearborn, President
Route A, P.O. Box 72
Palmer, AK 99645
(907) 745-3501
Supports chamber music, symphonic music.

Arizona

State Arts Agency:

Arizona Commission On The Arts And Humanities
Louise Tester, Executive Director
6330 North Seventh Street
Phoenix, AZ 85014
(602) 271-5884
Supports 20th century chamber music, new and experimental music, jazz, ethnic music.
Provides financial support. Sponsors a 20th century Mexican chamber music program in Tucson, Arizona. Works with American composers in preparing grant requests.
Music Budget: $10,000.00-$24,999.00; 10%-20% for 20th century music.

Arizona Cello Society, Ltd.
Takayori Atsumi, Executive Director
1872 East Concorda Circle
Tempe, AZ 85282
(602) 967-8167
A private foundation serving central and northern Arizona.
Supports chamber music, new and experimental music.
Provides financial support. Sponsors an annual 'Cello Ensemble Composition Competition, provides scholarships for student violoncellists. Acts as a violoncello music information center and hopes to acquire a library of music for violoncello.
Music Budget: $1,000.00-$4,999.00; 51%-60% for 20th century music.

Pima County Parks And Recreation Department
Gene Laos, Executive Director
1204 West Silverlake Road
Tucson, AZ 85713
(602) 792-8817
A county agency.
Supports jazz, popular music, folk music.
Provides financial support, performing facilities. Brings the arts to Pima County at the lowest possible cost.
Music Budget: $1,000.00-$4,999.00; Under 10% for 20th century music.

Scottsdale Fine Arts Commission*
Mrs. Dickson Hartwell, Executive Director
3839 Civic Center Plaza
Scottsdale, AZ 85251
(602) 994-2304
Supports chamber music, jazz, symphonic music, operatic music, ethnic music, popular music.

20th Century Chamber Theater Of The Performing Arts
Dr. Edward C. Garza, Executive Director
P.O. Box 3726
Tucson, AZ 85722
(602) 325-0463
A private foundation serving Arizona and Southwestern states.
Supports 20th century chamber music, new and experimental music, chamber orchestra music, theater music.
Sponsors presentations of the arts related to theater: music, drama, and dance. Presents concerts featuring contemporary composers from the U.S.A. and Mexico. Publishes a newsletter.

Music Budget: $500.00-$999.00; 91%-100% for 20th century music.

Arkansas

State Arts Agency:

Arkansas State Council On The Arts And Humanities
Dr. Sandra Perry, Executive Director
400 Train Station Square
Victory at Markham
Little Rock, AR 72201
(501) 371-2539
Supports 20th century chamber music, jazz.
Provides financial support. Gives grants to associations who sponsor music ensembles. Assists local non-profit organizations in developing the arts.
Music Budget: Over $100,000.00; Under 10% for 20th century music.

Arkansas Arts Center*
Townsend Wolfe, Executive Director
MacArthur Park
Little Rock, AR 72202
(501) 376-3671
Supports chamber music, jazz, operatic music, popular music.

Southeast Arkansas Art Center*
Phillip A. Klopfenstein, Director
200 East 8th Street
Pine Bluff, AR 71601
(501) 536-3375
Supports chamber music, jazz, symphonic music, operatic music, ethnic music, popular music.

Warfield Concerts
Helen C. Mosby, Executive Director
P.O. Box 127
Helena, AR 72342
(501) 572-6105
A private foundation serving Eastern Arkansas.
Presents free public concerts, the content of which is determined by a concert committee.
Music Budget: $10,000.00-$24,999.00.

California

State Arts Agency:

California Arts Commission
James D. Forward, Jr., Executive Director
808 O Street
Sacramento, CA 95814
(916) 445-1530
Supports 20th century chamber music, new and experimental music, jazz.
Provides financial support. Funds community arts projects, festivals, music performing ensembles, and sponsoring organizations.
Music Budget: Over $100,000.00.

American Conservatory Theatre
James B. McKenzie, Executive Director
450 Geary Street
San Francisco, CA 94102
(415) 771-3880
A non-profit organization.
Supports theatrical music.
Provides financial support, performing facilities. Supports performances of original music written and incorporated into new and classical plays.

American Institute For Cultural Development*
Charles L. Burns, President
345 Fulton Street
San Francisco, CA 94102
(415) 626-0468
Supports chamber music, symphonic music, operatic music, ethnic music, popular music.

Arrowhead Allied Arts Council
Mrs. Marye L. Miles, President
P.O. Box 103
San Bernardino, CA 92402
(714) 885-7515
A regional agency serving San Bernardino and surrounding area.
Publicizes concerts presented by member performing organizations, offers scholarships to high school students, and funds local high school band tours.
Music Budget: $100.00-$499.00; 31%-40% for 20th century music.

Atlantic Richfield Foundation*
W. Bruce Evans, Executive Director
515 South Flower Street
Los Angeles, CA 90071
H. A. Slack, President
Sponsors higher education, community funds, the arts, and hospitals. No grants to individuals.

79

California State University
Department of Music
Peter Gena, Executive Director
Fresno, CA 93740
(209) 487-2654
Supports 20th century chamber music, new and experimental music, multi-media.
Provides financial support, performing facilities, publicity. Sponsors the Spring Festival of Contemporary Music. The 1975 Festival will feature multi-media and other works by Morton Feldman, Kenneth Gaburo, and Mel Powell.

California State University
Dr. Clarence Wiggins, Executive Director
18111 Nordhoff Street
Northridge, CA 91324
(213) 885-3184
Supports 20th century chamber music, new and experimental music, jazz.
Provides performing facilities.

The Chamber Music Society
Martha Blaine, General Manager
1017 North La Cienega Boulevard, Suite 109A
Los Angeles, CA 90069
(213) 657-5883
Sponsors the Los Angeles Chamber Orchestra.

City Of Palo Alto Arts Department*
Allan Longacre, Director
250 Hamilton Avenue
Palo Alto, CA 94301
(415) 329-2218
Supports chamber music, jazz, operatic music, ethnic music, popular music.

Coleman Chamber Music Association
George Heussenstamm, Executive Director
202 South Lake Avenue, Room 201
Pasadena, CA 91101
(213) 793-4191
Supports chamber music.
Produces Coleman Chamber Concert Series, an annual series of performances by prominent chamber ensembles. Sponsors an annual chamber ensemble competition.

Community Art Center Of Ojai Valley, Inc.*
Nancy Fenster, Executive Director
113 South Montgomery
P.O. Box 331
Ojai, CA 83023
(805) 646-2769

Supports chamber music, jazz, ethnic music, popular music.

Fine Arts Commission Of City Of Buena Park*
David White, Chairman
6650 Beach Boulevard
Buena Park, CA 90620
(714) 521-9900 Ext. 77
Supports symphonic music, operatic music.

Foresthill Divide Arts League*
Mary R. Menchinella, Coordinator
P.O. Box 462
Foresthill, CA 95631
(916) 367-2680
Supports chamber music, jazz, ethnic music, popular music.

Humboldt Arts Council
Sally Arnot, President
P.O. Box 221
Eureka, CA 95501
Supports chamber music, operatic music.

James Irvine Foundation*
N. Loyall McLaren, President
111 Sutter Street, Suite 1520
San Francisco, CA 94104
A foundation serving California, giving preference to Orange County and the San Francisco Bay area.
Sponsors community projects not supported by the government. No grants to individuals or for operating expenses.

Los Angeles Theaseum Corporation
Dan Morehouse, Executive Director
6226 Santa Monica Boulevard
Hollywood, CA 90038
(213) 467-3288
A non-profit organization serving the U.S.A.
Supports new and experimental music, jazz.
Sponsors The Jazz Chronicles, a continuing series of educational radio shows concerned with jazz in America today. Provides performing facilities, counseling, and artistic guidance. Operates a modern music museum, provides a means by which new music or musicians can be recorded, and presents new music or musicians through radio, television, and films.
Music Budget: Over $100,000.00; 91%-100% for 20th century music.

McGroarty Cultural Art Center*
Evaline Carrie, Executive Director
7570 McGroarty Terrace
Tujunga, CA 91042
(213) 352-5285
Supports symphonic music.

Mendocino Art Center*
William Zacha, Executive Director
P.O. Box 7
Mendocino, CA 95460
(707) 937-5229
Supports chamber music, jazz, popular music.

Mills College
Center for Contemporary Music
Robert Ashley, Executive Director
MacArthur Boulevard and Seminary
Oakland, CA 94613
(415) 632-2700 Ext. 337
A non-profit organization, funded in part by Mills College, paying users, and private foundations.
Supports new and experimental music, jazz, electronic music, multi-media.
Provides instruction and experience in contemporary music techniques and related media, such as film and video.

Muckenthaler Center*
William J. Gravesmill, Executive Director
1201 West Malvern
Fullerton, CA 92633
(714) 879-6860
Supports chamber music, jazz, operatic music, ethnic music, popular music.

Palos Verdes Community Arts Association*
Marilyn G. Fowler, President
P.O. Box 1051
Palos Verdes Estates, CA 90274
(213) 373-6685
Supports symphonic music.

Rosenberg Foundation*
Mrs. Jackson Chance, Executive Director
210 Post Street
San Francisco, CA 94108
Mrs. Allan E. Charles, President
Sponsors programs, including music, concerned with youth. Funds projects in which older youth serve the community. No grants to individuals and no scholarships.

Sacramento Regional Arts Council, Inc.
Joan Kay Bibow, Executive Secretary
1930 T Street
Sacramento, CA 95814
(916) 452-1800
Rudolf H. Michaels, President
A regional agency serving Sacramento, Yolo, El Dorado, and San Joaquin Counties.
Supports 20th century chamber music, new and experimental music, jazz.
Provides financial support. A membership organization of music departments of local colleges. Aids and advises member organizations and coordinates their cultural arts promotional activities. Does not directly sponsor music performances. Publishes a newsletter.
Music Budget: $100.00-$499.00.

San Francisco Art Commission*
Martin Snipper, Director
165 Grove Street
San Francisco, CA 94102
(415) 558-3465
Supports chamber music, jazz, symphonic music, operatic music, ethnic music, popular music.

San Francisco Foundation*
John R. May, Executive Director
425 California Street
San Francisco, CA 94104
Llewellen White, Associate Director
A foundation serving San Francisco.
Sponsors welfare planning and equal opportunity programs, educational, and cultural projects.

San Francisco Symphony Association
Joseph A. Scafidi, General Manager
107 War Memorial Veterans Building
San Francisco, CA 94102
(415) 861-6240
A private endowment serving the San Francisco Bay area.
Provides financial support. Sponsors all performances of the San Francisco Symphony Orchestra, including some fall chamber music concerts. Funds a program with the San Francisco School District which often involves contemporary music.
Music Budget: Over $100,000.00; 31%-40% for 20th century music.

San Mateo County Chamber Music Society
Helen Beyer, Executive Director
730 Winchester Drive
Burlingame, CA 94010
(415) 347-9315
A non-profit organization serving San Mateo County and the greater San Francisco Bay area.
Supports chamber music.
Manages and publicizes concerts. Sponsors Artist-In-Residence Concert Series, featuring one work by a resident composer per concert.

Santa Barbara Foundation*
Harold W. Beard, President
11 East Carrillo Street
Santa Barbara, CA 93101
Sponsors the equipment acquisitions and scholarships of local music schools. Funds youth education projects of music performing organizations.

Sausalito Arts Association*
Francis Cuchlo, Executive Director
P.O. Box 124
Sausalito, CA 94965
(415) 332-4421
Supports chamber music, jazz, ethnic music, popular music.

The Skaggs Foundation*
Charles N. Whitehead, President
1123 Central Building
Oakland, CA 94612
A foundation serving the Oakland area.
Sponsors projects concerned with hospitals, including music performances.

Sonoma County Arts Council
Nancy N. Meier, Executive Director
1049 4th Street
Santa Rosa, CA 95404
(707) 528-8220
A non-profit organization.
Sponsors performances and workshops, including booking and paying outside groups. Coordinates visual and performing arts activities.
Music Budget: $1,000.00-$4,999.00; Under 10% for 20th century music.

Southern California Chamber Music Society
Dorrance Stalvey, Executive Director
Los Angeles County Museum of Art
Leo S. Bing Theater
Los Angeles, CA 90036
(213) 937-4250
Sponsors the Monday Evening Concert Series, featuring 20th century chamber music, new and experimental music.

Sufism Reoriented, Inc.
Murshida Ivy O. Duce, Executive Director
1300 Boulevard Way
Walnut Creek, CA 94596
A school established to teach the religious philosophy of Avatar Meher Baba.
Supports musical theater.
Presents original musical dramas written by organization members. Sponsors an annual Birthday Commemoration of Avatar Meher Baba on February 25.
Music Budget: $100.00-$499.00; 91%-100% for 20th century music.

Theatre Vanguard
Judith Stark, Executive Director
9014 Melrose Avenue
Los Angeles, CA 90069
(213) 278-0641
Leonard Stein, Music Director
A non-profit organization receiving private and public support.
Supports 20th century chamber music, new and experimental music, jazz, electronic music, multimedia.
Provides financial support, performing facilities.
Presents experimental music, dance, theater, and film. Acts as a center for the avant-garde arts in Los Angeles, presenting free performances and lectures. Encourages audience development.
Music Budget: $5,000.00-$9,999.00; 91%-100% for 20th century music.

University Of California At San Diego
Center For Music Experiment And Related Research
Roger Reynolds, Executive Director
P.O. Box 109
La Jolla, CA 92037
(714) 452-4383
Supports new and experimental music, electronic music.
Provides a center for experimental activity by musicians, other artists, and interested scientists.

Offers workshops, demonstrations, and occasional concerts. Concentrates exclusively on experimental music, using electronics, computers, improvisation, new instrumental resources, and vocal techniques.

Ventura City Parks And Recreation Department
William J. Kent, Director
P.O. Box 99
Ventura, CA 93001
(805) 648-7881 Ext. 246
A city agency.
Supports jazz, popular music.
Provides financial support, performing facilities, publicity.
Music Budget: $1,000.00-$4,999.00; 91%-100% for 20th century music.

Zellerbach Family Fund*
Edward Nathan, Executive Director
260 California Street, Room 1010
San Francisco, CA 94111
Harold L. Zellerbach, President
Serves the San Francisco Bay area.
Funds cultural and welfare projects.

Colorado

State Arts Agency:

Colorado Council On The Arts And Humanities
Robert N. Sheets, Executive Director
1550 Lincoln Street, Room 205
Denver, CO 80203
(303) 892-2617.

Boettcher Foundation*
John C. Mitchell, Executive Director
828 Seventeenth Street
Denver, CO 80202
E. Warren Willard, President
Chris Dobbins, Chairman
A foundation serving Colorado.
Sponsors scholarships and cultural activities. No grants to individuals.

Colorado Springs Fine Arts Center*
Milo M. Naeve, Director
30 West Dale Street
Colorado Springs, CO 80903
(303) 634-5581
Supports chamber music, jazz, symphonic music, ethnic music, popular music.

Moffot County Council Of The Arts And Humanities
Helen B. Loyd, President
P.O. Box 764
Craig, CO 81625
(303) 824-5817.

Ouray County Arts Council*
Mary L. Tjossem, Director
c/o Philip Icke
600 Main
Ouray, CO 81427
(303) 325-4415
Supports symphonic music.

Rockymount Arts And Humanities Foundation*
Dr. Donald W. Galvin, President
2480 West 26th Avenue, Suite 300B
Denver, CO 80211
(303) 458-8000
Supports chamber music, jazz, symphonic music, operatic music, ethnic music, popular music.

Western Colorado Center For The Arts, Inc.
Grace Purcell, President
1803 North 7th Street
Grand Junction, CO 81501
(303) 243-7337
Supports chamber music.

Connecticut

State Arts Agency:

Connecticut Commission On The Arts
Anthony S. Keller, Executive Director
340 Capitol Avenue
Hartford, CT 06106
(203) 566-4770
Elizabeth Mahaffey, Program Associate
Supports chamber music, new and experimental music, jazz, symphonic music, operatic music, folk music, popular music.
Acts as a source of information for opportunities available to Connecticut musicians. Co-sponsors New England Contemporary Music Circuit with arts councils of Massachusetts and Rhode Island. The Music Circuit presents concerts and lecture-demonstrations on contemporary music performed by the ensembles from the 3 states. The participating ensembles make their presentations in the 3 states at colleges which act as co-sponsors.

Commission On The Arts And Cultural Activities
Joyce Kirkpatrick, Chairman
Mayor's Office, Municipal Building
Middletown, CT 06457
(203) 347-4671
A city agency serving Middletown.
Supports 20th century chamber music.
Provides financial support, publicity. Promotes arts exposure and appreciation in the community.
Total annual budget: $5,000.00.

Connecticut Traditional Jazz Club, Inc.
P.O. Box 30
Wethersfield, CT 06109
(203) 529-4845
A non-profit educational organizational serving Connecticut.
Supports jazz.
Sponsors live and recorded performances and educational programs.
Music Budget: $10,000.00-$24,999.00; 91%-100% for 20th century music.

Darien Arts Council
c/o Jeanne Burt Tuller
P.O. Box 3096
Darien, CT 06820
(203) 655-0470
A private endowment.
Recently incorporated. Projects presently undetermined.

Fine Arts Commission Of The Town Of East Hartford
Dan Lyman Russell, Chairman
740 Main Street
East Hartford, CT 06108
(203) 289-2781
A city agency.
Supports 20th century chamber music, new and experimental music, jazz.
Sponsors concerts and demonstrations in order to interest the community in the fine arts.
Music Budget: $5,000.00-$9,999.00; Under 25% for 20th century music.
Alternate address:
Mr. Dawson
60 Washington Street
Hartford, CT 06106
(203) 525-4291.

Friends Of Music, Inc.
Ruth Steinkraus Cohen, Executive Director
P.O. Box 369
Westport, CT 06880
(203) 227-3345
Supports chamber music.
Provides financial support. Sponsors Friends of Music Concert Series, presenting 6 to 7 concerts per season featuring guest composers and pre-concert lecture-demonstrations for Friends of Music members.
Music Budget: $5,000.00-$9,999.00; 10%-20% for 20th century music.

Goshen Concert Committee Of Goshen Recreation Commission*
Dale W. Ives, Chairman
Goshen Town Offices
Goshen, CT 06756
(203) 491-2249
Supports chamber music, jazz, operatic music, popular music.

Greenwich Arts Council
6 West Putman Avenue
Greenwich, CT 06830
(203) 661-2788
A service organization promoting the arts by coordinating local arts activities.

Hartford Jazz Society, Inc.
Lucy Marsters, President
73 Lebanon Street
Hartford, CT 06112
(203) 242-6886
A non-profit organization serving Connecticut and Western Massachusetts.
Supports jazz.
Music Budget: $10,000.00-$24,999.00; 91%-100% for 20th century music.

The Howard And Bush Foundation, Inc.*
J. H. Bartholomew, Jr., President
77 Forest Street
Hartford, CT 06105
A foundation serving Hartford, Connecticut; and Troy, New York.
Sponsors programs concerned with hospitals, youth, urban problems, and the arts.

Armin Loos Memorial Fund
William L. Carnow, Executive Director
P.O. Box 1253
New Britain, CT 06050
A private foundation.
Supports 20th century chamber music. Promotes and supports premiere performances of the works of Armin Loos exclusively.
Music Budget: $1,000.00-$4,999.00; 91%-100% for 20th century music.

New England Contemporary Music Circuit
See Connecticut Commission on the Arts.

New Haven Arts Project
John Baringer, Executive Director
148 Orange Street
New Haven, CT 06510
(203) 865-8368
Supports 20th century chamber music, new and experimental music, jazz, folk music.
Presents local artists in theater, dance, music, poetry, crafts, and visual arts. The organization's goals are social, rather than artistic, fostering communications among people through the arts. Sponsors the summer theatre-in-the-park programs, which include local musicians. Refers musicians to jobs.

The New Haven Foundation*
Norman Harrower, Jr., Executive Director
1 State Street
New Haven, CT 06511
A foundation serving New Haven and the Lower Naugatuck Valley.
Sponsors projects concerned with youth, public welfare, and music.

Performers Of Southern Connecticut, Inc.
Heida Hermanns, President
P.O. Box 1134
Weston, CT 06880
(203) 227-6770
A private endowment serving Southern Connecticut.
Supports 20th century chamber music, jazz.
Provides financial support, promotion. Presents public and private concerts. Sponsors annual young artists competition, requiring inclusion of 20th century music in submitted repertoire. Its Talent Referral Service is a non-profit booking agency which provides outstanding local performers for benefits, meetings, and special events at moderate fees.

Music Budget: $1,000.00-$4,999.00; 21%-30% for 20th century music.

Suffield Council For The Arts*
Gail L. Sanderson, President
142 North Main Street
Suffield, CT 06078
(203) 668-5066
Supports chamber music, ethnic music, folk music.

Talent Referral Service
See Performers of Southern Connecticut.

University Of Bridgeport
Music Department
Dr. Harrison R. Valante, Executive Director
Bridgeport, CT 06602
(203) 576-4404
Supports 20th century chamber music, new and experimental music, jazz.
Provides financial support, performing facilities. Sponsors Annual Contemporary Composer Festival and numerous jazz concerts.

Valley Arts Council, Inc.
Patricia G. Edwards, Executive Director
350 East Main Street
Ansonia, CT 06401
(203) 735-8689
A regional agency serving Lower Naugatuck Valley.
Supports 20th century chamber music, new and experimental music, jazz.
Presents workshops, exhibits, concerts, and demonstrations in order to increase local appreciation of the arts.
Music Budget: $500.00-$999.00; 61%-70% for 20th century music.

Wesleyan University
Center for the Arts
Cynthia White, Executive Director
Middletown, CT 06457
(203) 347-9411
Supports 20th century chamber music, new and experimental music, jazz.
Provides performing facilities, technical and managerial assistance. Produces concerts.

Westport-Weston Arts Council Inc.*
Maryo Ewell, Acting Executive Director
The Seabury Center
45 Church Lane
Westport, CT 06880
(203) 226-3587(8)

Supports chamber music, jazz, operatic music, ethnic music, popular music.

Delaware

State Arts Agency:

Delaware State Arts Council
Sophie Consagra, Executive Director
1105 Market Street
Room 803 Wilmington Tower
Wilmington, DE 19801
(302) 571-3540
Supports 20th century chamber music, jazz, operatic music.
Provides financial support. Supports music programs in the public school system.
Music Budget: $50,000.00-$99,000.00; 31%-40% for 20th century music.

Cultural Arts Section, New Castle County Department Of Parks And Recreation
Ralph Cryder, Executive Director
3300 Faulkland Road
Wilmington, DE 19808
(302) 571-7730
A county agency.
Supports 20th century chamber music, new and experimental music, jazz.
Sponsors annual summer concert series in parks, presenting many kinds of music performed by local ensembles. Plans and supervises cultural programs, including performing arts workshops.
Music Budget: $5,000.00-$9,999.00; 71%-80% for 20th century music.

University Of Delaware
Cultural Programs Department
Patricia C. Kent, Coordinator
Continuing Education Division
Newark, DE 19711
(302) 738-2893
Supports 20th century chamber music, new and experimental music.
Provides financial support, performing facilities. Coordinates scheduling and promotion of performing arts events at the University of Delaware. Presents performing and visual arts experiences as part of the lifelong learning process encouraged by the University.

District of Columbia

State Arts Agency:

District of Columbia Commission On The Arts
Leroy A. Washington, Executive Director
Room 1023, Munsey Building
1329 E Street, N.W.
Washington, D.C. 20004
(202) 347-5905
Supports 20th century chamber music, new and experimental music, jazz.
Sponsors contemporary music concerts and gives funding and administrative advice in workshops.
Music budget: $5,000.00-$9,999.00.

Friday Morning Music Club, Inc.
Jane Ross Hammer, President
1649 K Street, N.W.
Washington, D.C. 20006
(202) 347-6750 or 966-7208
A non-profit organization.
Supports 20th century chamber music, new and experimental music, solo music, and vocal music.
Provides financial support. A performing arts organization whose performer members are auditioned in order to join and perform with it. Presents concerts with a composer's group. Offers composition awards for works for string orchestra, chorus and orchestra, voice, or solo instrument. Winners receive cash awards and a premiere performance by the organization's performer members.
Music Budget: $10,000.00-$24,999.00.

Eugene And Agnes E. Meyer Foundation*
James L. Kunen, President
1730 Rhode Island Avenue, N.W.
Suite 1212
Washington, D.C. 20036
A foundation serving the greater Washington, D.C. area.
Sponsors new and improved services, rather than existing programs. Supports the arts and education. No grants to individuals or to projects which are national or international in scope.

The National Council On The Aging, Inc.
Jacqueline T. Sunderland, Director
1828 L Street, N.W.
Washington, D.C. 20036
(202) 223-6250
Encourages inclusion of the aged in concert planning. Offers guidance to Arts and Aging Councils in planning performing arts projects. Stimulates employment opportunities for artists concerned with the field of aging.

National Endowment For The Arts
Nancy Hanks, Chairman
Washington, D.C. 20506
(202) 634-6369
Walter F. Anderson, Director, Music Program
Ralph Rizzolo, Assistant Director, Music Program
Supports 20th century chamber music, new and experimental music, jazz, folk music, ethnic music, operatic music, orchestral music.

Sponsors individual composers, state arts agencies, service organizations, performing ensembles. Guidelines to composer grants: individual musicians and librettists are eligible to apply. These funds do not cover production costs or fees of production personnel, recording costs, or commercial music. Jazz composers may apply for assistance under the Jazz/Folk/Ethnic Program.

Categories of composer/librettists support:

(1) Non-matching fellowship grants of up to $10,000.00 to exceptionally talented composers for the creation of new works or the completion of works in progress. Support will be inclusive of the individual's time, copying and reproduction costs, or other services necessary to complete the work.

(2) Non-matching fellowship grants of up to $7,500.00 to exceptionally talented librettists for the creation of new works or the completion of works in progress.

(3) Non-matching fellowship grants of up to $2,500.00 to aid the professional development of a composer or librettist of exceptional talent.

(4) A limited number of non-matching fellowship grants of up to $10,000.00 will be awarded to nationally recognized composers to allow the composer free time for working. This time might include experimenting in new media.

The Endowment is investigating the possibility of establishing contemporary performance institutes throughout the country to bring the composer, performer, conductor, and critic into a working relationship.

Music Budget: $11,200,000.00; Under 10% for 20th century music.

National Endowment For The Humanities
Dr. Ronald S. Berman, Chairman
806 15th Street, N.W.
Washington, D.C. 20506
(202) 382-5721
A federal agency affiliated with the National Endowment for the Arts. Supports music projects, only if related to the humanities.

National Gallery Of Art
Richard Bales, Music Director
6th Street and Constitution Avenue
Washington, D.C. 20565
(202) 737-4215
A federal agency.

Supports 20th century chamber music, new and experimental music, 20th century orchestral, choral, and vocal music.

Sponsors annual American Music Festival in the spring.

Organization Of American States
Harold Boxer, Managing Director
Washington, D.C. 20006
(202) 381-8353
Guillermo Espinosa, Music Director

An international organization serving member states of the Organization of American States.

Supports 20th century chamber music, new and experimental music, contemporary orchestral music.

Provides financial support, performing facilities. Sponsors Inter-American Music Festival in Washington, D.C. Promotes the exchange of music and musicians within the Americas.

Smithsonian Institution
Division of Performing Arts
James Morris, Executive Director
Washington, D.C. 20560
(202) 381-6525
Supports 20th century chamber music, new and experimental music, jazz.

Presents series entitled: Jazz Heritage, Jazz Connoisseur, American Popular Song, Women in Country Song, and Theater Chamber Players.

Smithsonian Resident Associate Program
Janet W. Solinger, Executive Director
900 Jefferson Drive, N.W.
Washington, D.C. 20056
(202) 381-5157

A membership organization of the Smithsonian Institution. Presents concerts of 20th century chamber music, new and experimental music, choral music.

Washington Ethical Society
Maxine Pineau, Executive Director
7750 16th Street, N.W.
Washington, D.C. 20012
(202) 882-6650
A humanistic religious organization serving the greater Washington, D.C. area.
Supports 20th century chamber music, new and experimental music.
Provides performing facilities, publicity, programs. Presents Third-Monday Concert Series, featuring works by living composers, rarely heard pieces, and premieres performed by the Contemporary Music Forum.
Music Budget: $100.00-$499.00; 10%-20% for 20th century music.

Florida

State Arts Agency

Fine Arts Council Of Florida
Division of Cultural Affairs
Leonard Pas, Jr., Director
The Capitol Building
Tallahassee, FL 32304
(904) 488-2417 Ext. 7
Supports 20th century chamber music, new and experimental music, jazz.

Osceola County Art And Culture Center*
Jean Grice, President
P.O. Box 1195
Kissimmee, FL 32741
(305) 846-6257
Supports symphonic music, choral music.

Georgia

State Arts Agency:

Georgia Council For The Arts
George Beattie, Jr., Executive Director
225 Peachtree Street, N.E.
Suite 706
Atlanta, GA 30303
(404) 656-3990
Supports 20th century chamber music, new and experimental music, jazz.
Provides grants to music ensembles for performances.
Music Budget: $25,000.00-$49,000.00.

Atlanta Arts Alliance, Inc.*
Charles Yates, President
1280 Peachtree Street, N.E.
Atlanta, GA 30309
(404) 892-3600
Supports chamber music, symphonic music, operatic music, ethnic music.

Columbus Arts Council*
Dr. Katherine H. Mahan, President
c/o Fine Arts Department
Columbus College
Columbus, GA 31907
(404) 561-5134
Supports chamber music, symphonic music, operatic music, folk music.

Creative Arts Guild*
Bernice Spigel, Executive Director
The Old Firehouse on Pentz Street
P.O. Box 375
Dalton, GA 30720
(404) 278-9624
Supports chamber music, symphonic music, folk music.

DeKalb Council For The Arts*
Jack B. Sartain, President
P.O. Box 875
Decatur, GA 30030
(404) 371-2172
Supports symphonic music, operatic music.

Glynn Art Association
J. S. Garrison, President
P.O. Box 673
St. Simons Island, GA 31522
(912) 638-8770
Supports chamber music, jazz.
Provides performing facilities, publicity. Sponsors and organizes the annual Golden Isles Arts Festival, a presentation of many art forms, including chamber music and jazz.

Habersham Arts Council*
Carolyn Hodges, President
P.O. Box 43
Clarkesville, GA 30523
(404) 754-2425
Supports chamber music.

Hawaii

State Arts Agency:

Hawaii-The State Foundation On Culture And The Arts
Alfred Preis, Executive Director
250 South King Street, Room 310
Honolulu, HI 96813
(808) 548-4145.

Juliette M. Atherton Trust*
P.O. Box 3170
Honolulu, HI 96802
Address mail to Executive Director
Serves Hawaii.
Sponsors programs concerned with the promotion of Protestant Christian principles.

Samuel N. And Mary Castle Foundation*
P.O. Box 3170
Honolulu, HI 96802
Address mail to Executive Director
Serves local area.
Sponsors projects concerned with youth and the Protestant Church.

Charles M. And Anna C. Cooke, Ltd.*
Richard A. Cooke, Jr., President
745 Fort Street, Suite 1212
Honolulu, HI 96813
Serves local area primarily.
Sponsors community funds, private elementary and secondary schools, and fine arts.

Kalihi Palama Culture And Arts Society, Inc.*
Virgil Jhoo, President
357 North King Street
Honolulu, HI 96817
(808) 521-6905
Supports symphonic music, ethnic music.

Lanai Community Association*
Aurelio Del Rosario, President
Lanai City, HI 96763
Supports jazz, ethnic music, popular music.

McInery Foundation*
Mrs. Marguerite Jackson, Secretary
P.O. Box 2390
Honolulu, HI 96804
Serves Hawaii exclusively.
Sponsors projects concerned with education, welfare, and capital improvements in cultural facilities.

Waianae Coast Culture And Arts Society, Inc.*
Alice L. Mole, Chairman
89-188 Farrington Highway
Nankuli, HI 96792
(808) 668-1540 or 668-1549
Supports symphonic music, operatic music, ethnic music, folk music.

Idaho

State Arts Agency:

Idaho State Commission On The Arts And Humanities
Suzanne D. Taylor, Executive Director
506 North 5th Street, Annex 3
Boise, ID 83720
(208) 384-2119.

Civic Arts, Inc.*
Charlotte Duley, President
P.O. Box 212
Lewiston, ID 83501
(208) 743-6907 or 743-2561
Supports chamber music.

Illinois

State Arts Agency:

Illinois Arts Council
Michele Brustin, Executive Director
111 North Wabash
Chicago, IL 60602
(312) 793-3520
Supports 20th century chamber music, new and experimental music, jazz.
Provides financial support. Sponsors ensembles based on their artistic merit. Excludes popular, commercial music from funding.
Music Budget: Over $100,000.00.

Action For The Arts
Phyllis C. Safman, Executive Director
Sangamon State University
Shepard Road
Springfield, IL 62708
(217) 786-6680
Supports 20th century chamber music, jazz.
Provides financial support, publicity. Presents concerts of works written or performed by staff members for community and students of Sangamon State University.

The Allstate Foundation*
John T. Murphy, Executive Director
Allstate Plaza, F-3
Northbrook, IL 60062
Archie R. Boe, President
Sponsors projects concerned with education.
Funds cultural activities.

Centralia Cultural Society*
W. W. Koelling, President
1254 East Rexford Street
Centralia, IL 62801
(618) 532-9734 or 532-2314
Supports symphonic music.

Central Illinois Cultural Affairs Consortium
Mrs. Norma C. Murphy, Executive Director
1501 West Bradley Avenue
Peoria, IL 61606
(309) 674-7355
A non-profit association of colleges, universities,
and arts organizations working in cooperation
with local communities and school districts in the
Central Illinois area. Coordinates programming,
publishes a calendar of arts activities and a
biographical artists directory, and serves as a
resource and referral agency for the region. Offers
cooperative booking of talent at a pro-rated cost,
artist-in-residence programs, and low-cost
community arts programs. Researches foundation,
corporation, and governmental funding
opportunities.
Supports 20th century chamber music, jazz.
Music Budget: $5,000.00-$9,999.00; Under 10%
for 20th century music.

The Chicago Community Trust*
Bruce L. Newman, Executive Director
208 South La Salle Street
Chicago, IL 60604
Serves Cook County.
Supports operating budgets for neighborhood
services and scholarships.

Decatur Area Arts Council
Ann Stanhope, President
P.O. Box 1607
Decatur, IL 60625
(217) 423-3189
Supports chamber music, operatic music.

Fine Arts Center Of Clinton
Mr. Robin McNeil, Executive Director
119 West Macon Street
Clinton, IL 61727
(217) 935-5055
A private endowment and membership
organization serving Central Illinois.
Supports 20th century chamber music, new and
experimental music, jazz.
Donates auditorium seating 65 for concerts.

Fromm Music Foundation At Harvard
Chicago Office
1028 West Van Buren Street
Chicago, IL 60607
For further information, see Fromm Music
Foundation at Harvard, Massachusetts.

Harris Bank Foundation*
Errett Van Nice, President
111 West Monroe Street
Chicago, IL 60690
Serves Chicago.
Supports community funds and higher education.

Illinois Wesleyan University
School Of Music
William Hipp, Executive Director
Bloomington, IL 61701
(309) 556-3061
Supports 20th century chamber music, new and
experimental music, jazz.
Provides financial support, performing facilities.
Sponsors annual Symposium of Contemporary
Music and annual Choral Commission Series.

Inland Steel-Ryerson Foundation, Inc.*
Robert J. Greenebaum, President
30 West Monroe Street
Chicago, IL 60603
Funds organizations concerned with higher
education. Does not fund research projects,
individual scholarships, and fellowships.

Lakeview Center For The Arts And Sciences*
Lowell G. Adams, Executive Director
1125 West Lake Avenue
Peoria, IL 61614
(309) 685-4028
Supports chamber music, symphonic music,
operatic music, ethnic music.

**Mt. Vernon Council For The Arts And
Humanities, Inc.***
Mrs. Larry Martin, Mrs. Jack Goldman,
Chairmen
c/o Demetri Hassakis, Attorney
306 King City Federal Building
Mount Vernon, IL 62864
Supports symphonic music, operatic music.

Quad Cities Arts Council*
Harriette R. Freeman, Executive Director
639 38th Street
Rock Island, IL 61201
(309) 793-1213
Supports jazz, popular music.

Quincy Society Of Fine Arts*
Gary F. Schaub, Executive Director
Warfield House
1624 Maine Street
Quincy, IL 62301
(217) 222-3432
Supports chamber music, symphonic music,
operatic music, ethnic music, folk music.

Ravinia Festival Association
Edward Gordon, Executive Director
22 West Monroe Street, Number 1404
Chicago, IL 60610
(312) 782-9696
A non-profit organization serving the
metropolitan Chicago area.
Supports 20th century chamber music, orchestral
music, popular music, ballet, art, theater.
Sponsors a summer performing arts festival at
Ravinia Park.
Music Budget: Over $100,000.00.

Dr. Scholl Foundation*
Edward L. Scholl, President
111 West Washington Street
Suite 2137
Chicago, IL 60602
Funds projects concerned with higher and
secondary education, and cultural activities.

The Siragusa Foundation*
John R. Siragusa, Secretary
c/o Daniel J. De Marco
3800 Cortland Street
Chicago, IL 60647
Sponsors projects concerned with music, higher
education, religion, community funds. No grants
to individuals.

Wieboldt Foundation*
Robert M. Johnson, Executive Director
111 South La Salle Street
Chicago, IL 60603
Funds projects concerned with community
development, welfare, and education.

Woods Charitable Fund*
Mrs. Carl H. Rohman, President
59 East Van Buren Street, Room 1500
Chicago, IL 60605
Serves Illinois and Nebraska.
Sponsors fine arts projects concerned with arts
education in the community. No grants to
individuals or endowments.

Woodstock Fine Arts Association
Val Gitlin, President
P.O. Box 221
Woodstock, IL 60098
(815) 338-1891
Serves McHenry County and Northern Illinois.
Supports chamber music, operatic music.
Promotes local cultural activities, including arts
education and community participation. Sponsors
and maintains the Woodstock Opera House.
Presents chamber music concerts.
Music Budget: $1,000.00-$4,999.00.

Indiana

State Arts Agency:

Indiana Arts Commission
John M. Bitterman, Executive Director
155 East Market Street
Suite 614
Indianapolis, IN 46204
(317) 633-5649.

Anderson Fine Arts Center-Alford House*
Glenn A. Anderson, Executive Director
266 West Historical 8th Street
Anderson, IN 46016
(317) 649-1248
Supports chamber music, jazz, ethnic music,
popular music.

Arts For Rush County, Inc.
Muriel P. Moore, Arts Coordinator
P.O. Box 5
Arlington, IN 46104
(317) 663-2655
A county agency.
Supports jazz.

Provides financial support, performing facilities. Encourages music performances in Rush County. Music Budget: $500.00-$999.00; Under 10% for 20th century music.

Bluffon-Wells Performing Arts Council*
Dr. Jack T. Collins, Executive Director
Mayor's Office
Bluffon, IN 46714
(219) 824-1520
Supports chamber music, jazz, operatic music, symphonic music, popular music.

The Center For Contemporary Celebration
Reverend Kent Schneider, Executive Director
320 North Street
West Lafayette, IN 47906
(317) 743-4821
A religious arts organization.
Supports new and experimental music, jazz, electronic music, multi-media.
Sponsors performances of works composed for religious services. Intends to provide opportunities, resources, publications, and workshops which facilitate creativity.
Music Budget: $1,000.00-$4,999.00; 91%-100% for 20th century music.

Civic Arts Guild, Inc.*
Parvin Lambertus, President
P.O. Box 242
Seymour, IN 47274
(812) 522-3244
Supports chamber music, symphonic music, folk music.

Contemporary Music Foundation, Inc.
A. Paul Johnson, Executive Director
4105 Devon Drive
Indianapolis, IN 46226
(317) 547-2822
A non-profit foundation serving Indiana and Illinois.
Supports 20th century chamber music, new and experimental music, jazz, music theater, ballet, plays.
Provides financial support, performing facilities, advertising. Sells tickets and the *New Art Review*. Produces performances and tours, and sponsors television broadcasts of contemporary music, emphasizing Indiana composers. Publishes calendars and criticisms of contemporary music.
Music Budget: $10,000.00-$24,999.00; 91%-100% for 20th century music.

Cummins Engine Foundation*
James A. Joseph, Executive Director
1000 Fifth Street
Columbus, IN 47201
Sponsors programs in the area of race, and interdenominational religious projects. Funds architectural fees for local public buildings. Sponsors projects of local performing ensembles.

DePauw University
School of Music
Donald H. White, Executive Director
DePauw University
Greencastle, IN 46135
(317) 653-9721
Supports 20th century chamber music, new and experimental music, jazz.
Provides performing facilities. Presents Annual Festival of Contemporary Music and 90 annual concerts, many featuring contemporary works.

Driftwood Valley Arts Council*
Burdell H. Sell, Executive Director
422 1/2 Fifth Street
Columbus, IN 47201
(812) 379-4192
Supports chamber music, jazz, symphonic music, operatic music, popular music.

Festival Players Guild*
James R. Myers, Managing Director
P.O. Box 157
Michigan City, IN 46360
(219) 874-4269
Supports chamber music, jazz, symphonic music, popular music.

Fort Wayne Fine Arts Foundation, Inc.*
Ralph E. Kohloff, Executive Director
132 The Landing
Fort Wayne, IN 46802
(209) 743-8075
Supports chamber music, jazz, symphonic music, operatic music, ethnic music, popular music.

Greater Gary Arts Council, Inc.*
Mrs. James W. Curtis, President
504 Broadway, Suite 1037
Gary, IN 46402
(219) 885-8444
Supports symphonic music, operatic music.

Indianapolis Foundation*
Jack Killen, Managing Director
P.O. Box 24152
Speedway, IN 46224
Serves Marion County.
Funds local cultural programs, including operating costs of performing groups.

Irwin-Sweeney-Miller Foundation*
Richard B. Stoner, President
552 Franklin Street
Columbus, IN 47201
Mrs. Robert S. Tangeman, Chairman
Sponsors projects concerned with racial and social justice, religion, and the arts.

Kankee Valley Area Fine Arts Council*
Doris B. Myers, President
Wheatfield, IN 46392
(219) 956-3707
Supports chamber music, folk music.

Lilly Endowment*
Eugene N. Beesley, President
2801 North Meridan
Indianapolis, IN 46208
Sponsors projects concerned with cultural improvements, concentrating on needs in Indiana. Funds creative undertakings to advance Christian faith through mass media communications. Sponsors community programs educating minority children in the arts.

Madison-Ohio Valley Arts Council*
Carolyn Neal, President
419 Broadway
Madison, IN 47250
(812) 265-2757
Supports chamber music, jazz, symphonic music, popular music.

Northern Indiana Art Association, Inc.
Anthony Radich, Executive Director
5448 Hohman
Hammond, IN 46320
(219) 931-0018
A private endowment serving Lake and Porter Counties.
Supports 20th century chamber music, new and experimental music.
Provides performing facilities, publicity. Promotes the arts in Northern Indiana.
Music Budget: $10,000.00-$24,999.00; Under 10% for 20th century music.

Owen County Committee For The Performing Arts, Inc.
Janet B. Wardlaw, Executive Director
207 West Hillside
Spencer, IN 47460
(812) 829-4266
A county agency.
Supports 20th century chamber music, new and experimental music, jazz.
Provides financial support. Brings live performances to Owen County.
Music Budget: $500.00-$999.00; 51%-60% for 20th century music.

University Of Notre Dame
Reverend David E. Schlaver, C.S.C., Director of Collegiate Jazz Festival
P.O. Box 523
Notre Dame, IN 46556
(219) 283-7308
Sponsors Collegiate Jazz Festival at the University.

Iowa

State Arts Agency:

Iowa State Arts Council
Jack Olds, Executive Director
State Capitol Building
Des Moines, IA 50319
(515) 281-5297
Supports 20th century chamber music, new and experimental music, jazz, folk music, electronic music.
Provides financial support. Sponsors artists and arts service organizations.
Music Budget: $25,000.00-$49,000.00; 10%-20% for 20th century music.

Burlington Area Fine Arts Council*
Mrs. William C. Steele, President
172 Gold Lane
Burlington, IA 52601
(319) 754-8576
Supports chamber music, symphonic music.

Cass County Arts Council*
Bette L. Newbold, President
P.O. Box 11
Atlantic, IA 50022
(712) 243-5110
Supports symphonic music, ethnic music.

Cedar Rapids-Marion Fine Arts Council*
David J. Spatola, Executive Director
127 Third Street, N.E.
Cedar Rapids, IA 52402
(319) 362-3001
Supports operatic music, ethnic music.

Central Iowa Art Association*
Gary Eason Eige, Executive Director
Fisher Community Center
Marshalltown, IA 50518
(515) 753-9013
Supports chamber music, jazz, popular music, ethnic music.

Fort Dodge Area Fine Arts Council
Dorothy S. Anderson, President
Blandon Memorial Art Gallery
Fort Dodge, IA 50501
(515) 573-3076
A private foundation serving Fort Dodge.
Supports various types of music, emphasizing country music. Sponsors annual arts festival.

Keokuk Community Fine Arts Council*
Mrs. Alan F. Lee, President
925 Grand Avenue
Keokuk, IA 52632
(319) 524-3357
Supports chamber music, symphonic music, ethnic music, folk music.

LeMars Arts Council, Inc.
Mrs. William Sturges, Executive Director
35 Ninth Street, S.W.
LeMars, IA 51031
(712) 546-5431
A city agency serving Northwestern Iowa.
Supports 20th century operatic music.
Provides financial support, performing facilities.
Encourages community interest in the arts.
Music Budget: $1,000.00-$4,999.00; 21%-30% for 20th century music.

Sioux Center Recreation And Arts Council
James Koldenhoven, Executive Director
City Offices
Sioux Center, IA 51250
(712) 722-0761
A city agency.
Provides performing facilities. Attempts to enrich the life of the community through recreation and the arts.

Music Budget: $100.00-$499.00; 51%-60% for 20th century music.

Kansas

State Arts Agency:

Kansas Arts Commission
Jonathan Katz, Executive Director
117 West 10th Street, Suite 100
Topeka, KS 66612
(913) 296-3335.

Coffeyville Cultural Arts Council*
Kenneth H. Burchinal, Executive Director
1302 West 2nd
Coffeyville, KS 67337
(316) 251-3118
Supports symphonic music, operatic music, ethnic music, folk music, popular music.

Hays Arts Council*
Kate Mohollon, Executive Director
P.O. Box 831
Hays, KS 67601
(913) 625-7522
Supports chamber music, jazz, orchestral music, ethnic music, popular music.

Kansas Cooperative College Composer's Project
Peter Ciurczak, Executive Director
Emporia State College
Emporia, KS 66801
(316) 343-1200
A state agency administered by Emporia Kansas State College.
Sponsors a composer-in-residence who writes works for student ensembles from Butler County Junior College, Dodge City Community Junior College, Emporia Kansas State College, and Kansas City Junior College. The resident composer regularly visits these schools to conduct rehearsals and performances of his works, to lecture on 20th century music, and to give private composition lessons.
Music Budget: $10,000.00-$24,999.00; 91%-100% for 20th century music.

Manhattan Arts Council
Mary Knecht, Executive Director
P.O. Box 74
Manhattan, KS 66502
(913) 539-3276
A city agency and private endowment.

Supports 20th century chamber music, new and experimental music, jazz.
Provides financial support, performing facilities. Presents American performing ensembles and soloists to the community and encourages community involvement in arts activities.
Music Budget: $10,000.00-$24,999.00; 31%-40% for 20th century music.

Musical Arts Of Kansas, Inc.
John Reed, Executive Director
Wichita State University
School of Music
Wichita, KS 67208
(913) 296-3335
A non-profit organization serving Kansas.
A coordinating and booking agency for professional chamber ensembles, which are primarily from Kansas state colleges and universities. Supports mini-residencies, workshops, clinics, concert series, and elementary school programs, and a series of in-depth programs designed particularly for young audiences.
Music Budget: $10,000.00-$24,999.00.

Neodesha Arts Association
Mrs. Leon Faweet, Executive Director
P.O. Box 65
Neodesha, KS 66757
(316) 325-3239
Mrs. W. C. Gausman, Music Chairman
A city agency serving Southwest Kansas.
Supports chamber music, new and experimental music, jazz.
Provides financial support, performing facilities.
Music Budget: Under $100.00.

Neosho Valley Arts Council*
Doris Dalton, President
P.O. Box 429
Chanute, KS 66720
Supports chamber music, symphonic music, operatic music, folk music.

Western Plains Art Council*
Ms. Dewey Nelle Classi, President
P.O. Box 56
Brewster, KS 67732
(913) 694-2794
Supports chamber music, symphonic music, operatic music.

Kentucky

State Arts Agency:

Kentucky Arts Commission
Ms. Nash Cox, Executive Director
Louisville Gas and Electric
311 West Chestnut Street
Louisville, KY 40202
(502) 582-3511.

Lexington Philharmonic Society
Betsy Kennedy, Executive Director
P.O. Box 3838
Lexington, KY 40501
(606) 266-0311
A non-profit organization.
Supports chamber music, jazz.
Provides financial support. Sponsors one world premiere performance per year by Lexington Philharmonic Orchestra.
Music Budget: $500.00-$999.00; 31%-40% for 20th century music.

Living Arts And Science Center*
James E. Seidelman, Executive Director
362 Walnut
Lexington, KY 40508
(606) 252-5222
Supports chamber music.

Louisiana

State Arts Agency:

Louisiana Council For Music And Performing Arts
Mrs. Edwin H. Blum, President
611 Gravier Street
Suite 804 International Building
New Orleans, LA 70130
(504) 527-5070 or 525-7241.

Council Of Arts For Children In New Orleans*
Ann Melser, Executive Director
624 Louisiana Avenue
New Orleans, LA 70115
(504) 899-0203
Supports chamber music, jazz.

Louisiana State University
School of Music
Everett Timm, Dean
Baton Rouge, LA 70803
(504) 388-3261
Supports 20th century chamber music, new and experimental music, jazz, symphonic music, choral music, operatic music.

95

Provides performing facilities. Sponsors Festival of Contemporary Music, concerts, and recitals.

Rapides Arts Council*
Mrs. LeDoux R. Provosty, Jr., President
P.O. Box 1086
Alexandria, LA 71301
(318) 443-3219
Supports symphonic music, popular music.

Maine

State Arts Agency:

Maine State Commission On The Arts And Humanities
Alden C. Wilson, Executive Director
State House
Augusta, ME 04330
(207) 289-2724
Supports 20th century chamber music, new and experimental music, jazz, symphonic music, popular music.
Provides financial support.
Music Budget: $25,000.00-$49,000.00; 91%-100% for 20th century music.

Augusta Music Society
Myrtle D. Willey, President
P.O. Box 2105
Augusta, ME 04330
(207) 582-5350
A private endowment serving Augusta, Winthrop, and Lewiston.
Supports jazz.
Presents monthly jazz concerts by Society members and hired groups.
Music Budget: $1,000.00-$4,999.00; 21%-30% for 20th century music.

The Coastal Arts Council*
Mary Sullivan, President
P.O. Box 155
Camden, ME 04843
(207) 236-2451
Supports symphonic music, operatic music, folk music.

Forum-A
James R. Floyd, Community Arts Coordinator
University of Maine
Augusta, ME 04330
(207) 622-7131 Ext. 212
Supports 20th century chamber music, new and experimental music, jazz, popular music.

Joint arts organization of the University and community. Sponsors musical events and coordinates arts programs for the area.

Maryland

State Arts Agency:

Maryland Arts Council
James Backas, Executive Director
15 West Mulberry Street
Baltimore, MD 21201
(301) 685-7470
Supports 20th century chamber music, new and experimental music, jazz.
Provides financial support. Funds performing organizations and sponsoring organizations. Supports university cultural arts series and music department programs.

Academy Of The Arts*
John Donoho, Chairman
P.O. Box 605
Easton, MD 21601
(301) 822-0455
Supports chamber music.

Anne Arundel Arts Association*
Heannett Stanford, Chairman
Department of Parks and Recreation
Room 415 Arundel Center
Annapolis, MD 21401
(301) 268-4300 Ext. 255
Supports symphonic music, operatic music, ethnic music.

The Chamber Music Society Of Baltimore, Inc.
Randolph S. Rothschild, President
2909 Woodvalley Drive
Baltimore, MD 21208
(301) 486-7566
A non-profit organization.
Supports chamber music.
Provides financial support, performing facilities. Produces concerts of new and old chamber works, assists in the commissioning of new works, sponsors recordings.
Music Budget: $5,000.00-$9,999.00; 61%-70% for 20th century music.

Charles County Parks And Recreation Department*
Edward R. Corley, Director
P.O. Box 368
LaPlata, MD 20646
(301) 934-9305
Supports symphonic music.

Massachusetts

State Arts Agency:

Massachusetts Council On The Arts And Humanities
Louise G. Tate, Executive Director
14 Beacon Street
Boston, MA 02108
(617) 727-3668
Clement Van Buren, Public Information
Supports 20th century chamber music, new and experimental music, jazz.
Provides grants to performing ensembles and artists for college residencies. Provides grants to composers through the Massachusetts Arts and Humanities Foundation Creative Artists Services Fellowships. Sponsors arts service organizations. Co-sponsors New England Contemporary Music Circuit with arts councils of Connecticut and Rhode Island. The Music Circuit presents concerts and lecture-demonstrations on contemporary music performed by ensembles from the 3 states. The participating ensembles make their presentations in the 3 states at colleges which act as co-sponsors.
Music Budget: Over $100,000.00; 10%-20% for 20th century music.

Berkshire Music Center
Gunther Schuller, Director
Lenox, MA 01240
(413) 637-1600
Daniel Gustin, Administor
Supports 20th century chamber music, new and experimental music.
Co-sponsors with the Fromm Music Foundation at Harvard the annual Tanglewood Festival of Contemporary Music. Commissions works which are performed at the Festival.

Cape Cod Conservatory*
Richard Casper, Director
P.O. Box 637
Barnstable, MA 02630
(617) 362-2772
Supports chamber music, symphonic music.

Committee Of The Permanent Charity Fund*
Donald J. Hurley, President
1 Boston Place, Room 3005
Boston, MA 02106
Serves metropolitan Boston.
Funds the operating costs of new and established institutions when they are planning new or experimental projects. Funds educational programs.

Community Music Center Of Boston
Michael L. Garroway, Executive Director
48 Warren Avenue
Boston, MA 02116
(617) 482-7494
A non-profit educational organization serving the greater Boston area.
Supports 20th century chamber music, new and experimental music, jazz, contemporary choral music.
Music Budget: $500.00-$999.00; 10%-20% for 20th century music.

Council For The Arts At Massachusetts Institute Of Technology*
Alice McHugh, Executive Director
Cambridge, MA 02108
(617) 723-4045
Supports symphonic music.

Creative Artists Services
See Massachusetts Arts and Humanities Foundation, Inc.

Creative Media, Inc.
Christopher Yavelow, Executive Director
P.O. Box 74
Nahant, MA 01908
(617) 354-1139
A non-profit organization serving New England.
Supports 20th century chamber music, new and experimental music, dance, mime, theater.
Umbrella organization for Annex Players, The Atlantic Arts Association, Boston Bach Ensemble, Kinesis, and Outstanding Artists Chamber Music Series. Holds an annual competition for new music, dance, and film. Winning work is

97

performed by Kinesis, and a new work by winner is commissioned. Entry deadline: April 1.
Music Budget: $1,000.00-$4,999.00; 71%-80% for 20th century music.

Lincoln And Therese Filene Foundation, Inc.*
George E. Ladd, Jr., President
c/o Nutter, McClennen and Fish
75 Federal Street, 8th Floor
Boston, MA 02110
Sponsors projects concerned with higher education, music, and the performing arts.

Fogg Art Museum
Seymour Slive, Executive Director
Harvard University
32 Quincy Street
Cambridge, MA 02138
(617) 495-2397
Janet Cox, Public Relations
Supports chamber music.
Provides financial support to performers, performing facilities.
Sponsors several free public concert series.
Music Budget: $500.00-$999.00; Under 10% for 20th century music.

Fromm Music Foundation At Harvard
Elliot Forbes, Paul Fromm, Gunther Schuller, Directors
Harvard University
Music Building
Cambridge, MA 02138
(617) 495-2791
A private foundation serving the U.S.A.
Supports 20th century chamber music, new and experimental music.
Sponsors contemporary music composition and performance. Commissions works. Sponsors performances of single concerts, series, and festivals. Funds performing projects which create conditions under which contemporary music can become an integral part of concert life, including recording and radio projects. Co-sponsors with the Berkshire Music Center the annual Tanglewood Festival of Contemporary Music. Funds seminars and publications concerned with contemporary music.
Reply Address: Fromm Music Foundation at Harvard
Chicago Office
1028 West Van Buren Street
Chicago, IL 60607.

Goethe Institute
Dr. Erhard Stadtler, Executive Director
170 Beacon Street
Boston, MA 02116
(617) 262-6050
A West German agency serving New England.
Supports 20th century chamber music, new and experimental music.
Provides financial support, performing facilities. Sponsors performers from Boston and West Germany who present concerts, workshops, and master classes which promote German culture in the U.S.A.
Music Budget: $1,000.00-$4,999.00; 21%-30% for 20th century music.

Harvard University
Department of Music
Elliot Forbes, Chairman
Music Building
Cambridge, MA 02138
(617) 495-2791
Supports 20th century chamber music.
Co-sponsors with the Fromm Music Foundation at Harvard a series of free public concerts of contemporary music.

Godfrey M. Hyams Trust*
Richard Erlich, Chairman
1 Boston Place, 33rd Floor
Boston, MA 02108
Serves Massachusetts charitable corporations.
Sponsors projects concerned with Jewish welfare, youth agencies, community funds, and recreation.
Contributes to operating funds of Massachusetts cultural institutions.

Massachusetts Arts And Humanities Foundation, Inc.
Creative Artists Services
Susan Channing, Coordinator
14 Beacon Street
Boston, MA 02108
(617) 723-3851
Creative Artists Services is a program of the Massachusetts Council on the Arts and Humanities. It assists individual Massachusetts artists in their work through direct fellowships awarded on the basis of artistic excellence.
Eligibility: Creative artists committed to careers in music composition, photography, film, video, poetry, fiction, playwrighting, and choreography may apply. Applicants must be Massachusetts residents over 18 years of age who can submit a

representative body of work which demonstrates a high level of accomplishment in the field in which the application is made. Fellowships are $3,000.00.

Massasoit Community College
c/o Director of Student Activities
290 Thatcher Street
Brockton, MA 02402
(617) 588-9100
Supports 20th century chamber music, new and experimental music.
Provides financial support. Sponsors touring ensembles offering concerts and lecture-demonstrations on contemporary music.

Merrimack Valley Council On The Arts And Humanities
George C. Capron, Executive Director
4 Summer Street, Room 303
Haverhill, MA 01830
(617) 373-0421
A regional agency serving Northern Essex and Eastern Middlesex Counties.
Supports 20th century chamber music, new and experimental music, jazz.
Provides publicity, ticket sales. Promotes the arts locally by making artistic events available at a low cost to as many people as possible.
Music Program Budget: $500.00-$999.00; 10%-20% for 20th century music.

Metropolitan Cultural Alliance
Alice McHugh, Executive Director
37 Newbury Street
Boston, MA 02116
(617) 247-1460
A membership organization serving metropolitan Boston.
Organizes community cultural projects, such as placing performer members in school workshops. Books members who perform music, dance, and drama with members who act as sponsors in offering their performing facilities.

Museum of Fine Arts Musical Instruments Collection
Barbara Lambert, Keeper of Musical Instruments
Huntington Avenue
Boston, MA 02115
(617) 267-9300 Ext. 340
A private endowment.
Presents 20th century chamber music, new and experimental music.

Provides financial support, performing facilities. Presents Collage Concert Series, featuring Collage-Contemporary Music Ensemble of Boston. Presents Music Here and Now Series, featuring works played on instruments from the Museum's Musical Instruments Collection.

New England Contemporary Music Circuit
See Massachusetts Council on the Arts and Humanities.

Performing Arts Council of Franklin County, Inc.*
John Francis Bednarski, President
Newell Pond Place
Greenfield, MA 01301
(413) 772-0961
Supports symphonic music, ethnic music.

Rowland Foundation*
Edwin H. Land, President
P.O. Box 13
Cambridge, MA 02138
Serves local area.

William E. And Bertha E. Schrafft Charitable Trust*
c/o Hazen H. Ayer
50 Congress Street
Boston, MA 02109
Serves charitable corporations within Massachusetts.
Sponsors community funds and youth agencies. Funds performing organizations and cultural programs at educational institutions.

Nathaniel And Elizabeth P. Stevens Foundation*
c/o Caroline S. Rogers
2 Johnson Street
North Andover, MA 01845
Serves Massachusetts.
Sponsors projects concerned with local public and private elementary and secondary schools, and community funds. Sponsors performing organizations with youth education programs.

Walpole Arts Council*
Mrs. Wayne O. Stacy, President
South Holly Road
Walpole, MA 02081
(617) 668-6572
Supports chamber music, symphonic music.

Michigan

State Arts Agency:

Michigan Council For The Arts
E. Ray Scott, Executive Director
10125 East Jefferson Avenue
Detroit, MI 48214
(313) 256-3731.

Albion Community Arts Program*
Elsie Munro, Executive Director
P.O. Box 588
Albion, MI 49224
(517) 629-2543
Supports chamber music, jazz, popular music.

Algonac Sponsors Of The Arts
Bonnie Potter, Chairman
820 Golf View
Algonac, MI 48001
(313) 794-3728
A regional agency.
Promotes local arts activities.
Music Budget: $1,000.00-$4,999.00; 21%-30% for 20th century music.

Cadillac Area Council For The Arts*
David E. Naylor, Chairman
2951 West M55
Cadillac, MI 49601
(616) 775-5055
Supports symphonic music, folk music.

Cheboygan Area Arts Council*
Mrs. August Tranquilla, President
P.O. Box 95
Cheboygan, MI 49721
Supports symphonic music.

Chrysler Corporation Fund*
T. Killefer, President
Chrysler Center
12000 Oakland Avenue
Highland Park, MI 48203
Sponsors cultural projects, race relations programs, and community funds. Supports established music performing organizations and music festivals.

Delta Iota Chapter
Phi Mu Alpha Sinfonia
See Phi Mu Alpha Sinfonia

Detroit Adventure, Inc.
Mrs. Alacoque D. Barrow, Executive Secretary
100 West Kirby
Detroit, MI 48202
(313) 577-2330
An association of schools, local arts councils, and libraries serving metropolitan Detroit.
Promotes cultural activities of members by publishing a calendar of events. Administers the Excursions in Music Program which presents professional performing ensembles in public schools.

The DeWaters Charitable Trust*
James R. Kettler, Executive Director
Michigan National Bank
503 South Saginaw Street
Flint, MI 48502
Serves Genesee County.
Sponsors projects concerned with elementary and secondary education. Funds scholarships and cultural institutions.

Eaton Rapids Fine Arts Council
Mary Minnich, President
202 State Street
Eaton Rapids, MI 48827
Sponsors an annual Children's Art Show, prepares an arts programs calendar, and coordinates plans of other local arts organizations.
Music Budget: Under $100.00.

Fenton Living Theatre Series*
Jack T. Winegarden, President
715 Worchester Drive
Fenton, MI 48430
(313) 629-5152
Supports chamber music, jazz, symphonic music, ethnic music, popular music.

Henry Ford Centennial Library
Audio-Visual Division
Rollin P. Marquis, Librarian
16301 Michigan Avenue
Dearborn, MI 48126
(313) 271-1000
A public library serving the Detroit area.
Supports jazz, popular music.
Provides performing facilities. Sponsors free public concerts.

Gogebic Council For the Arts*
Carl Mockross, President
P.O. Box 255
Ironwood, MI 49938
(906) 932-4101
Supports chamber music, symphonic music, operatic music, ethnic music.

Grand Haven Community Arts Council*
Bernard Boyink, Executive Director
421 Columbus Street
Grand Haven, MI 49417
(616) 842-2550
Supports chamber music, jazz, symphonic music, operatic music, ethnic music, popular music.

Jackson Coordinating Committee For Michigan Outreach*
Bernice R. Otis, Director
Jackson Community College
2111 Emmons Road
Jackson, MI 49201
(517) 787-0800
Supports chamber music, jazz, ethnic music, popular music.

Kresge Foundation*
William H. Baldwin, President
1500 North Woodward Avenue
Birmingham, MI 48011
Funds building construction or renovation, music, and institutions of higher education.

Menominee Arts Council, Inc.
John B. Henes, Executive Director
1502 First Street
Menominee, MI 49858
(906) 863-2524
A private endowment serving Menominee.
Promotes the arts locally.
Music Budget: Under $100.00; Under 10% for 20th century music.

Midland Center For The Arts*
Don Jaeger, Executive Director
1801 West St. Andrews
Midland, MI 48640
(517) 631-5930
Supports chamber music, operatic music, symphonic music, ethnic music, folk music.

Charles Stewart Mott Foundation*
Charles Stewart Mott, Honorary Chairman and Treasurer
500 Mott Foundation Building
Flint, MI 48602
Provides grants for adult education, music education, recreation, and community schools.
Offers fellowship grants to universities for community education centers.

Peninsula Arts Appreciation Council*
John Pontti, President
1010 North 2nd Street
Ishpeming, MI 49849
(906) 485-5227 or 486-4326
Supports chamber music, jazz, symphonic music, popular music.

Phi Mu Alpha Sinfonia
Delta Iota Chapter
Western Michigan University
Maybee Music Hall
Kalamazoo, MI 49001
(616) 383-0910
A professional music fraternity serving Lower Michigan.
Supports 20th century chamber music, new and experimental music, jazz.
Provides financial support, performing facilities, publicity for concerts.
Music Budget: $1,000.00-$4,999.00; 71%-80% for 20th century music.

The Henry Reichhold Foundation*
Henry H. Reichhold, President
1657 City National Bank Building
Detroit, MI 48226
Supports community funds, music, and education.

Space In South Haven*
V. C. M. Anderson, President
615 Williams Street
South Haven, MI 49090
(616) 637-9914
Supports chamber music, jazz, ethnic music, popular music.

Steelcase Foundation*
c/o Trustee David D. Hunting
Old Kent Bank and Trust Company
Grand Rapids, MI 49502
Sponsors community funds, higher education, and youth agencies.

Thunder Bay Arts Council*
Stanley C. Beck, President
3167 U.S. 23 South
Alpena, MI 49707
(616) 354-8728
Supports symphonic music, operatic music.

Tibbits Opera Foundation And Arts Council, Inc.*
John Milnes, President
14 South Hanchett Street
Coldwater, MI 49036
(517) 278-6029
Supports chamber music, symphonic music.

Warren Cultural Commission
Tom Carey, Executive Director
29500 Van Dyke Avenue
Warren, MI 48093
(313) 772-8919
A city agency.
Supports jazz, musical theater, popular music.
Promotes and develops local arts programs.
Music Budget: $5,000.00-$9,999.00; 10%-20% for
20th century music.

Minnesota

State Arts Agency:

Minnesota State Arts Council
Louis Janson, Executive Director
100 East 22nd Street
Minneapolis, MN 55404
(612) 874-1335
Supports 20th century chamber music, new and
experimental music, jazz.
Sponsors contemporary concerts at the Walker Art
Center in Minneapolis. Funds a composer-in-
residence program which brings a composer to
Minnesota to work extensively with performing
ensembles.

F. A. Bean Foundation, Inc.*
H. G. McConnell, Managing Director
1200 Investors Building
Minneapolis, MN 55415
Serves local area.
Sponsors cultural, religious, and community
welfare projects.

The Bush Foundation*
Humphrey Doermann, Executive Director
W-962 First National Bank Building
St. Paul, MN 55101
Sponsors higher education and the performing
arts. Funds local orchestras and opera companies.

Cedar-Riverside Arts Council*
Ann Payson, Chairman
1812 South 6th Street
Minneapolis, MN 55404
(612) 336-9130
Supports chamber music, jazz, popular music,
ethnic music.

Edwin W. And Catherine M. Davis Foundation*
Mrs. Bette D. Moorman, President
W-2191 First National Bank Building
St. Paul, MN 55101
Offers grants for higher education, medical
research, youth agencies, local community funds,
music, race relations projects, and social agencies.
No grants to individuals.

Dayton Hudson Foundation*
Wayne E. Thompson, President
777 Nicollet Mall
Minneapolis, MN 55402
Supports social and cultural programs aimed at
improving urban environment in areas of the
corporation's operation. Sponsors established
cultural institutions such as orchestras and opera
companies. Funds construction of performing
halls.

The First Unitarian Society
Uri Barnea, Music Director
900 Mt. Curve Avenue
Minneapolis, MN 55403
(612) 377-6608
Supports 20th century chamber music, new and
experimental music, vocal and solo instrumental
recitals.
Sponsors the Unitarian Chorus and Orchestra in
its Divertimento Concert Series. Also sponsors the
Divertimento Recital Series, featuring 20th
century works, and Composer Sunday, featuring a
contemporary composer every other year.
Music Budget: $1,000.00-$4,999.00; 21%-40% for
20th century music.

General Mills Foundation*

Thomas M. Crosby, President

9200 Wayzata Boulevard

Minneapolis, MN 55426

Sponsors projects concerned with civic and cultural activities. Funds local orchestras.

Minnesota Composers Forum, Inc.

Stephen Pauls, Elizabeth Larsen, Directors

University of Minnesota

104C Scott Hall

Minneapolis, MN 55455

(612) 373-3452

A non-profit organization serving Minnesota.

Supports 20th century chamber music, new and experimental music, jazz, new church music, theater music.

Provides financial support, performing facilities. Promotes the creation and performance of new works by Minnesota composers. Presents Minnesota Composers Forum New Music Series at Walker Art Center in Minneapolis. Presents lectures and encourages Minnesota performing organizations to play new works. Helps composers to secure commissions and acts as an information center.

Music Budget: $1,000.00-$4,999.00; 91%-100% for 20th century music.

Plymouth Congregational Church

Philip Brunelle, Music Director

1900 Nicollet Avenue

Minneapolis, MN 55403

(612) 871-7400

Supports 20th century liturgical music.

Provides financial support, performing facilities. Sponsors Plymouth Music Series, featuring premieres of commissioned works and performances of neglected works.

Music Budget: $5,000.00-$9,999.00; 71%-80% for 20th century music.

St. Paul Council Of Arts And Sciences*

Marlow G. Burt, Executive Director

30 East 10th Street

St. Paul, MN 55701

(612) 227-8241

Supports chamber music, symphonic music.

Southwest Minnesota Arts And Humanities Council

Phyllis Stibler, Executive Director

P.O. Box 583

Marshall, MN 56258

(507) 537-6201(2)

A private, non-profit organization.

Supports 20th century chamber music, new and experimental music, jazz.

Sponsors local composers, regional performing groups, and touring ensembles. Coordinates performance schedules and publishes a quarterly arts calendar and magazine.

Music Budget: $10,000.00-$24,999.00; 41%-50% for 20th century music.

Walker Art Center

Martin Friedman, Executive Director

Vineland Place

Minneapolis, MN 55403

(612) 377-7500

Supports 20th century chamber music, new and experimental music, jazz.

Provides performing facilities, promotion, and funds costs. Presents concerts, workshops, and lectures concerning contemporary music, visual arts, crafts, and drama.

West Bank School Of Music

Warren Park, Executive Director

1813 6th Street South

Minneapolis, MN 55404

(612) 336-6651

Supports 20th century chamber music, new and experimental music, jazz, folk music, popular music.

Organizes and promotes concert series.

Mississippi

State Arts Agency:

Mississippi Arts Commission

Mrs. Shelby Rogers, Executive Director

P.O. Box 1341

301 North Lamar Street

Jackson, MS 39205

(601) 354-7336

Supports 20th century music.

Provides grants for programs in community arts development and personnel development of arts organizations. Funds guest and resident artists. Coordinates arts activities, touring performances, arts appreciation programs for youth, and arts information and communications programs. Presents arts conferences on subjects neglected by educational institutions. Provides consultants to work with arts organizations. Publishes *Directory of Performing Arts Organizations in Mississippi.*

Greater Gulf Coast Arts Council*
Mrs. O. Z. Culler, Chairman
15 Mockingbird Lane
Gulfport, MS 39501
(601) 896-1600
Supports symphonic music, operatic music, ethnic music, folk music.

Hattiesburg Civic Arts Council*
Mrs. Stewart Gammill III, President
P.O. Box 693
Hattiesburg, MS 39401
(601) 544-3969
Supports symphonic music, operatic music.

Laurel Arts Council
James D. Bowne, Executive Director
c/o Laurew Rogers Museum
Laurel, MS 39440
(601) 425-1722
Supports 20th century chamber music, folk music, choral music, popular music.
Provides financial support, performing facilities. Offers the town a varied music program in conjunction with art exhibits.
Music Budget: $500.00-$999.00; 31%-40% for 20th century music.

Missouri

State Arts Agency:

Missouri State Council On The Arts
Emily Rice, Executive Director
111 South Berniston
St. Louis, MO 63105
(314) 721-1672
Supports all types of music.
Provides financial support. Funds performing, sponsoring, and service organizations.
Music Budget: Over $100,000.00.

Allied Arts Council Of St. Joseph*
Madeline Barlow, Executive Director
510 Francis Street
St. Joseph, MO 64501
(816) 233-0231
Supports symphonic music, operatic music.

Art Research Center
Thomas M. Stephens, President
922 East 48th Street
Kansas City, MO 64110
(816) 531-2067
A public foundation funded by federal and state goverments.
Supports 20th century chamber music, new and experimental music, electronic music, jazz.
Provides financial support, performing facilities. Sponsors collaboration of professional musicians, dancers, visual artists, actors, and film makers. Presents performances of works by member musicians and local composers on traditional and experimental instruments.
Music Budget: $1,000.00-$4,999.00; 91%-100% for 20th century music.

Arts And Education Council Of Greater St. Louis
Anthony B. Turney, Executive Director
607 North Grand
St. Louis, MO 63103
(314) 531-6450
Serves the Greater St. Louis area.
Provides publicity on a monthly calendar.

Arts And Recreation Council Of The Cape Girardeau Area
Sharon Dow, Executive Director
P.O. Box 901
Cape Girardeau, MO 63701
(314) 334-4061
A local arts council serving Southeast Missouri and Southern Illinois.
Supports new and experimental music.
Produces community arts events, encouraging community participation and patronage.
Music Budget: $100.00-$499.00; 51%-60% for 20th century music.

Florissant Fine Arts Council*
Marvin Standley, President
955 Rue St. Francois
Florissant, MO 63135
(314) 921-5700 Ext. 34
Supports symphonic music.

H.E.L.P. Inc.*
Cultural Enrichment School
Harry Rhetta, Executive Director
4290 Natural Bridge
St. Louis, MO 63115
(314) 531-3285

Supports chamber music, ethnic music, folk music.

Nodaway Arts Council*
David A. Shestak, President
P.O. Box 55
Maryville, MO 64468
Supports chamber music, symphonic music, folk music.

Ozark Foothills Arts Council*
Margaret Harwell, President
315 Oak Street
Popular Bluff, MO 63901
(314) 785-3138
Supports chamber music.

Parkville Fine Arts Association*
Mrs. Jay W. Burnett, President
P.O. Box 12082
Parkville, MO 64152
(816) 741-7270
Supports symphonic music.

Montana

State Arts Agency:

Montana Arts Council
David E. Nelson, Executive Director
235 East Pine
Missoula, MT 59801
(406) 543-8286.

Flathead Valley Art Association, Hockaday Center*
Karen J. Lauder, President
P.O. Box 83
2nd Avenue East and 3rd Street
Kalispell, MT 59901
(406) 756-9371
Supports chamber music, operatic music, folk music.

Montana State University
Department of Music
Creech Reynolds, Executive Director
Bozeman, MT 59715
(406) 994-3561
Supports 20th century chamber music, new and experimental music, jazz.
Provides performing facilities. Sponsors Annual Jazz Festival and Annual Contemporary Music Festival.

Yellowstone Art Center*
John A. Armstrong, Director
401 North 27th Street
Billings, MT 59101
(406) 259-1869
Supports chamber music.

Nebraska

State Arts Agency:

Nebraska Arts Council
Gerald L. Ness, Executive Director
Oak Park
7367 Pacific Street
Omaha, NE 68114
(402) 391-1835
Supports 20th century chamber music, new and experimental music, jazz.
Provides matching grants. Stimulates the study and presentation of the arts in Nebraska.

McCook Area Arts Council*
Mrs. John T. Harris, Chairman
Defender's Townhouse
McCook, NE 69001
(305) 345-3739
Supports chamber music, symphonic music, choral music.

Nevada

State Arts Agency·

Nevada State Council On The Arts
Merle L. Snider, Acting Executive Director
560 Mill Street
Reno, NV 89502
(702) 784-6231.

Northern Nevada Arts Council*
Merle L. Snider, Executive Director
1962 Harmony Road
Winnemucca, NV 89445
(702) 623-2491
Supports ethnic music.

University of Nevada
Music Department
4505 Maryland Parkway
Las Vegas, NV 89154
(702) 739-3332
Supports 20th century chamber music, new and experimental music.
Provides financial support, performing facilities,

administrative support. Sponsors the Annual Contemporary Music Festival.

New Hampshire

State Arts Agency:

New Hampshire Commission On The Arts
John G. Loe, Executive Director
40 North Main Street
Concord, NH 03301
(603) 271-2780
Supports 20th century chamber music, new and experimental music.
Provides financial support. Promotes, stimulates, and encourages presentations of the arts to New Hampshire citizens. Sponsors community residencies for performing ensembles. Supports Experimental Arts In Education, a school and performance center dedicated to 20th century music instruction and performance.
Music Budget: $25,000.00-$49,000.00; Under 10% for 20th century music.

Arts And Science Center
Ronald Deane, Executive Director
14 Court Street
Nashua, NH 03060
(603) 883-1506
Supports 20th century chamber music, new and experimental music, jazz.
Provides performing facilities. Promotes musical performances in Southern New Hampshire.
Music Budget: $1,000.00-$4,999.00.

Arts Council Of Greater Concord
Dennis Metnick, Executive Director
40 North Main Street
Phenix Hall
Concord, NH 03301
(603) 225-6911
A local arts council serving the greater Concord area.
Supports 20th century chamber music, jazz.
Provides performing facilities, publicity. Brings arts programs to the area.
Music Budget: $1,000.00-$4,999.00; 21%-30% for 20th century music.

Dartmouth College
Department of Music
Jon Appleton, Christian Wolff, Directors
P.O. Box 746
Hanover, NH 03755
(603) 646-2520
Supports 20th century chamber music, new and experimental music, jazz, electronic music.
Provides financial support, performing facilities. Has an electronic music studio. Offers guest composer lectures and has a resident composer program.

Greater Concord Arts Council
Kate Torres, Executive Director
40 North Main Street
Phenix Hall
Concord, NH 03301
(603) 225-6911
A regional agency serving Concord and Southern New Hampshire.
Supports 20th century chamber music, new and experimental music.
An arts center providing financial assistance, free performing facilities, and free publicity to local creative and performing artists. Sponsors the Noon-Time Concert Series of 20th century chamber music on 20 Fridays each season.
Music Budget: $500.00-$999.00; 41%-50% for 20th century music.

Manchester Institute Of Arts And Sciences*
James K. Boatner, Executive Director
148 Concord Street
Manchester, NH 03104
(603) 623-0313
Supports chamber music, jazz, symphonic music, operatic music, ethnic music, popular music.

St. Anselm's College*
Eugene D. Rice, Director of Student Activities
St. Anselm's Drive
Manchester, NH 03102
(603) 668-1030
Supports chamber music, jazz, symphonic music, popular music, ethnic music.

Sharon Arts Center, Inc.
Carl Jackson, Managing Director
Route 2
Peterborough, NH 03458
(603) 924-3582
A private, non-profit organization serving South Central New Hampshire and Northern Massachusetts.
Supports 20th century chamber music, jazz.
Provides performing facilities. Primarily a visual art instruction and display facility, with a secondary goal of providing interesting programs in all the arts.

New Jersey

State Arts Agency:

New Jersey State Council On The Arts
Brann J. Wry, Executive Director
27 West State Street
Trenton, NJ 08625
(609) 292-6130
Supports 20th century chamber music, new and experimental music, jazz.
Provides financial support. Provides grants for non-profit organizations. Matching grants of up to $15,000.00 available to non-profit community groups and arts organizations. Matching funds may be in the form of money, contributed services, or memberships. Awards to individual artists, including commissions to composers of up to $3,000.00.
Music Budget: Over $100,000.00.

Art Center Of Northern New Jersey*
Byron Kelley, Executive Director
10 Jay Street
Tenafly, NJ 07670
(201) 871-3373
Supports chamber music.

Arts Council Of The Morris Area
Barbara Keefauver, Executive Director
Hannan House
Drew University
Madison, NJ 07940
(201) 377-6622
A non-profit service organization providing calendar coordination, mailing, promotion, and program planning. Has arts resources files.

Arts Council Of Princeton, Inc.*
Philetus H. Holt III, President
44 Nassau Street
Princeton, NJ 08540
(609) 921-7676
Supports chamber music.

Burlington County Cultural And Heritage Commission
Keith W. Betten, Executive Director
49 Rancocas Road
Mount Holly, NJ 08060
(609) 267-3300 Ext. 228
A county agency.
Provides publicity. Advises Burlington County's artists and arts organizations and coordinates arts activities.

Music Budget: $100.00-$499.00.

Camden County Cultural And Heritage Commission
Gail Greenberg, Executive Director
Courthouse, 10th Floor
Camden, NJ 08101
(609) 966-1844
A county agency.
Supports various types of music.
Provides financial support. Develops programs which promote public interest in local and county history. Promotes interest in the arts.
Music Budget: $1,000.00-$4,999.00.

Clinton Historical Museum
Gloria Lazor, Executive Director
56 Main Street
P.O. Box 5005
Clinton, NJ 08809
(201) 735-4101
A private, non-profit organization serving Hunterdon, Somerset, and Morris Counties.
Supports 20th century chamber music, new and experimental music, jazz, folk music.
Provides financial support, performing facilities. Produces and sponsors the summer Concerts in the Park Series, presenting various performing ensembles in order to raise money for the Museum.
Music Budget: $1,000.00-$4,999.00; 31%-40% for 20th century music.

Composer's Forum Project
c/o Jeffrey Kaufman
200 Winston Drive
Cliffside Park, NJ 07010
(201) 224-6376
A non-profit organization.
Sponsors Composer's Forum Radio Series, featuring contemporary composers in interviews with Martin Bookspan on non-commercial public radio.

Highland Park Arts Commission*
Irving Klaus, Chairman
Borough Hall
21 South Fourth Avenue
Highland, NJ 08904
(201) 572-3400
Supports chamber music, jazz, symphonic music, operatic music, ethnic music, popular music.

107

Ernest Christian Klipstein Foundation*
Kenneth H. Klipstein, President
Village Road
New Vernon, NJ 07976
Supports projects concerned with higher education, music, hospitals, and public welfare.

Mercer County Cultural And Heritage Commission
Catherine Makowicz, Executive Director
640 South Broad Street
Trenton, NJ 08607
(609) 989-8000 Ext. 293
A county agency.
Supports 20th century chamber music, new and experimental music.
Provides financial support. Fosters public knowledge, appreciation, and participation in cultural activities.
Music Budget: $1,000.00-$4,999.00; 10%-20% for 20th century music.

The Merck Company Foundation*
Grace M. Winterling, President
Rahway, NJ 07065
Sponsors state and regional associations of independent colleges, community charities, orchestras. No grants for research projects.

Monmouth County Arts Council, Inc.
Eduardo Garcia, Executive Director
99 Monmouth Street
Red Bank, NJ 07701
(201) 842-9000
A county agency.
A service organization which will make available a performing facility to member organizations at reduced rates.

New Jersey Jazz Society
P.O. Box 302
Pluckemin, NJ 07978
A non-profit organization.
Supports jazz.
Sponsors 6 to 8 annual jazz parties, hiring ensembles that perform jazz of all styles.
Music Budget: $1,000.00-$4,999.00; 100% for 20th century music.

Paterson Free Public Library
Leo Fichtelberg, Executive Director
250 Broadway
Paterson, NJ 07501
(201) 279-4200
A city agency.
Supports 20th century chamber music, new and experimental music.
Presents Always on Sunday Series and a chamber music series.

Turrell Fund*
Vincent J. Riggio, Executive Director
15 South Munn Avenue
East Orange, NJ 07018
S. Whitney Landon, President
Sponsors only organizations dedicated to service or care of youth, with emphasis on needy, maladjusted, and socially, physically, or mentally handicapped. Sponsors performing ensembles presenting youth concerts.

Victoria Foundation*
2 Russell Terrace
Montclair, NJ 07042
Serves Northern New Jersey primarily.
Sponsors orchestras. Gives special consideration to pilot projects meeting urban problems when a limited amount is needed to begin the project and the eventual goal is to be self-supporting.

John Jay And Eliza Jane Watson Foundation*
507 Westminster Avenue
Elizabeth, NJ 07208
Serves New York Metropolitan area.
Sponsors educational programs of music performing organizations. Gives priority to institutions meeting important public needs. No long term support of operating budgets.

YM-YWHA Of Metropolitan New Jersey
Zev Hymowitz, Executive Director
760 Northfield Avenue
West Orange, NJ 07052
(201) 736-3200
Supports chamber music, new and experimental music, jazz, electronic music.
A social service agency with an arts department serving Metropolitan New Jersey. Presents concerts and donates performing facilities.
Music Budget: $10,000.00-$24,999.00; Under 10% for 20th century music.

New Mexico

State Arts Agency:

New Mexico Arts Commission
John E. Wyant, Executive Director
Lew Wallace Building
Capitol Complex
Santa Fe, NM 87501
(505) 827-2061.

Carlsbad Arts Council*
Mrs. Roy H. Carey, Jr., Chairman
1308 Gamma Street
Carlsbad, NM 88220
(505) 885-5904
Supports chamber music, folk music.

Los Alamos Arts Council*
Carol Ann Mullaney, President
P.O. Box 284
Los Alamos, NM 87544
Supports chamber music, jazz, symphonic music, operatic music, popular music, ethnic music.

Socorro Art League*
507 Fitch Avenue
Socorro, NM 87801
(505) 835-0217
Supports chamber music.

Taos School Of Music
Chilton Anderson, Executive Director
P.O. Box 1879
Taos, NM 87571
(505) 776-2388
Supports chamber music.
Presents a concert series which include 20th century works.

New York State

Excluding New York City

State Arts Agency:

New York State Council On The Arts
Joan Davidson, Chairman
250 West 57th Street
New York, NY 10019
(212) 397-1700
Arthur Bloom, Music Associate
Supports 20th century chamber music, new and experimental music, jazz.
Eligibility for grants: all ensembles with more than 2 years continuity providing quality performances for the New York State public, which apply to the Council for deficit funds.
Music Budget: $6,500,000.00; Under 10% for 20th century music.

Artpark
David Midland, Acting Executive Director
P.O. Box 371
Lewiston, NY 14092
(716) 745-3377
Christopher Keene, Music Director
A park dedicated to the arts, serving Western New York and Southern Ontario.
Supports 20th century chamber music, new and experimental music, jazz.
Contact David Midland concerning the artist-in-residence program.

Arts And Humanities Council Of St. Lawrence Valley*
Dr. Fritz H. Grupe, Chairman
State University of New York
Crane Building
Potsdam, NY 13676
(315) 265-2795
Supports chamber music, jazz, symphonic music, operatic music, popular music.

The Arts Center
Annette T. Corvatta, Director
1069 New Scotland Road
Albany, NY 12208
(518) 438-7895
A non-profit organization.
Supports 20th century chamber music, new and experimental music.
Provides financial support, performing facilities. Sponsors the Composer's Forum in Albany Concert Series which presents works by contemporary composers who discuss their music with the audience. Commissions works to be performed in the Series.
Music Budget: Over $100,000.00; Under 10% for 20th century music.

Arts Development Services, Inc.
Maxine N. Brandenburg, Executive Director
237 Main Street
Buffalo, NY 14203
(716) 856-7520
Joanne M. Allison, Project Director
Supports new and experimental music, jazz, orchestral music.
A service organization which promotes the arts in

Western New York. Serves member arts organizations located in Western New York by coordinating scheduling, offering workshops and seminars, and providing technical and managerial assistance. Sponsors a Performing Arts Voucher designed to increase attendance at performing arts events. Individuals may purchase vouchers for $1.00 to be redeemed at the box office for the full ticket price; performing organizations receive $2.50 per voucher. The Volunteer Lawyers For The Arts Program offers free legal representation and services to individual and arts organizations unable to afford private attorneys.

Voucher System Budget: $100,000.00; 61%-70% for musical groups.

Associated Colleges Of The Mid-Hudson Area

Jeanne Rodewald, Arts Coordinator
6 Vassar Street
Poughkeepsie, NY 12601
(914) 471-8923
A regional agency serving 7 counties in the Mid-Hudson area.
Provides, through regional coordination, programs in the arts for area colleges.
Music Budget: Over $100,000.00; 71%-80% for 20th century music.

Association For Jazz Performance

Phil Di Re, Executive Director
P.O. Box 1640
Buffalo, NY 14216
A non-profit organization serving Western New York.
Supports jazz, multi-media.
Encourages community exposure and involvement in jazz performance. Prepares programs in conjunction with an educational awareness project in Buffalo, New York.

Buffalo Foundation*

George C. Letchworth, Chairman
312 Genesee Building
Buffalo, NY 14202
Serves the Buffalo area.
Sponsors trust funds for charitable, educational, and civic purposes. Offers grants to educational institutions, music performing organizations, family and child welfare programs, hospitals, and community development projects. Offers scholarships to local residents only.

Caramoor Center For Music And The Arts

Michael Sweeley, Executive Director
Katonah, NY 10536
(914) 232-4206
A private foundation.
Supports 20th century chamber music, operatic music, symphonic music.
Produces the annual Caramoor Festival.
Music Budget: Over $100,000.00; 10%-20% for 20th century music.

Mary Flagler Cary Charitable Trust*

c/o Herbert J. Jacobi
P.O. Box 289
Millbrook, NY 12545
Serves New York State.
Gives grants to music schools, performing organizations for operating expenses and educational programs. Supports production costs of opera performances. Sponsors conservation projects.

Center Of The Creative And Performing Arts

See State University of New York, Buffalo.

Central New York Community Arts Council, Inc.

Philippa G. Kennedy, Executive Director
800 Park Avenue
Utica, NY 13501
(315) 798-5039
An arts service organization.
Coordinates and promotes the arts in Central New York. Operates Stanley Performing Arts Center.

Clinton-Essex Counties Council On The Arts*

Mary Louise Perkins, President
4 Mason Drive
Plattsburgh, NY 12901
(518) 563-1620
Supports chamber music, jazz, symphonic music, popular music.

Community Arts Council Of The South Shore*

Lynn Abrams, Lois Applebaum, Jean Kromenberg, Associate Chairmen
P.O. Box 382
Valley Stream, NY 11582
(516) 872-6324
Supports chamber music, jazz, operatic music, popular music, ethnic music.

Corning Glass Works Foundation*
Community Relations
Corning, NY 14830
Gives grants to improve the quality of life through cultural institutions, especially in communities where Corning Glass has manufacturing plants.

Council For The Arts In Westchester
Polly F. Siwek, Executive Director
White Plains Railroad Station, Mezzanine
White Plains, NY 10606
(914) 428-4220
A non-profit organization serving Westchester County.
Publishes a monthly calendar on county arts activities. Presents workshops and conferences concerned with arts programs and economics. Does not directly fund performances.

East End Arts And Humanities Council
Mardy Di Pirro, Executive Director
300 Pulaski Street
Riverhead, NY 11901
(516) 727-8080 Ext. 82
Supports 20th century music.
Provides performing facilities, and publicity, distributes tickets, and secures grants. Acts as a clearing house for local artists, bringing artistic events to the area.
Music Budget: $5,000.00-$9,999.00; 10%-20% for 20th century music.

Folk Art Gallery
Dr. Harry Morgan, Executive Director
2233 South Salina Street
Syracuse, NY 13210
(315) 423-4302
Affiliated with Syracuse University Afro-American Studies Program.
Supports jazz. Provides financial support, performing facilities. Presents music ensembles with art show openings. Sponsors symposiums, workshops, and lectures in order to provide Third World artists with a forum. Encourages appreciation of these artists by other Third World people in their own environment.
Music Budget: $500.00-$999.00; 91%-100% for 20th century music.

Free Music Store
See State University of New York, Albany.

Friends Of Brentwood Public Library
Seymour Berman, Executive Director
Second Avenue and Fourth Street
Brentwood, NY 11717
(516) 273-7883
Supports jazz.
Sponsors free community concerts.
Music Budget: $1,000.00-$4,999.00; 21%-30% for 20th century music.

Friends Of Music
Dr. Abel Moreinis, Executive Director
220 South State Road
Briarcliff Manor, NY 10510
(914) 941-2954
Presents 4 concerts per year of chamber music of all eras.

Fulton County Arts Council
Leonard L. Crawford, Executive Director
40 North Main Street
Gloversville, NY 12078
(518) 725-0641
A county agency.
Supports 20th century chamber music, choral music.
Provides financial support, performing facilities. Sponsors and develops educational and cultural activities.
Music Budget: $500.00-$999.00; 51%-60% for 20th century music.

Greater Newburgh Arts Council
N. Terry Holbert, President
427 Grand Street
Newburgh, NY 12550
(914) 562-9028
An educational corporation under the Regents of the State of New York.
Supports chamber music. Promotes performing, visual, and literary arts. Offers guidance to those planning arts activities locally or on tour. Sponsors and arranges for performances.
Music Budget: Under $100.00; Under 10% for 20th century music.

Greater Westbury Arts Council, Inc.
Kayla Kazahn Zalk, Executive Director
454 Rockland Street
Westbury, NY 11590
(516) 334-5148
A regional agency.
Encourages community exposure to the arts.

Greenburgh Arts And Culture Committee
See Town of Greenburgh

Hempstead
See Town of Hempstead

High Winds Fund, Inc.*
Lila Acheson Wallace, Chairman
Byram Lake Road
Mount Kisco, NY 10549
Sponsors higher education, music, conservation, religious projects, art museums, historic restoration, and community funds.

Hornell Area Arts Department*
Dr. David Davidson, President
P.O. Box 94
Canisteo, NY 14823
(607) 678-2722
Supports chamber music, jazz, symphonic music, popular music.

International Art Of Jazz, Inc.
Ann H. Sneed, Executive Director
5 Saywood Lane
Stony Brook, NY 11790
(516) 246-6125
A non-profit organization.
Supports jazz.
Provides financial support. Produces and raises funds for jazz performances throughout the year. Performances supported include free summer concerts, a subscription winter series, and special programs for libraries, civic, and governmental groups. Presents performance-demonstrations, artist-student forums, and workshops in public schools and colleges. Intends to perpetuate the art of jazz through audience development and education.
Music Budget: $25,000.00-$49,000.00; 91%-100% for 20th century music.

Long Island Composers' Alliance
H. A. Deutsch, Marga Richter, Directors
12 New Street
Huntington, NY 11743
(516) 421-5315 or 427-4050
Supports 20th century chamber music, new and experimental music, jazz, multi-media, electronic music.
Performs and sponsors works by Long Island composers. Encourages student composers.

The Charles E. Merrill Trust*
Charles E. Merrill, Jr., Chairman
P.O. Box 488
Ithaca, NY 14850
Sponsors higher education, music and the performing arts, religious institutions, health and welfare agencies.

Mid-Hudson Jazz Society
Michael Krasnov, Executive Director
14 Parkside Drive
Great Neck, NY 11021
(516) 487-8824
A non-profit organization.
Supports jazz.
Organizes and finances concerts and workshops.
Music Budget: $5,000.00-$9,999.00; 91%-100% for 20th century music.

Music Teachers Council Of Westchester
Verena Kossodo, Executive President
15 Vermont Avenue
White Plains, NY 10606
(914) 948-0007
Supports 20th century chamber music, new and experimental music.
Promotes performances of contemporary music by presenting programs and workshops for teachers and students. Maintains a library of contemporary compositions.
Music Budget: $100.00-$499.00; 31%-40% for 20th century music.

Nassau County Office Of Cultural Development
John W. Maerhofer, Director
P.O. Box D
Northern Boulevard
Roslyn, NY 11567
(516) 484-9333
A county agency.
Supports chamber music, jazz.
Provides financial support, performing facilities, publicity.

Niagara Council Of The Arts, Inc.
M. Jacquie Allen, Executive Director
1022 Main Street
Niagara Falls, NY 14301
(716) 284-8881
A local arts council serving Niagara County.
Supports 20th century chamber music, new and experimental music, jazz.
Provides financial support, performing facilities,

publicity. Sponsors concerts in Niagara Art Center. Cultivates and promotes the arts.
Music Budget: $1,000.00-$4,999.00; 10%-20% for 20th century music.

Night Kitchen Community Cultural Center
Peter Rossi, Executive Director
Lake Drive
Lake Peekskill, NY 10537
(914) 528-9704
A non-profit organization serving Upper Westchester and Lower Putnam.
Supports new and experimental music, jazz, folk music.
A community cultural center with a coffee house. Provides arts courses and weekend concerts, including free Sunday concerts.
Music Budget: $1,000.00-$4,999.00; 10%-20% for 20th century music.

Northport Public Library
Victoria Wallace, Executive Director
151 Laurel Avenue
Northport, NY 11768
(516) 261-6930
Presents concerts of 20th century chamber music, new and experimental music, jazz, folk music.
Provides performing facilities.
Music Budget: $1,000.00-$4,999.00; 41%-50% for 20th century music.

Olean Public Library
Maureen Curry, Director
Second and Laurens Street
Olean, NY 14760
(716) 372-0200
Robert Taylor, Arts Coordinator
Supports chamber music, jazz.
Sponsors ensembles by finding them halls in which to perform.

Performing Arts Committee Of Wellsville*
Mickey Martelle, President
c/o The Air Preheater Company
Wellsville, NY 14895
(716) 593-2700
Supports chamber music, jazz, popular music, symphonic music, operatic music, ethnic music.

Performing Arts Society, Inc.
Jena Smith, Artistic Director
Healy Avenue South
Scarsdale, NY 10583
(914) 472-6717 or 725-3777
A non-profit organization serving Westchester County.
Supports chamber music, vocal chamber music, contemporary operatic music.
Promotes music performance in Westchester County.
Music Budget: $10,000.00-$24,999.00; Under 10% for 20th century music.

Putnam Arts Council
Nancy Maier Greenwood, President
P.O. Box 156
Mahopac, NY 10541
(914) 628-3664
A non-profit educational organization.
Supports jazz.
Provides publicity. Sponsors performances by Concert Society of Putnam and Northern Westchester. Donates performing facility for privately sponsored jazz performances. Promotes various forms of creative art.
Music Budget: $100.00-$499.00; Under 10% for 20th century music.

Rensselaer County Council For The Arts*
Janice Harriman, Executive Secretary
189 Second Street
Troy, NY 12180
(518) 273-0552
Supports chamber music, jazz, symphonic music, operatic music, popular music.

Roberson Center For The Arts And Sciences*
Keith Martin, Director
30 Front Street
Binghamton, NY 13905
(607) 772-0660
Supports chamber music, jazz, ethnic music, popular music.

Rome Council On History And The Arts*
Edward C. Scott, Chairman
c/o Rome Chamber of Commerce
218 West Dominick Street
Rome, NY 13440
(315) 337-1700
Supports chamber music, jazz, symphonic music, operatic music, popular music, ethnic music.

113

Sleepy Hollow Community Concerts Association
Mrs. Roland Glasser, President
44 Whitetail Road
Irvington, NY 10533
(914) 591-7404
A non-profit membership organization serving the Hudson River Valley.
Supports chamber music, solo performances.
Produces the annual Sleepy Hollow Community Concerts Association Series to be attended by subscriber members of the Association.

Society For New Music
Neva S. Pilgrim, Vice President
102 Hillcrest Road
Syracuse, NY 13224
(315) 446-4025
A non-profit organization serving the city of Syracuse and the county of Onondaga.
Supports 20th century chamber music, new and experimental music.
Plans concerts and books performers for them.
Sponsors annual concert series at the Everson Museum, Syracuse.

South Huntington Public Library
Peter Draz, Executive Director
2 Melville Road
Huntington Station, NY 11746
(516) 549-4411
Affiliated with School District 13 of South Huntington.
Supports 20th century chamber music, new and experimental music, jazz, folk music, popular music.
Provides financial support, performing facilities, publicity in Library *Newsletter*. Presents community concerts.

State University Of New York
Free Music Store
Joel Chadabe, Coordinator
1400 Washington Avenue
Albany, NY 12222
(518) 457-2147
Supports 20th century chamber music, new and experimental music, jazz, electronic music, multimedia.
With funds from the University Student Association, provides financial support, performing facilities, fulfills technical production needs for performances. Produces Free Music Store Concert Series. Sponsors small ensembles

and produces recitals, lectures, and events dealing with technology.

State University Of New York
Center Of The Creative And Performing Arts
Renee Levine, Managing Director
Buffalo, NY 14214
(716) 831-9000
Jan Williams, Music Director
Supports 20th century chamber music, new and experimental music.
Offers annual resident fellowships to young professionals in new music and the contemporary performing arts. Presents Evenings For New Music Concert Series at the Albright-Knox Art Gallery in New York.

State University Of New York
Concert Office
Terry Charles Schwarz, Executive Director
108 Baird Hall
Buffalo, NY 14214
(716) 831-3408 or 831-3425
Supports 20th century chamber music, new and experimental music, jazz.
Provides financial support, performing facilities.
Co-sponsors concerts with the Center of Creative Performing Arts, Buffalo. Co-sponsors with University Symphony Band composer-conductor presentations.

State University Of New York
Music Department
Geneseo, NY 14454
(716) 245-5424
Supports chamber music of all eras.
Provides performing facilities, publicity. Presents Sunday Afternoon Concert Series of chamber music, featuring works of the 20th century.

Studio Arena Theatre
Neal DuBrock, Executive Producer
681 Main Street
Buffalo, NY 14203
(716) 856-8025
A non-profit theater.
Supports 20th century chamber music, new and experimental music, jazz, theater music.
Provides financial support, performing facilities, publicity. Presents concerts in cooperation with local churches and the State University of New York, Buffalo.

Syracuse Friends of Chamber Music
Louis Krasner, Music Director
521 Scott Avenue
Syracuse, NY 13224
(315) 446-1527
A non-profit organization.
Supports chamber music.
Presents an annual concert series.
Music Budget: $10,000.00-$24,999.00; 10%-20% for 20th century music.

Tappan Zee Concert Society
Rockland Center For The Arts
Marlene Kleiner, Executive Director
Old Greenbush Road
West Nyack, NY 10994
(914) 358-0877
Abba Bogin, Music Director
Supports chamber music.
Provides financial support, performing facilities. Produces concerts performed by American chamber ensembles combining contemporary and earlier works. At least one American work is performed per concert.
Music Budget: $10,000.00-$24,999.00; 31%-40% for 20th century music.

Temple Israel Of New Rochelle
Nathan Emanuel, Executive Director
1000 Pinebrook Boulevard
New Rochelle, NY 10804
(914) 235-1800
Supports 20th century chamber music, liturgical music.
Sponsors concerts and services that feature Israeli performing ensembles and Jewish American composers. Presents experimental religious services such as David Benedict's *Dance Service*.
Music Budget: $10,000.00-$24,999.00; 10%-20% for 20th century music.

Town Of Greenburgh
Arts and Culture Committee
Madeline Gutman, Executive Director
P.O. Box 205
Elmsford, NY 10523
(914) 592-6200 or 478-3559
A town agency.
Supports 20th century chamber music, new and experimental music, jazz, non-Western music.
Provides financial support, performing facilities.
Presents community concerts, using local musicians. Sponsors poetry readings, lecture-demonstrations of dance, and theater and visual arts presentations.
Music Budget: $1,000.00-$4,999.00.

Town Of Hempstead
Roger A. Malfatti, Jr., Executive Director
50 Clinton Street, Room 706
Hempstead, NY 11550
(516) 489-5000 Ext. 388
A regional agency.
Supports 20th century chamber music, new and experimental music, jazz.
Provides financial support, performing facilities. Sponsors local music ensembles performing in Hempstead concerts, workshops, and festivals.
Music Budget: $50,000.00-$99,000.00; 41%-50% for 20th century music.

Utica College Social/Cultural Committee
Domenick B. Sicilia, Executive Director
Burrstone Road
Utica, NY 13502
(315) 792-3038
Supports 20th century chamber music, new and experimental music, jazz, popular music.
Provides financial support, performing facilities, publicity. Brings professional performing ensembles to campus concerts. Coordinates and develops social and cultural activities at Utica College of Syracuse University.

Volunteer Lawyers For The Arts
Maxine Brandenburg, Executive Director
Arts Development Services, Inc.
237 Main Street
Buffalo, NY 14203
(716) 856-7520
Offers free legal representation and services to individuals and arts organizations unable to afford private attorneys.

WBFO Public Radio
Marvin Granger, General Manager
3435 Main Street
Buffalo, NY 14214
(716) 831-5393
Marsha Alvar, Program Director
A public radio station supported by the State University of New York at Buffalo and the Corporation for Public Broadcasting.
Supports 20th century chamber music, new and experimental music, jazz.
Provides performing facilities. Presents live jazz

115

and new music concerts on the air. Interviews performers of new music on the air. Coordinates bi-annual New Music Festival and initiates experimental arts events.

Westbury Memorial Public Library
W. F. Lollis, Executive Director
454 Rockland Street
Westbury, NY 11590
(516) 333-0176
A city agency.
Supports 20th century chamber music, new and experimental music, jazz.
Provides cultural programs for the community in addition to standard public library services.
Music Budget: $100.00-$499.00.

Westchester Chamber Music Society
Richard E. Grunebaum, President
50 Coralyn Avenue
White Plains, NY 10605
(914) 948-8165
A non-profit organization.
Supports chamber music.
Hires chamber music performing ensembles to present concerts.
Music Budget: $5,000.00-$9,999.00; 10%-20% for 20th century music.

New York City

Bronx

Bronx Council On The Arts
Irma L. Fleck, Executive Director
57 East 184th Street
Bronx, NY 10468
(212) 733-2100
A non-profit organization supported by city, state, and federal government.
Supports 20th century chamber music, jazz.
Provides financial support. Distributes funds from the New York City Department of Parks, Recreation, and Cultural Affairs to performing groups in the Bronx.
Music Budget: $5,000.00-$9,999.00; 61%-80% for 20th century music.

Riverdale-Yonkers Society For Ethical Culture
Mrs. Lee Louis, Executive Secretary
4450 Fieldston Road
Bronx, NY 10471
(212) 548-4445
A religious, humanistic institution serving Northwest Bronx and Lower Westchester.

Supports 20th century chamber music, new and experimental music, jazz.
Sponsors a religious fellowship educational program. Sponsors the Bronx Arts Ensemble by donating concert and rehearsal facilities. Provides community services.
Music Budget: Under $100.00.

Brooklyn

Arise Records
Denis Baggi, Executive Director
373 Henry Street
Brooklyn, NY 11201
(212) 834-8142
An independent record company.
Supports jazz.
A non-commercial recording company of independent musicians intended to allow performers free expression in experimental jazz.
Music Budget: $100.00-$499.00; 91%-100% for 20th century music.

Brooklyn Arts And Culture Association, Inc.
Charlene Victor, Executive Director
200 Eastern Parkway
Brooklyn, NY 11238
(212) 783-4469 or 783-3077
Supports 20th century chamber music, new and experimental music, jazz.
Provides financial support, performing facilities, publicity, public relations, technical assistance.
Sponsors performing ensembles in Brooklyn.

The Brooklyn Heights Music Society
T. Denton Carman, Executive Director
105 State Street
Brooklyn, NY 11201
(212) 624-6475
Supports chamber music, new and experimental music.
Provides financial support. Sponsors community concerts using local musicians.
Music Budget: $1,000.00-$4,999.00; 10%-20% for 20th century music.

Manhattan

Advocates For The Arts
John B. Hightower, Chairman
1564 Broadway, Suite 820
New York, NY 10036
(212) 586-3731
A program of Associated Councils of the Arts.
Disseminates information on precedent-setting

court cases, takes legal action, researches legislation, maintains an advocacy library, engages in public issues affecting the arts, and testifies before congressional committees.

American Academy Of Arts And Letters
Margaret M. Mills, Executive Director
633 West 155th Street
New York, NY 10032
(212) 286-1480

A private foundation serving the U.S.A. Parent organization is the National Institute of Arts and Letters.

Awards four annual $3,000.00 prizes to American composers selected by members of the organization. Prize recipients are also funded in a recording of one work. Promotes the performance and publication of the works of Charles Ives. No grant applications accepted.

Music Budget: $25,000.00-$49,000.00; 91%-100% for 20th century music.

American Brass Chamber Music Association, Inc.
Edward Birdwell, Executive Director
1860 Broadway
New York, NY 10023
(212) 581-2198

A private foundation.

Supports 20th century chamber music.

Provides financial support. Commissions new brass works and promotes research in early brass music in order to further the art of brass playing.

Music Budget: $50,000.00-$99,000.00; 41%-50% for 20th century music.

American Federation Of Musicians
Hal C. Davis, President
1500 Broadway
New York, NY 10036
(212) 869-1330

A labor union.

Provides financial support. Offers scholarships to student string players, ages 16-23, in annual summer Congress of Strings. The Congress of Strings meets at one Eastern and one Western College, each with 60 students. Scholarship recipients are selected by Union locals. Promotes the economic and professional welfare of professional musicians in the U.S.A. and Canada.

American Guild Of Organists
James Bryan, Executive Director
630 Fifth Avenue
New York, NY 10020
(212) 265-5611

A non-profit organization serving the U.S.A. Supports organ music of all eras.

Provides financial support. Awards cash prizes to winners of National Open Competition. Competitors are required to present one 20th century American work among other pieces. In order to elevate the status of church musicians, the Guild awards achievement certificates to organists who pass examinations.

Music Budget: Over $100,000.00.

American Landmark Festivals, Inc.
Francis L. Heilbut, Executive Director
26 Wall Street
New York, NY 10005
(212) 264-4451

A non-profit organization serving New York State.

Supports 20th century chamber music, new and experimental music, jazz.

Provides financial support, performing facilities, volunteer staff support. Presents concerts at community and national landmarks. Concerts include works by contemporary composers who are often present to perform and explain their music.

Music Budget: $5,000.00-$9,999.00; 10%-20% for 20th century music.

American Society Of University Composers
Bruce J. Taub, Chairman, Executive Committee
250 West 57th Street, Suite 626-7
New York, NY 10019
(212) 347-3122

A non-profit organization serving the U.S.A. and Canada.

Supports 20th century chamber music, new and experimental music.

A professional organization of composers and other musicians interested in contemporary American music. Presents concerts and discussions on contemporary music at national and regional conferences, distributes radio broadcasts of members' works, and publishes a *Journal of Music Scores* by members.

Music Budget: $10,000.00-$24,999.00; 91%-100% for 20th century music.

117

Associated Councils Of The Arts
Michael Newton, President
1564 Broadway
New York, NY 10036
(212) 586-3731
A membership organization of state and community arts agencies, acting as a service organization for these agencies. Acts as a spokesman for the arts. The Advocates for the Arts Program investigates and takes action on legal issues affecting the arts.

The Vincent Astor Foundation*
Mrs. Vincent Astor, President
405 Park Avenue
New York, NY 10022
Serves New York City.
Supports cultural institutions and projects, educational programs, community services for young people. No grants or loans to individuals. Discourages small grant requests.

The Howard Bayne Fund*
G. B. Wattles, President
c/o Simpson, Thacher, and Bartlett
One Battery Park Plaza
New York, NY 10004
Sponsors the arts, emphasizing music. Funds hospital programs, education, and conservation.

The Mary Duke Biddle Foundation*
Mrs. Mary D. B. T. Semans, Chairman
30 Rockefeller Plaza, Suite 4300
New York, NY 10020
Serves New York State and North Carolina, particularly Duke University.
Sponsors formation of new performing organizations, purchase of musical instruments, artist-in-residence programs, music education. Funds ticket price reduction programs of performing ensembles.

Booth Ferris Foundation*
C/O Robert Murtagh
40 Exchange Place
New York, NY 10005
Sponsors music education, operas, theological seminaries, higher education, urban programs, minority education.

Bruner Foundation*
Edith Friedman, Executive Director
60 East 42nd Street
New York, NY 10017
Martin C. Barell, Chairman
Sponsors projects which apply knowledge, rather than create it through research. Emphasizes innovative, experimental programs. Funds no individuals, operating budgets of educational or welfare institutions, or building construction.

Florence V. Burden Foundation*
William A. M. Burden, President
630 Fifth Avenue
New York, NY 10020
Serves New York State and California.
Sponsors projects concerned with music education, the elderly, secondary education, health, and youth. Funds museums. No support for building programs, endowments, general scholarship funds, or individuals.

Louis Calder Foundation*
Ten Rockefeller Plaza, Room 601
New York, NY 10020
Sponsors only agencies known to the Foundation or of interest to the donor. Funds projects concerned with health, relief to needy, music education. No grants to individuals, endowments, building funds, or capital development programs.

Center For New Music
Gregory Reeve, Executive Director
1841 Broadway, Suite 1007
New York, NY 10023
(212) 757-3025
Serves New York State.
A non-profit membership organization of performing ensembles and individuals interested in new music.
Supports 20th century chamber music, new and experimental music.
Promotes concerts of member performing ensembles by publishing and distributing a monthly calendar of events and other literature concerning 20th century music activities.

The Clarion Music Society, Inc.
John L. Hurley, Jr., Executive Director
415 Lexington Avenue, Room 1110
New York, NY 10017
(212) 697-3862
A private foundation.
Supports chamber music.

Is dedicated to the research and performance of master works of the 17th and 18th centuries as well as contemporary music. Produces annual Clarion Concerts Series. Commissions new works. Music Budget: $50,000.00-$99,000.00; Under 10% for 20th century music.

Robert Sterling Clark Foundation, Inc.*
Scott McVay, Executive Director
100 Wall Street
New York, NY 10005
Eugene W. Goodwillie, President
Sponsors community music programs and educational projects. Supports established cultural institutions. No grants to individuals.

Collective Black Artists, Inc.
Ms. Cobi Narita, Executive Director
P.O. Box 94 Times Square Station
New York, NY 10036
(212) 255-4814
A non-profit service, communications, educational, and performance organization.
Supports jazz, African-American music.
Provides information, resource material, and technical assistance to the creative artist community. Publishes *Expansions*, a news forum which provides a link between artists, their community, and their audience. Sponsors classes for professional and aspiring musicians. Sponsors lecture-demonstrations in public schools and other institutions. Presents single concerts and a series annually. The performing arm of the organization is the CBA Ensemble: see Performing Ensembles/Manhattan, New York.

Composer's Forum, Inc.
William Hellermann, General Manager
111 Amsterdam Ave.
New York, NY 10023
(212) 666-8307
Supports 20th century chamber music, jazz.
Presents Composers' Forum, a concert series at WBAI Free Music Store, Manhattan. These concerts provide young composers with New York debuts. Each program presents several chamber works by two composers who are selected by a jury. After the concert, a discussion with the composers is moderated by a distinguished member of the music profession.

Composers' Showcase
Charles Schwartz, Executive Director
Whitney Museum
Madison Avenue at 75th Street
New York, NY 10021
Also known as Contrasts in Contemporary Music.
A non-profit corporation.
Presents 20th century chamber music, new and experimental music, jazz, dance, operatic music, multi-media, electronic music.
Provides performers, advertising. Sponsors the annual Composers' Showcase Concert Series at the Whitney Museum. This series features composers who are often present to explain or conduct their works.

Composers Theatre
John Watts, Executive Director
25 West 19th Street
New York, NY 10011
(212) 989-2230
Supports 20th century chamber music, new and experimental music, jazz.
A division of Composers and Choreographers Theatre, Inc., a non-profit cultural and educational organization serving the greater New York area.
Provides financial support, performing facilities. A cooperative of composers, performing musicians, and audiences working toward an improved performance environment for 20th century American music. Produces annual May Festival of Contemporary American Music. Promotes collaborations between composers, choreographers, and related artists. Maintains a master tape and record library, containing recordings of live performances of contemporary works. Conducts lecture-demonstrations. Publishes *Composers and Choreographers Review*.
Music Budget: $10,000.00-$24,999.00; 91%-100% for 20th century music.

Concerned Citizens For The Arts
Amyas Ames, Chairman
P.O. Box 755 Ansonia Station
New York, NY 10023
(212) 246-4962.

Concert Artists Guild, Inc.
Wendy Sharp, Administrator
154 West 57th Street
New York, NY 10019
(212) 757-8344
David Black, President

119

A non-profit organization serving New York State.

Supports 20th century chamber music.

Provides performing facilities. Sponsors and organizes performances by young musicians.

Music Budget: Over $100,000.00; 21%-30% for 20th century music.

Congress Of Strings

See American Federation of Musicians.

Contrasts In Contemporary Music

See Composers' Showcase.

Creative Artists Public Service Program (CAPS)

Isabelle Fernandez, Executive Director

250 West 57th Street

New York, NY 10019

(212) 247-7701

Supports 20th century chamber music, new and experimental music, jazz, 20th century orchestral music.

Funds creative artists in playwrighting, poetry, fiction, graphics, music composition, painting, video, photography, sculpture, choreography, mixed-media, and film. Eligibility: applicants must be New York State residents. Matriculating students may not apply. Awards grants of $3,500.00-$5,000.00 to composers for the completion of a work. The Exposure and Indirect Aid Program publicizes the work completed on a CAPS grant and finds new audiences for the artists. The 1975 Music Exposure Project is a record album featuring the works of CAPS composers. The CAPS Community Service Program pays artists fees for engaging in activities beneficial to the community.

Music Budget: $25,000.00-$49,000.00; 91%-100% for 20th century music.

Charles E. Culpeper Foundation, Inc.*

Mrs. Helen D. Johnson, President

866 United Nations Plaza, Room 4087

New York, NY 10017

Sponsors educational programs of music performing organizations. Supports projects concerned with children, American Indians, ecology, and the physically handicapped.

Alice M. Ditson Fund Of Columbia University

Jack Beeson, Executive Director

Columbia University

703 Dodge Hall

New York, NY 10027

(212) 280-3825

A private endowment serving the U.S.A.

Supports 20th century chamber music, new and experimental music.

Provides financial support. Encourages musicians involved with 20th century music programs. Supports recordings and publications that aid American composers who have not yet been recognized. Presents Annual Ditson Conductor's Award to a conductor who has consistently programmed a quantity of works by neglected American composers.

East And West Artists

Andolovni P. Acosta, Executive Director

310 Riverside Drive, Room 313

New York, NY 10025

(212) 222-2433

A non-profit organization.

Supports 20th century chamber music.

Provides secretarial services, ticket sales. Auditions and presents young musicians in Carnegie Recital Hall debuts. Holds a solo and chamber music composition contest and presents winning works at Carnegie Recital Hall.

Music Budget: $1,000.00-$4,999.00; 31%-40% for 20th century music.

Experimental Intermedia Foundation, Inc.

Elaine Summers, Executive Director

537 Broadway

New York, NY 10012

(212) 966-3367

A private foundation serving New York State.

Supports new and experimental music.

Provides financial support, performing facilities, mailing lists. A service center for film makers, choreographers and their companies, composers, performing musicians, video and mixed-media artists.

Music Budget: $5,000.00-$9,999.00; 91%-100% for 20th century music.

The Ford Foundation*

McGeorge Bundy, President

320 East 43rd Street

New York, NY 10017

Supports contemporary music, jazz.

Has sponsored the American Branch of

International Contemporary Music Exchange which screens and selects contemporary musical works in order to increase their chances of performance in various countries. Sponsors experimental and electronic music projects, jazz education and appreciation programs. Funds experimental and developmental efforts, including curriculum experimentation in education, and community development projects.

Herman Goldman Foundation*

Stanley T. Gordon, Executive Director
120 Broadway, Room 2915
New York, NY 10005
Serves New York State.
Sponsors local, innovative arts programs. No grants to individuals.

Harlem Cultural Council

Geonie Faulkner, Executive Director
2341 Seventh Avenue
New York, NY 10030
(212) 862-3000
A community cultural council serving New York City.
Supports 20th century chamber music, new and experimental music, jazz.
Provides financial support, performing facilities. Aids professional minority artists and brings artistic programs to the community. Created the Jazzmobile, a touring jazz performance group. Sponsors community seminars, using improvisational jazz to educate the community in health and consumer affairs. Sponsors the Songmobile, a float on which singers perform in the summer.
Music Budget: $10,000.00-$24,999.00; 21%-30% for 20th century music.

Charles Hayden Foundation*

William T. Wachenfeld, President
140 Broadway
New York, NY 10005
Serves the New York and Boston metropolitan areas.
Sponsors music schools in acquiring equipment. Sponsors projects concerned with youth and education. Funds acquisition and renovation of organizations concerned with youth. No grants to individuals.

The Heckscher Foundation For Children*

Mrs. Ruth Smadbeck
52 Vanderbilt Avenue, Room 2005
New York, NY 10017
Promotes child welfare. Supports projects concerned with health, hospitals, music. No grants to individuals.

Jazz Interactions, Inc.

527 Madison Avenue, Suite 306
New York, NY 10022
(212) 866-6316
Supports jazz.
Sponsors lecture-demonstrations and workshops in schools and free outdoor concerts. Presents Jazz Interactions In Residence at Hunter College Series, offering lecture-discussions on various jazz styles. Publishes *Jazzline*, a weekly schedule of jazz events in the greater New York City area. Provides a recorded telephone schedule of local jazz events. The telephone schedule may be reached at: (212) 421-3592.

Jazzmania Society, Inc.

Michael Morgenstern, Executive Director
14 East 23rd Street
New York, NY 10010
(212) 677-1737 or 852-2722
Supports jazz.
Membership organization which presents public jam sessions open to professional and amateur musician members.
Music Budget: $5,000.00-$9,999.00; 91%-100% for 20th century music.

Jazzmobile, Inc.

S. David Bailey, Executive Director
361 West 125th Street
New York, NY 10027
(212) 866-4900
Supports jazz.
A traveling jazz organization that presents prominent jazz ensembles in free public concerts in the streets of New York. Gives public school programs discussing the history of jazz as a unique American art form. Offers instruction in harmony, sight reading, instrumental technique, and ensemble work.

Jewish Music Council Of The National Jewish Welfare Board
Irene Heskes, Executive Director
15 East 26th Street
New York, NY 10010
(212) 532-4949
A private philanthropic community service organization.
Promotes the performance and appreciation of Jewish music by disseminating information concerning it. Sponsors annual Jewish Music Festival, lasting from Purim to Passover. 1975 Festival theme: American Jewish Music - A Bicentennial Celebration 1776-1976. During the Festival, the organization promotes active national participation in Jewish music by encouraging commissioning projects, concerts, lectures, and displays in American communities. Publishes educational literature and musical anthologies.

The Kitchen
Robert Stearns, Executive Director
59 Wooster Street
New York, NY 10012
(212) 925-3615
A non-profit organization serving New York State.
Supports new and experimental music, multi-media.
Provides financial support, performing facilities, technical assistance. Presents programs of works by living composers who often perform their own compositions. Features recent developments in video, music, and non-objective performance.
Music Budget: $10,000.00-$24,999.00; 91%-100% for 20th century music.

The Koussevitzky Music Foundation, Inc.
Mrs. Serge Koussevitzky, President
30 West 60th Street
New York, NY 10023
Supports 20th century music.
Commissions eminent composers to write new works.

League Of Composers-International Society For Contemporary Music, U.S. Section, Inc. (League-ISCM)
Hubert S. Howe, Jr., Executive Director
250 West 57th Street, Suite 626-7
New York, NY 10019
(212) 247-3121
Supports 20th century chamber music, new and experimental music, electronic music.

Encourages the dissemination of new musical works by sponsoring the League-ISCM Concert Series, and World Music Days in 1976. Sponsored the International Electronic Music Competitions in 1975 for works not employing live performers or special staging directions. Winners were awarded a premiere in the League-ISCM Concert Series and a commemorative recording.
Music Budget: $10,000.00-$24,999.00; 91%-100% for 20th century music.

Lincoln Center For The Performing Arts, Inc.
John W. Mazzola, Managing Director
1865 Broadway
New York, NY 10023
(212) 765-5100
Supports 20th century chamber music, new and experimental music.
Provides performing facilities. Operates community arts programs designed to reach new audiences, produces special performing arts activities, sells student tickets at reduced rates.
Music Budget: Over $100,000.00; Under 10% for 20th century music.

Lower Manhattan Cultural Council
Florence Barnett, Executive Director
15 State Street
New York, NY 10004
(212) 269-2710
A private foundation serving the area of Canal Street to the Battery in New York City.
Supports 20th century chamber music, new and experimental music, jazz.
Provides performing facilities.
Music Budget: $1,000.00-$4.999.00.

Meet The Composer
John Duffy, Executive Director
American Music Center
250 West 57th Street, Suite 626-7
New York, NY 10019
(212) 247-4082(3)
A non-profit organization serving New York State. An American Music Center Project.
Supports 20th century chamber music, new and experimental music, jazz, operatic music, music theater, symphonic music.
Provides financial assistance to sponsors who wish to invite composers into their communities to perform, direct, lecture, and exchange ideas on their music. Schools, churches, libraries, community orchestras, choruses, museums, civic organizations, unions, and local arts centers

throughout New York State may request any composer and assisting artists, if needed, for a single engagement or extended visit. Meet The Composer provides 20% to 50% of the total cost of each program depending on extent of sponsor support, amount charged for admission, and size of audience. Total financial assistance for any single program may not exceed $1,500.00.
Music Budget: $50,000.00-$99,000; 91%-100% for 20th century music.

Andrew W. Mellon Foundation*
Nathan M. Pusey, President
140 East 62nd Street
New York, NY 10021
Albert O. B. Andrews, Vice President
Supports contemporary music.
Sponsors music commissioning programs, International Contemporary Music Exchange, performing organizations, and music education. Funds projects concerned with health, community service, and the arts. No grants or loans to individuals.

Music Performance Trust Funds
Kenneth E. Raine, Trustee
1501 Broadway, Room 810
New York, NY 10036
A public service organization created and financed by the Recording Industries under agreements with the American Federation of Musicians, serving the U.S.A. and Canada.
Supports instrumental music of all eras.
Pays musicians union scale wages to perform in free public concerts. The Trust pays musicians recommended by union locals and community sponsors. Funds summer outdoor concert series and school concerts. Events sponsored must be primarily musical in nature, rather than events using music as an accompaniment, such as political rallies.

National Institute Of Arts And Letters
Margaret M. Mills, Executive Director
633 West 155th Street
New York, NY 10032
(212) 286-1480
A private foundation serving the U.S.A.
Parent organization of the American Academy of Arts and Letters.
Supports 20th century music.
Awards four annual $3,000.00 prizes to American composers selected by members of the organization. Prize recipients are also funded in a

recording of one work. Promotes the performance and publication of the works of Charles Ives. No grant applications accepted.
Music Budget: $25,000.00-$49,000.00; 91%-100% for 20th century music.

New Music Distribution Service
Michael Mantler, Executive Director
6 West 95th Street
New York, NY 10025
(212) 749-6265
A non-profit organization.
Supports 20th century chamber music, new and experimental music, jazz.
Distributes independently produced recordings of new music. Affiliated with Jazz Composer's Orchestra Association, Inc.
Music Budget: Over $100,000.00; 91%-100% for 20th century music.

New Music For Young Ensembles, Inc.
Claire Rosengarten, Executive Director
490 West End Avenue
New York, NY 10024
(212) 724-1603
Supports 20th century chamber music.
Provides financial support. Sponsors annual composition contest for intermediate level chamber works. Contest eligibility: open to all resident American composers; entries to be works for 3 to 5 instruments. Prize: $300.00 and performances of winning works.
Music Budget: $1,000.00-$9,999.00; 91%-100% for 20th century music.

New Wilderness Foundation
Charlie Morrow, Executive Director
365 West End Avenue, Apartment 8C
New York, NY 10024
(212) 799-0636
Supports cross-cultural arts programs.
Provides organizational advice and coordinates events. Helps secure matching grants for performance projects concerned with the aural arts of poetry, music, and sound sculpture. Encourages rural and urban performances of American Indian music, Tibetan chants, and sacred rituals.

123

Sponsoring Organizations

New York Community Trust*
Herbert B. West, Director
415 Madison Avenue
New York, NY 10017
Gives grant priority to projects having particular significance for the New York City area.

New York Composers Collective
John Fischer, Executive Director
83 Leonard Street
New York, NY 10013
(212) 431-5786
A non-profit organization serving New York State.
Supports new and experimental music, jazz.
Presents chamber concerts. Offers recording and performing facilities at low rates.
Music Budget: $5,000.00-$9,999.00; 91%-100% for 20th century music.

New York Foundation*
D. John Heyman, President
Four West 58th Street
New York, NY 10019
Supports jazz.
Sponsors projects concerned with community music education, disadvantaged youth, young audience development. Funds inner city music performing ensembles. Supports programs in health, education, and welfare.

The New-York Historical Society
James J. Heslin, Executive Director
170 Central Park West
New York, NY 10024
(212) 873-3400
A private endowment serving metropolitan New York.
Supports chamber music.
Provides performing facilities, programs, publicity. Sponsors a series of free concerts.
Music Budget: $100.00-$499.00.

New York University Loeb Program Board
Ernest L. Roab, Executive Director
566 La Guardia Place
New York, NY 10012
(212) 598-2027
Supports new and experimental music, jazz.
Provides performing facilities, publicity. Sponsors composer workshops and individual showcases for jazz composer-performers.

Park Avenue Synagogue
Cantor David J. Putterman
50 East 87th Street
New York, NY 10028
(212) 369-2600
Supports liturgical music for the synagogue. Commissions works to be presented in annual New Liturgical Music By Contemporary Composers Service.
Music Budget: $50,000.00-$99,000.00; 41%-50% for 20th century music.

The Participation Project Foundation, Inc.
Nelson Howe, President
P.O. Box 2020 Grand Central Station
New York, NY 10017
(212) 431-4125
Mark Ross, Executive Director
A non-profit organization.
Supports new and experimental music.
Provides administrative and organizational assistance to arts groups. Sponsors experimental performing arts events, facilities presenting these events, and publications concerned with experimental arts. Funds participation events such as Participation Arts Festival in Brooklyn, New York. Affiliated with International Carnival of Experimental Sound (ICES) in Edinburgh and London; *Source, Music of the Avant-Garde* Magazine; *Assembling Press*; and Charlotte Moorman's Annual Avant-Garde Festival in New York.
Music Budget: Over $100,000.00; 41%-50% for 20th century music.

Performing Artservices, Inc.
Mimi Johnson, Associate Director
463 West Street
New York, NY 10014
(212) 989-4953
A non-profit agency.
Provides cooperative management and administrative services to paying clients. Clients are experimental performing ensembles in dance, theater, and music.

Rockefeller Brothers Fund*
Dana S. Creel, President
30 Rockefeller Plaza
New York, NY 10020
Supports community music schools. Funds projects promoting cooperation in the music community. Sponsors symphony orchestras. No

grants to individuals, hospitals, churches, or community centers.

Rockefeller Foundation*
John H. Knowles, M.D., President
111 West 50th Street
New York, NY 10020
Has supported the American Music Recording Project. Funds music workshops and performances in neglected rural areas. Sponsors performing and educational organizations in youth music education projects. No grants to establish, build, or operate local institutions. No grants to individuals.

The JDR 3rd Fund, Inc.*
Kathryn Bloom, Porter A. McCray, Program Directors
50 Rockefeller Plaza, Room 1034
New York, NY 10020
Encourages communication, understanding, and cooperation between peoples in Asia and the U.S.A. through exchanges in the visual and performing arts. The Arts In Education Program supports selected projects designed to make arts an integral part of education in lower schools. Provides grants to assist arts organizations helping with this education. The Youth Task Force Program encourages communication between youth and the establishment. Supports musician residencies and exchanges in Asia and America. Supports American ethnomusicology programs concerned with Asian music.

The Martha Baird Rockefeller Fund For Music, Inc.
Maude E. Brogan, Executive Director
1 Rockefeller Plaza, Room 3315
New York, NY 10020
A private foundation serving the U.S.A.
Supports 20th century chamber music, new and experimental music.
Provides financial support. Contributes toward programs featuring the music of younger or lesser known composers, played by non-profit incorporated groups of professional musicians. Favors projects which develop music ensembles, and projects which increase new music audiences, such as recordings and radio broadcasts. Gives priority to performing organizations presenting concerts to audiences or geographical areas inadequately served. Sponsors ensembles wishing to take a step toward advancement or consolidation. Funds composer service organizations, individual performers, and Ph.D. candidates in musicology. Application requirements: representative of organizations may write to the Fund, stating the history and goals of their organizations, purposes for which the aid is requested, estimated cost, and the organization's general budget. Proof of tax-exempt status is required, and classification according to the Internal Revenue Code as amended after the Tax Reform Act of 1969.
Music Budget: Over $100,000.00; 21%-30% for 20th century music.

Helena Rubinstein Foundation*
Harold Weill, President
261 Madison Avenue
New York, NY 10016
Oscar Kolin, Executive Vice President
Funds conservatory music scholarships. Aims to benefit women and children throughout the world. Supports projects concerned with health, education, and medical research and rehabilitation.

The Scherman Foundation, Inc.*
Axel G. Rosin, President
280 Park Avenue
New York, NY 10017
Supports projects concerned with music and the performing arts, Jewish welfare funds, conservation, population control, higher education, and international studies. No grants to individuals.

Studio Museum In Harlem
Edward S. Spriggs, Executive Director
2033 Fifth Avenue
New York, NY 10035
(212) 427-5959
A non-profit organization serving the New York-New Jersey area.
Supports jazz, gospel music, traditional African music.
Provides financial support, performing facilities. Sponsors concerts of improvisational ensembles, blues singers, gospel choirs, and African performers.
Music Budget: $1,000.00-$4,999.00; 51%-60% for 20th century music.

William Matheus Sullivan Musical Foundation, Inc.*
c/o Hugh Ross
410 East 57th Street
New York, NY 10022
Andrew Y. Rogers, President
Advances the careers of gifted young singers, either directly or by finding engagements for them through assistance given to orchestras, operatic societies, or other musical groups. No support for the general fields of music education and vocal or instrumental training.

Surdna Foundation*
John E. Andrus III, Chairman
200 Park Avenue
New York, NY 10017
Edward F. McGee, President
Supports community music schools. Sponsors projects concerned with higher education, medicine, child welfare, youth, community welfare, and mental health.

Trope Incorporated
Joseph Fennimore, Executive Director
463 West Street, Number 350D
New York, NY 10014
(212) 691-1347
A non-profit organization serving New York City.
Supports 20th century chamber music, new and experimental music, jazz, American music.
Provides financial support. Sponsors Hear America First Concert Series at the Museum of Natural History in Manhattan. Promotes the performance of American music by demonstrating its uniqueness to audiences and encouraging performers to include it in their repertoires.
Music Budget: $10,000.00-$24,999.00; 81%-90% for 20th century music.

Young Concert Artists
Susan Wadsworth, Director
75 East 55th Street
New York, NY 10022
(212) 759-2541
A non-profit artists management serving the U.S.A.
Supports 20th century chamber music, new and experimental music.
Provides financial support, performing facilities, publicity, and administrative services. Established to discover and promote the careers of young musicians. Sponsors a concert series in which ensembles managed by the organization perform.

Commissions works to be premiered by performer clients.
Music Budget: $50,000.00-$99,000.00; 10%-20% for 20th century music.

Queens

Jamaica Arts Center
Paul Waters, Executive Director
161-04 Jamaica
Jamaica, NY 11432
(212) 658-7400
A community agency serving the Jamaica area of Queens.
Supports 20th century chamber music, new and experimental music, jazz, folk music, popular music.
Provides financial support, performing facilities, publicity. Presents Chamber-Jazz Series of 10 concerts featuring ensembles performing 17th to 20th century music.
Music Budget: $10,000.00-$24,999.00; 61%-70% for 20th century music.

New York Free Music Committee
Steven Tintweiss, Executive Director
P.O. Box 509
Middle Village, NY 11379
(212) 894-7231
A non-profit organization serving metropolitan New York and Southern Vermont.
Supports new and experimental music, jazz, electronic music.
Provides financial support, performing facilities. Sponsors free public concerts in parks during the summer. Encourages development of new musical forms by performing ensembles and composers. Promotes public awareness and appreciation of contemporary arts, including poetry, dance, visual video art.
Music Budget: $5,000.00-$9,999.00; 91%-100% for 20th century music.

Queens Council On The Arts*
Wallace M. West, Executive Director
218-14 Jamaica Avenue
Queens Village, NY 11428
(212) 479-3666
Supports chamber music, jazz, operatic music, symphonic music, popular music, ethnic music.

Staten Island

Staten Island Council On The Arts*
Melisande Charles, Executive Director
15 Beach Street
Staten Island, NY 10304
(212) 448-7877
Supports chamber music, jazz, operatic music, popular music, ethnic music.

North Carolina

State Arts Agency:

North Carolina Arts Council
Halsey M. North, Executive Director
North Carolina Department of Cultural Resources
Raleigh, NC 27611
(919) 829-7897.

The Arts Council, Inc.*
Milton Rhodes, Executive Director
610 Coliseum Drive
Winston-Salem, NC 27106
(919) 722-2585
Supports jazz, popular music.

Clay County Historical And Arts Council
Mrs. Edgar Price, President
Route 1
Hayesville, NC 28904
(704) 389-8977
A local arts council serving Clay County.
Supports contemporary music, jazz.
Provides performing facilities. Sponsors and encourages cultural education and activities in Clay County and surrounding area, emphasizing local history and the arts.
Music Budget: Under $100.00; 10%-20% for 20th century music.

Community Arts Council Of Goldsboro*
Danielle K. Withrow, Executive Director
P.O. Box 826
Goldsboro, NC 27530
(919) 736-3335
Supports chamber music, symphonic music.

Duke University
Department of Music
Frank P. Tirro, Executive Director
6695 College Station
Durham, NC 27708
(919) 684-2534
Supports 20th century chamber music, new and experimental music, jazz.

Provides financial support, performing facilities. Offers composer residencies. Resident performing organizations regularly commission and program new works. Provides electronic music studio.

Greenville Art Center*
Edith G. Walker, Executive Director
802 Evans Street
Greenville, NC 27834
(919) 758-1946
Supports chamber music.

North Carolina School Of The Arts
Robert Suderberg, Chancellor
P.O. Box 4657
Winston-Salem, NC 27107
(919) 784-7170
Supports 20th century chamber music, new and experimental music, jazz, multi-media.
Sponsors performances of contemporary music.

Rocky Mount Arts And Crafts Center*
Mrs. W. L. Thorp, Chairman
P.O. Box 4031
Rocky Mount, NC 27801
(919) 442-5181 Ext. 257
Supports chamber music, jazz, operatic music, popular music, ethnic music.

Southeastern North Carolina Arts Council
Ann A. Hood, Executive Director
Route 2, P.O. Box 211
Elizabethtown, NC 28337
(919) 588-4898
A state agency serving 8 Southeastern North Carolina counties.
Supports 20th century chamber music, jazz, folk music, ethnic music.
Provides promotion, publicity, and performing facilities when possible. Promotes and encourages the arts in Southeastern North Carolina by sponsoring performances.

Surry Arts Council*
Donald A. Nance, Executive Director
P.O. Box 141
Mount Airy, NC 27030
(919) 786-7998
Supports jazz, symphonic music, popular music.

127

Toe River Arts Council at Maryland Technical Institute
Bill Wilson, Executive Director
P.O. Box 547
Spruce Pine, NC 28777
(615) 765-7549
A tri-county arts council serving Mitchell, Avery, and Yancey Counties.
Supports new and experimental music, jazz.
Provides performing facilities, scheduling, and accommodations. Presents Music In The Mountains Concert Series in Burnsville, North Carolina. Exposes arts and crafts in the counties which it serves.

North Dakota

State Arts Agency:

North Dakota Council On The Arts And Humanities
Dr. John Hove, Executive Director
North Dakota State University
320 Minard Hall
Fargo, ND 58102
(701) 237-7143
Intends to make the arts available to all citizens of North Dakota.
Music Budget: $25,000.00-$49,000.00; 21%-30% for 20th century music.

Ohio

State Arts Agency:

Ohio Arts Council
James Edgy, Executive Director
50 West Broad Street, Room 2840
Columbus, OH 43215
(614) 466-2613
Supports 20th century chamber music, new and experimental music, jazz.
Provides financial support, publicity, ticket sales. Co-sponsors, with local arts councils, touring arts activities and concert series. Grants given primarily to non-profit organizations, not individuals. Funds sponsoring organizations and provides major matching grants. Provides consultants for arts organizations.

Akron Community Trusts*
John L. Feudner, Executive Director
One Cascade Plaza
Akron, OH 44308
Robert C. Brouse, President
Serves Summit County, Ohio.
Supports charitable, educational, recreational, health, cultural, and public welfare activities.

Bowling Green State University
College of Musical Arts
James Paul Kennedy, Dean
123 Hall of Music
Bowling Green, OH 43403
(419) 372-2181
Supports 20th century chamber music, new and experimental music, jazz.
Provides performing facilities. Sponsors hundreds of concerts annually, emphasizing American music.

Cleveland Area Arts Council
Nina Gibans, Executive Director
140 The Arcade
Cleveland, OH 44114
(216) 781-0045
A local arts council serving the greater Cleveland area.
Supports chamber music, jazz, symphonic music, operatic music, popular music, ethnic music.
Provides matching grants. Supports and promotes 20th century music performance in the community.

Cleveland Foundation*
Barbara H. Rawson, Interim Director
700 National City Bank Building
Cleveland, OH 44114
Raymond Armington, Chairman
A foundation serving the greater Cleveland area.
Supports community music schools. Assists public charitable institutions concerned with education, science research, and public recreation. No grants for sectarian or religious activities.

The Cleveland Institute Of Music
Grant Johannesen, Music Director
11021 East Boulevard
Cleveland, OH 44106
(216) 791-5165
Supports 20th century chamber music, new and experimental music.
Produces an annual public concert series. Sponsors the annual Cleveland Chamber Music Seminar.

Corbett Foundation*
J. Ralph Corbett, President
1501 Madison Road, Suite 410
Cincinnati, OH 45206
A foundation serving local needs primarily.
Sponsors operatic productions. Sponsors projects with charitable and scientific purposes, emphasizing music.

Firman Fund*
Pamela H. Firman, President
100 Erieview Plaza, 36th Floor
Cleveland, OH 44114
Supports projects concerned with music, hospitals, health, secondary education, youth, and the community.

French Art Colony*
Donald M. Thaler, Chairman
530 First Avenue
Gallipolis, OH 45631
(614) 446-3834
Supports chamber music.

George Gund Foundation*
James P. Lipscomb, Executive Director
One Erieview Plaza
Cleveland, OH 44114
Frederick K. Cox, President
Serves Ohio.
Supports music education programs, emphasizing new concepts of teaching and learning. Supports projects concerned with social problems, economics, ecology, medicine, public health, and cultural affairs. No grants for building programs, endowments, or normal operating budgets. No grants to individuals.

Martha Holden Jennings Foundation*
Arthur S. Holden, Jr., President
1100 National City Bank Building
Cleveland, OH 44114
Serves Ohio primarily.
Sponsors music education projects of performing organizations. Fosters the developmental capabilities of young people by encouraging and improving the quality of teaching in secular elementary and secondary schools. Sponsors awards for outstanding teaching. No grants for capital funds.

Lorain County Arts Council, Inc.*
Betty L. Stringer, Executive Director
247 Temple Court
Elyria, OH 44035
(513) 225-5433
Supports chamber music, symphonic music.

Louise Foundation*
Louise Ireland Humphrey, President
100 Erieview Plaza, 36th Floor
Cleveland, OH 44114
Serves Ohio.
Supports projects concerned with music, education, communities, hospitals, and social welfare.

Marietta Area Arts Council*
Ray H. Rosenblum, President
c/o WMOA Radio
P.O. Box 708
Marietta, OH 45750
(614) 373-1490
Supports chamber music, symphonic music, operatic music.

Orange Community Arts Council*
Mrs. William A. Johnson, President
32000 Chagrin Boulevard
Pepper Pike
Cleveland, OH 44124
(216) 831-8600
Supports jazz, symphonic music, popular music.

Portsmouth Area Arts Council*
Robert A. Fuller, President
2138 Timlin Hill
Portsmouth, OH 45662
(614) 353-6389
Supports chamber music, jazz, symphonic music, operatic music, popular music.

Springfield Arts Council*
J. Chris Moore, Executive Director
P.O. Box 745
Springfield, OH 45506
Supports jazz, popular music.

Upper Arlington Cultural Arts Commission*
Charles Ritter, Chairman
3600 Tremont Road
Upper Arlington, OH 43221
(614) 457-5080 Ext. 274
Supports chamber music, jazz, symphonic music, popular music, ethnic music.

Oklahoma

State Arts Agency:

Oklahoma Arts And Humanities Council
William McKenzie Andres, Executive Director
Jim Thorpe Building, 6th Floor
P.O. Box 53553
Oklahoma City, OK 73105
(405) 521-2931
Supports 20th century chamber music, new and experimental music, jazz.
Provides financial support. Awards matching grants only: matching funds may not be from a federal agency. Sponsors touring performance programs and community presentations of local artists. Funds arts organizations concerned with commissioning and performing new compositions, festivals, education, and cooperative facilities or services. Ineligible: individuals, most projects involving travel outside Oklahoma, and projects involving purchase of permanent equipment.
Music Budget: $50,000.00-$99,000.00.

Arts And Humanities Council Of Tulsa
Mark Ross, Executive Director
2210 South Main
Tulsa, OK 74114
(918) 583-5794
Supports 20th century chamber music, new and experimental music, jazz.
Provides financial support, performing facilities. Sponsors television programs on 20th century music.

Black Liberated Arts Center, Inc.
P.O. Box 11014
Oklahoma City, OK 73111
(405) 424-2616
A non-profit organization serving Oklahoma and Texas.
Supports jazz.
Provides financial support, performing facilities. Encourages the performance of jazz in public schools and churches in an effort to develop and perpetuate the black creative arts.
Music Budget: $1,000.00-$4,999.00.

Bristow Arts And Humanities Council
Mrs. Harry M. McMillan, Executive Director
P.O. Box 444
Bristow, OK 74010
(918) 367-2536
Serves Northeast Oklahoma.

Supports new and experimental music, symphonic music.
Presents concerts. Promotes the cultural and educational organizations of the Bristow area. Coordinates cultural activities and assists in the establishment of new cultural facilities.
Music Budget: $10,000.00-$24,999.00; Under 10% for 20th century music.

Henryette Arts And Humanities Council*
Mrs. K. W. Durarvay, President
703 West Broadway Street
Henryette, OK 74437
(918) 652-4256
Supports symphonic music, folk music.

Lawton Arts And Humanities Council*
Chester L. Wells, Executive Director
P.O. Box 1332
Lawton, OK 73501
(405) 357-8721
Supports chamber music.

Living Arts Of Tulsa, Inc.
Virginia Myers, Executive Director
1436 South Oswego
Tulsa, OK 74112
(918) 936-6772
A non-profit organization.
Supports 20th century chamber music, new and experimental music, multi-media.
Provides financial support. Presents concerts and workshops on new music, including electronic compositions. Organized in order to develop and present contemporary art forms.
Music Budget: $10,000.00-$24,999.00; 91%-100% for 20th century music.

Stillwater Arts And Humanities Council, Inc.*
Mrs. Richard Powell, President
P.O. Box 135
Stillwater, OK 74074
(405) 372-7185
Supports chamber music, folk music.

Tahlequah Area Arts And Humanities Council
Paul Grover, President
P.O. Box 494
Tahlequah, OK 74464
(918) 456-2289
A non-profit organization serving Northeastern Oklahoma.
Brings cultural events to Tahlequah with the assistance of the Oklahoma Arts and Humanities

Council and the National Endowment for the Arts. Assists arts organizations in producing and publicizing arts and humanities programs.
Music Budget: $500.00-$999.00.

Oregon

State Arts Agency:

Oregon Arts Commission
Terry Melton, Executive Director
328 Oregon Building
494 State Street
Salem, OR 97301
(503) 378-3625.

Coos Bay Museum*
Maggie Karl, Executive Director
515 Market Avenue
Coos Bay, OR 97420
(503) 267-3901
Supports folk music.

Corvallis Arts Center
Corrine Woodman, Executive Director
700 Southwest Madison
Corvallis, OR 97330
(503) 752-0186
Serves Benton and Linn Counties.
Supports 20th century chamber music, new and experimental music, jazz.
Provides performing facilities, coordinates community cultural activities.
Music Budget: $500.00-$999.00; 81%-90% for 20th century music.

McMinnville Association Of The Arts
Mrs. Sigrid Gould, Executive Director
P.O. Box 265
McMinnville, OR 97128
A non-profit organization.
Supports 20th century chamber music, new and experimental music, jazz.
Promotes awareness and appreciation of the arts.

North Coast Friends Of Music
Bernice Smith, President
P.O. Box 1016
Seaside, OR 97138
A non-profit organization.
Supports 20th century chamber music.
Provides financial support, advertising, ticket sales. Brings concerts to the area.

Portland State University
Music Department
S. John Trudeau, Executive Director
P.O. Box 751
Portland, OR 97207
(503) 229-3011
Supports 20th century chamber music, new music, jazz.
Provides performing and rehearsal facilities, publicity. Sponsors annual Portland Composers Concerts, a 3-day presentation of works by Portland composers.

Pennsylvania

State Arts Agency:

Commonwealth Of Pennsylvania Council On The Arts
Robert Bernat, Executive Director
503 North Front Street
Harrisburg, PA 17101
(717) 787-6883
Supports 20th century chamber and full orchestral music, new music, jazz, multi-media.
Sponsors Pennsylvania Composers Project, a series of 4 concerts at Drexel University presenting works by Pennsylvania composers. Works performed are selected from compositions submitted to a panel of judges. Supports radio broadcasts of contemporary music.
Music Budget: Over $100,000.00; 10%-20% for 20th century music.

Arts Council Of Washington County*
Larry L. Koehler, President
Citizen's Library
55 South College Street
Washington, PA 15301
(412) 222-2400.

Bethlehem Fine Arts Commission*
James F. Braden, Chairman
City Hall
10 East Church Street
Bethlehem, PA 18018
Supports jazz, symphonic music, operatic music, popular music, ethnic music.

Blair County Arts Foundation*
J. Richard Ward, Chairman
Mishler Theatre
1208 12th Avenue
Altoona, PA 16601
(814) 944-9434

Supports jazz, symphonic music, operatic music, popular music.

Butler Arts Council*
Thomas George Crane, President
234 West Fulton Street
Butler, PA 16001
(412) 287-3836
Supports symphonic music, ethnic music.

Cheltenham Art Center*
Gersley Kieserman, President
439 Ashbourne Road
Cheltenham, PA 19012
(215) 379-4660
Gladys Wagner, Education Director
Supports jazz, popular music.

Samuel S. Fels Fund*
Dale Phalen, Executive Director
Two Penn Center Plaza
Philadelphia, PA 19102
Supports contemporary music.
Sponsors premiere performances of works by Pennsylvania composers, concerts on college campuses, and musical theater productions. Owns and operates the Fels Research Institute for the study of Human Development in Yellow Springs, Ohio. Provides grants for continuing support of major projects instituted by the Fels Fund. Offers additional grants in fields of education, the arts, and community service.

Fulton Opera House Foundation*
Dr. Robert W. Tolan, Executive Director
12 North Prince Street
Lancaster, PA 17603
(717) 394-7133
Supports chamber music, jazz, symphonic music, operatic music, popular music, ethnic music.

Haas Community Fund
See William Penn Foundation

Howard Heinz Endowment*
Alfred W. Wishart, Jr., Executive Director
P.O. Box 926
Pittsburgh, PA 15230
Serves Pennsylvania.
Sponsors music performing organizations. Supports projects concerned with music and the arts, community planning, education, health, welfare, and religion. Provides education grants for Pittsburgh colleges only.

Hillman Foundation*
Ronald Wertz, Executive Director
2000 Grant Building
Pittsburgh, PA 15219
Henry L. Hillman, President
Serves Pittsburgh and Western Pennsylvania.
Sponsors innovative arts programs. Supports projects concerned with education, community welfare and development. No grants to individuals.

INA Foundation*
Algernon Roberts, Director
1600 Arch Street
Philadelphia, PA 19101
John T. Gurash, Chairman and President
Sponsors orchestras. Supports projects concerned with health, welfare, civic and cultural causes, community welfare, and education.

Johnstown Area Arts Council
Mrs. Herbert B. Schloss, Executive Secretary
P.O. Box 402
Johnstown, PA 15905
(814) 536-1333
A private foundation serving the greater Johnstown area.
Supports jazz.
Helps secure grants. Meets clerical and publicity needs of local arts organizations.
Music Budget: $100.00-$499.00; under 10% for 20th century music.

A. W. Mellon Educational And Charitable Trust*
Theodore L. Hazlett, Jr., President
224 Oliver Building
Pittsburgh, PA 15222
Serves Pittsburgh.
Supports jazz, musical theater, choral music, operatic music, symphonic music.
Sponsors tours and foreign residencies. Sponsors projects concerned with local performing organizations. Funds youth orchestras and music festivals, education of the gifted, civic planning, and conservation. No grants for individuals, nor usually to endowment or building funds.

William Penn Foundation*
John C. Haas, Chairman
330 Boulevard Building
Philadelphia, PA 19103
Formerly Haas Community Fund.
Supports Philadelphia area primarily. Sponsors

contemporary music performances, concert series in schools and colleges, public school audience development programs, and tours made by performing organizations. Supports projects concerned with education, culture, health, conservation, and social welfare.

Philadelphia '76, Inc.
Len Alexander, Program Director
12 South 12th Street, Suite 1700
Philadelphia, PA 19107
(215) 629-1776
A city agency.
Provides financial support, performing facilities. Established to organize American Bicentennial activities in Philadelphia.
Music Budget: Over $100,000.00.

Pittsburgh Council On Higher Education
J. G. K. Miller, Executive Director
222 Craft Avenue
Pittsburgh, PA 15213
(412) 683-7905
Supports 20th century chamber music, new and experimental music.
A consortium of the colleges and universities in the Pittsburgh area. Sponsored and initiated the first Pittsburgh Colloquium for Contemporary Music in November, 1974. Plans to make this an annual event, with Pittsburgh Symphony Chamber Orchestra as a resident ensemble.

Pittsburgh Foundation*
Alfred W. Wishart, Jr., Director
301 Fifth Avenue, Suite 1417
Pittsburgh, PA 15222
John T. Ryan, Jr., Chairman
Sponsors Pittsburgh area opera productions, youth concerts, professional and youth orchestras, concert tours of university performing organizations. Supports projects concerned with child care, education, hospitals, and community planning. Grants are generally non-recurring. No support for operating budgets.

The Presser Foundation*
John Ronald Ott, President
Presser Place
Bryn Mawr, PA 19010
Provides grants to accredited colleges and universities for undergraduate music student scholarships. Encourages music education and music teaching profession. No grants to individuals.

University Of Pennsylvania
Music Department
Nancy Adams Drye, Performance Coordinator
3680 Walnut Street
Philadelphia, PA 19174
(215) 243-6244
Provides financial support, performing space, publicity, and administration. Presents 2 concert series of contemporary music.

Puerto Rico

State Arts Agency:

Institute Of Puerto Rican Culture
Luis H. Rodriguez-Morales, Executive Director
Apartado Postal 4184
San Juan, PR 09005
(809) 723-2686
Supports 20th century chamber music, new and experimental music, mixed-media.
Sponsors experimental, aleatoric, and mixed-media concerts. Encourages preservation and development of Puerto Rican culture.
Music Budget: $25,000.00-$49,000.00; Under 10% for 20th century music.

Rhode Island

State Arts Agency:

Rhode Island State Council On The Arts
Ann Vermel, Executive Director
4365 Post Road
East Greenwich, RI 02218
(401) 884-6410
Supports 20th century chamber music, new and experimental music, jazz.
Provides grants-in-aid to composers and sponsors composition and performance workshops. Co-sponsors New England Contemporary Music Circuit with arts councils of Connecticut and Massachusetts. The Music Circuit presents concerts and lecture-demonstrations on contemporary music performed by ensembles from the 3 states. The participating ensembles make their presentations in the 3 states at colleges which act as co-sponsors.
Music Budget: $25,000.00-$49,000.00; Under 10% for 20th century music.

New England Contemporary Music Circuit
See Rhode Island State Council on the Arts

Westerly Arts Council*
Gail F. Forbes, President
P.O. Box 130
Westerly, RI 02891
Supports chamber music, jazz, operatic music, popular music, ethnic music.

South Carolina

State Arts Agency:

South Carolina Arts Commission
Rick George, Executive Director
829 Richland Street
Columbia, SC 29201
(803) 758-3442
Supports 20th century chamber music, new and experimental music, jazz, 20th century orchestral music.
Provides financial support. Emphasizes educational and community programs. The Arts In Motion Project places actors, composers, poets, and dancers in community residencies to perform and present workshops, helping to integrate the arts into the school curriculum. Project Tap (Total Arts Program) integrates professional artists and craftsmen into local educational, recreational, and community programs. The Arts-In-Prison Program involves artists, musicians, and actors who conduct studios in various art forms in state correctional institutions. The Ensemble Residency Program enables professional music performing ensembles to settle in a community or college and present concerts and workshops. The Commission publishes the *South Carolina Directory of Performing Musicians* and *Eye On The Arts*, a calendar of arts events.
Music Budget: Over $100,000.00; 71%-80% for 20th century music.

The Arts Council Of Spartanburg County*
Georgia Allen, Executive Director
151 North Fairview Avenue
Spartanburg, SC 29302
(803) 583-2776
Supports chamber music, jazz, symphonic music, popular music, operatic music.

Columbia Museum Of Art*
Dr. John Richard Craft, Executive Director
Senate and Bull Streets
Columbia, SC 29201
(803) 254-2791
Supports chamber music, jazz, popular music.

Columbia Music Festival Association*
Leon Harrelson, Executive Director
1527 Senate Street
Columbia, SC 29201
(803) 256-2230 or 254-5640
Supports chamber music, symphonic music, operatic music.

Easley Arts Council*
Joseph B. Thornton, President
P.O. Box 68
Easley, SC 29640
(803) 859-8481
Supports symphonic music.

Laurens County Arts Council, Inc.*
Mrs. Charles Allen, President
P.O. Box 923
Laurens, SC 29360
Supports symphonic music.

Marlboro Area Arts Council*
Joel David Russell, Chairman
927 East Main Street
Bennettsville, SC 29512
(803) 479-2192
Supports symphonic music, operatic music, ethnic music.

South Dakota

State Arts Agency:

South Dakota State Fine Arts Council
Charlotte Carver, Executive Director
108 West 11th Street
Sioux Falls, SD 57102
(605) 339-6647.

Community College Arts Association*
Joyce Domorski, President
P.O. Box B
Madison, SD 57042
(605) 256-2378
Supports chamber music, operatic music, folk music.

Rapid City Fine Arts Council*
Ruth Brennan, President
P.O. Box 872
Rapid City, SD 57701
(605) 342-4997
Supports chamber music.

Sioux Nation Arts Council
Sidney J. Keith, Executive Director
P.O. Box 73
Eagle Butte, SD 57625
(605) 964-2811 Ext. 50
A state agency.
Supports new and experimental music, jazz.
Provides matching funds for concerts. Promotes music, art, and theater in the community.

Tennessee

State Arts Agency:

Tennessee Arts Commission
Norman Worrell, Executive Director
222 Capitol Hill Building
Nashville, TN 32719
(615) 741-1701
Supports 20th century chamber music, new and experimental music, jazz, folk music, electronic music.
Provides financial support. Sponsors Peabody College Electronic Music Symposium.
Music Budget: $10,000.00-$24,999.00.

Arts Council Of Oak Ridge*
V. Louise Mixon, President
P.O. Box 324
Oak Ridge, TN 37830
Supports chamber music, jazz, operatic music, symphonic music, popular music.

Arts Guild Of Sparta*
Joseph G. Geer, Director
P.O. Box 305
Sparta, TN 38583
Supports jazz, popular music, choral music.

Kingsport Fine Arts Center*
Anthony U. Garton, Executive Director
Church Circle
Kingsport, TN 37660
(615) 246-9351
Supports chamber music, jazz, symphonic music, operatic music, popular music.

League Of Women Composers
Nancy Van de Vate, Chairperson
5610 Holston Hills Road
Knoxville, TN 37914
(615) 522-2459
Seeks expanded opportunities for women composers. Intends to obtain commissions, grants,

recordings, and orchestral performances of women's works.

Manchester Municipal Arts Commission*
T. Evans Baird, Chairman
Route 2, P.O. Box 354
Manchester, TN 37355
(615) 728-2968
Supports chamber music, symphonic music.

McNairy County Arts Association*
Harry H. Hickman, President
P.O. Box 262
Selmer, TN 38375
(901) 645-6155
Supports chamber music, symphonic music.

Oak Ridge Civic Music Association
Mrs. A. E. Cameron, Executive Director
P.O. Box 271
Oak Ridge, TN 37830
(615) 483-7037
A private foundation serving Anderson, Roane, and Knox Counties.
Supports chamber music, symphonic music, choral music.
Presents Chamber Series and free Coffee Concerts Series.
Music Budget: $10,000.00-$24,999.00.

Texas

State Arts Agency:

Texas Commission On The Arts And Humanities
Maurice Coats, Executive Director
P.O. Box 13406 Capitol Station
Austin, TX 78711
(512) 475-6593
Provides financial support.

Arts Council Of Brazos Valley*
Dr. A. G. McGill, President
914 Park Lane
Bryan, TX 77801
(713) 244-8883
Supports chamber music, jazz, symphonic music, operatic music, popular music.

Dallas Public Library
Fine Arts Division
George Henderson, Executive Director
1954 Commerce
Dallas, TX 75201
(214) 748-9071
Supports 20th century chamber music, new and
experimental music.
Provides performing facilities. Sponsors Dallas
Public Library Composer Festival, which includes
the Dallas Symphony Orchestra and Dallas
Chamber Music Society.

Eastfield College
Dr. John D. Stewart, Executive Director
3737 Motley Drive
Mesquite, TX 75149
(214) 746-3132
Supports 20th century chamber music, new and
experimental music, jazz.
Sponsors annual Festival of 20th Century Music,
concerts, lecture-demonstrations, and master
classes.

Ewing Halsell Foundation*
Gilbert M. Denman, Jr., Chairman
Travis Park West, Suite 537
San Antonio, TX 78205
Serves Texas.
Supports operatic productions. Sponsors projects
concerned with educational and charitable goals.
No grants to individuals.

Houston Endowment*
J. Howard Creekmore, President
P.O. Box 52338
Houston, TX 77052
Supports operatic music, symphonic music, choral
music.
Sponsors charitable, educational, and religious
undertakings. Funds cultural programs, including
museums, music, and other performing arts. No
grants to permanent endowment funds.

Lubbock Cultural Affairs Council*
John A. Logan, Executive Director
P.O. Box 561
Lubbock, TX 79408
(806) 763-4666
Supports symphonic music.

Moody Foundation*
Robert E. Baker, Administrator
704 Moody National Bank Building
Galveston, TX 77550
Serves Texas.
Sponsors arts projects which advance community
communication and education. Supports projects
concerned with churches, hospitals, health,
science, education, and the advancement of
knowledge.

Pampa Fine Arts Association
Mrs. Homer D. Johnson, President
P.O. Box 818
Pampa, TX 79065
(806) 669-3517
Supports chamber music, operatic music,
symphonic music.

Texas Technical University
Department of Music
Dr. Jeanne Van Appledorn, Executive Director
P.O. Box 4239
Lubbock, TX 79409
(806) 742-1121
Supports 20th century chamber music, new and
experimental music, jazz.
Sponsors Symposium of Contemporary Music, an
annual festival featuring guest composers, panel
discussions, and lectures.

Volunteer Lawyers For The Arts
c/o Jay M. Vogelson
2200 Fidelity Union Tower
Dallas, TX 75201
(214) 748-9312
Provides legal services for performing and visual
arts organizations in the Southwestern U.S.A.

U.S. Virgin Islands

State Arts Agency:

Virgin Islands Council On The Arts
Stephen J. Bostic, Executive Director
Caravelle Arcade
Christiansted
St. Croix, U.S.V.I. 00801
(809) 773-3075 Ext. 3.

Utah

State Arts Agency:

Utah State Institute Of Fine Arts
Ruth R. Draper, Executive Director
609 East South Temple Street
Salt Lake City, UT 84102
(801) 328-5895
Supports 20th century chamber music.
Provides grants-in-aid to over 60 performing ensembles, service organizations, and arts projects. Sponsors out-of-state tours by professional performing ensembles from Utah. Acts as a clearing house for grants to groups in Utah.
Music Budget: $50,000.00-$99,000.00.

Chamber Music Society Of Salt Lake City
B. Gale Dick, Executive Director
1377 Butler Avenue
Salt Lake City, UT 84102
(801) 581-6408
A non-profit organization serving the Salt Lake City area.
Supports chamber music.
Provides financial support. Produces a concert series which includes some works from the 20th century.
Music Budget: $5,000.00-$9,999.00; 21%-30% for 20th century music.

Vermont

State Arts Agency:

Vermont Council On The Arts
Peter Fox Smith, Executive Director
136 State Street
Montpelier, VT 05602
(802) 828-3291
Supports 20th century chamber music, new and experimental music, jazz.
Provides consultation. The Touring Artists Program offers matching grants to sponsors and hosts of public performances. The sponsors and hosts may apply for up to 50% of the artist's fee at least one week before the event. Applications for aid exceeding $500.00 must be submitted 6 weeks prior to the event. To facilitate this program, the Council publishes the *Touring Artists Register*, which lists available touring ensembles and soloists in music, theater, mime, puppetry, dance, poetry, and film.
Music Budget: $25,000.00-$49,000.00; Under 10% for 20th century music.

Burlington Friends Of Music For Youth, Inc.*
Janet D. Rood, President
415 South Willard Street
Burlington, VT 95401
(802) 863-3310
Supports chamber music, symphonic music, operatic music, folk music.

Crossroads Arts Council*
Sandra Cohen, President
Mountain View Drive
Rutland, VT 05701
(802) 773-7276
Louise McCoy, Chairman
Supports chamber music, jazz, symphonic music, operatic music, popular music, ethnic music.

Norwich Arts Association
Susan Hastings, Executive Director
P.O. Box 144
Norwich, VT 05055
(802) 649-1069
A volunteer non-profit organization.
Supports electronic music, choral music.
Supports local artists.
Music Budget: $1,000.00-$4,999.00.

Virgin Islands
See U.S. Virgin Islands

Virginia

State Arts Agency:

Virginia Commission On The Arts And Humanities
Frank R. Dunham, Executive Director
1215 State Office Building
Richmond, VA 23219
(804) 770-4492
Supports 20th century chamber music, new and experimental music.
Provides financial support. Funds performing ensembles and arts service organizations.
Music Budget: $50,000.00-$99,000.00; 10%-20% for 20th century music.

Arlington County Performing Arts*
Norman Kaderlan, Performing Arts Supervisor
300 North Park Drive
Arlington, VA 22203
(703) 558-2161
Supports chamber music, jazz, popular music, ethnic music.

137

Fairfax County Council Of Arts
M. W. Pellettieri, Executive Director
2944 Patrick Henry Drive
Falls Church, VA 22003
(703) 532-0304
A non-profit organization.
Promotes the cultural life in Fairfax County.

Lynchburg Fine Arts Center, Inc.*
J. Clayton Chapman, Chairman
1815 Thomson Drive
Lynchburg, VA 24501
(804) 846-8451
Supports chamber music, jazz, symphonic music, operatic music, popular music, ethnic music.

Norfolk Foundation*
R. L. Sheetz, Executive Director
400 Royster Building
Norfolk, VA 23510
Serves Virginia.
Sponsors symphonic and choral music. Funds scholarships for Virginia colleges. Supports hospitals, schools, community funds, cultural, and civic programs.

Virginia Museum
James M. Brown, Executive Director
Boulevard and Grove Avenue
Richmond, VA 23221
(804) 770-6380
A state agency.
Provides financial support.
Music Budget: $1,000.00-$4,999.00; 41%-50% for 20th century music.

The Wolf Trap Foundation
John M. Ludwig, General Director
1624 Trap Road
Vienna, VA 22180
(703) 938-3810
A private foundation which does not award grants. Sponsors educational programs, especially for young performers. Presents a summer festival at Wolf Trap Farm Park for the Performing Arts, featuring chamber music, new and experimental music, jazz, operatic music, ballet, and popular music.
Music Budget: Over $100,000.00.

Washington

State Arts Agency:

Washington State Arts Commission
James L. Haseltine, Executive Director
1151 Black Lake Boulevard
Olympia, WA 98504
(206) 753-3860
Supports 20th century chamber music, new and experimental music, jazz, electronic music.
Music Budget: $25,000.00-$49,000.00.

Allied Arts Council Of Mid-Columbia Region*
Jacqueline H. Munson, Executive Director
P.O. Box 735
Richland, WA 99352
Supports chamber music, jazz, symphonic music, popular music.

Allied Arts Council Of The Yakima Valley, Inc.*
Jeanne R. Crawford, Executive Secretary
5000 West Lincoln Avenue
Yakima, WA 98902
(509) 966-0930
Gary F. Chambers, Chairman
Supports symphonic music, operatic music.

Burien Arts Association-Burien Arts Gallery*
Mrs. Robert Monroe, Gallery Director
15619 Fourth Avenue S.W.
Seattle, WA 98166
(206) 244-7808
Allen Reamer, Associate President
Supports symphonic music, ethnic music, folk music.

Creative Arts League*
Donna Schill, Chairman
620 Market Street
Kirkland, WA 98033
(206) 822-7161
Beverly Mattson, Executive Secretary
Supports chamber music.

Federal Way Library Arts Commission*
Rosalie Luce, President
848 South 320th Street South
Federal Way, WA 98002
Supports chamber music, jazz, symphonic music, operatic music, popular music, ethnic music.

King County Arts Commission*
Patricia K. Brunton, Chairman
400 King County Courthouse
Seattle, WA 98104
(206) 344-4040
Supports jazz, symphonic music, operatic music, popular music, ethnic music.

Pacific Lutheran University
Department of Music
Dr. Richard Jungkuntz, Provost
Tacoma, WA 98447
(206) 531-6900
Supports 20th century chamber music.
Provides financial support, performing facilities. Presents An Evening of Contemporary Music Concert Series; Composers Forum; and a Festival of Contemporary Music, featuring a guest composer, discussions, and lectures.

Ruby Arts Of Lake Chelan*
Donovan Gray, Executive Director
P.O. Box 1495
Lake Chelan, WA 98816
(506) 582-5041
Supports chamber music, jazz, popular music, symphonic music, ethnic music.

Seattle Arts Commission
John Blaine, Executive Director
305 Harrison Street
Seattle, WA 98109
(206) 583-6420
A city agency.
Supports 20th century chamber music, new and experimental music, jazz, orchestral music.
Sponsors free public performances, including children's concerts.
Music Budget: Over $100,000.00; Under 10% for 20th century music.

Tacoma-Pierce County Civic Arts Commission
Richard J. Trapp, Executive Director
County-City Building, Room 338
Tacoma, WA 98402
(206) 593-4494
A city and county agency serving Tacoma and Pierce County.
Supports new and experimental music, popular music.
Provides financial support, publicity, technical support. Sponsors free popular music concerts.
Music Budget: $50,000.00-$99,000.00; 21%-30% for 20th century music.

West Virginia

State Arts Agency:

West Virginia Arts And Humanities Council
Norman Fagan, Executive Director
State Office Building Number 6
1900 Washington Street East, Room B-531
Charleston, WV 25305
(304) 348-3711.

Parkersburg Fine Arts Council, Inc.*
Mrs. Noel Wheaton, President
P.O. Box 4338
Parkersburg, WV 26101
Supports symphonic music, operatic music.

Wisconsin

State Arts Agency:

Wisconsin Arts Council
Jerrold Rouby, Executive Director
1 West Wilson Street
Madison, WI 53702
(608) 266-0190.

John Michael Kohler Arts Center*
Ruth DeYoung Kohler, Director
608 New York Avenue
Sheboygan, WI 53081
(414) 458-6144
Supports chamber music, jazz, symphonic music, operatic music, popular music, ethnic music.

Marquette University
The University Committee on the Fine Arts
Dr. John Pick, President
Milwaukee, WI 53233
(414) 244-7263
Supports chamber music, jazz, symphonic music, operatic music, popular music, ethnic music.

Faye McBeath Foundation*
110 East Wisconsin Avenue
Milwaukee, WI 53202
Serves Wisconsin.
Sponsors youth music education projects. Funds public health projects, nursing homes, and scientific research. Promotes improvement in local government.

Milwaukee Art Center
Tracy Atkinson, Director
750 North Lincoln Memorial Drive
Milwaukee, WI 53202
(414) 271-9508
A non-profit organization.
Supports 20th century chamber music.
Provides financial support, performing facilities.
Presents Milwaukee Art Center Concert Series.
Music Budget: $100.00-$499.00; 91%-100% for
20th century music.

Milwaukee Foundation*
James O. Wright, Chairman
110 East Wisconsin Avenue
Milwaukee, WI 53202
Serves Milwaukee.
Sponsors light opera productions. Supports
cultural projects, scholarships, health facilities,
care of the aged, and mental health programs. No
grants to individuals.

Rock Prairie Arts Council
O. U. Shaffer, President
P.O. Box 313
Beloit, WI 53511
(608) 365-3391
A regional agency serving Beloit and Jonesville.
Supports 20th century chamber music, new and
experimental music.
Coordinates activities and communications of
local arts organizations.

**Wisconsin College-Conservatory Women's
League**
Sylvia L. Miller, President
1584 North Prospect Avenue
Milwaukee, WI 53202
(414) 276-4350

Supports 20th century chamber music.
Promotes the Conservatory by informing the
surrounding community of the school's cultural
value. Supports the Conservatory financially.
Music Budget: $1,000.00-$4,999.00; 91%-100%
for 20th century music.

Wyoming
State Arts Agency:

Wyoming Council On The Arts
Michael Haug, Executive Director
200 West 25th Street
Cheyenne, WY 82002
(307) 777-7742
Supports 20th century chamber music, new and
experimental music, jazz.
Provides financial support. Sponsors arts activities,
emphasizing innovative programs.
Music Budget: $25,000.00-$49,000.00; 51%-60%
for 20th century music.

University of Wyoming Department of Music
Department of Music
David Tomatz, Chairman
P.O. Box 3037 University Station
Laramie, WY 82071
(307) 766-5242
Supports 20th century chamber music, new and
experimental music, jazz.
Provides financial support, performing facilities.
Sponsors Western Arts Music Festival, featuring
courses in performance and composition
techniques, chamber music workshops, and choral
workshops. During the Festival, one week called
*Composers Symposium: New American Music:
Tangents* is devoted to contemporary music,
featuring intensive workshops, lectures,
discussions, and performances.

Performing Facilities

The facilities listed here were selected for their availability to contemporary music performers. Most are small and intimate spaces that are particularly suited to small chamber groups, jazz ensembles, and chamber orchestras.

For a broader, more general listing of performing facilities, consult *The National Directory for the Performing Arts and Civic Centers*, edited by Bea Handel, Janet Spencer, and Nolanda Turner (Dallas: Handel and Co., Inc., 1975). Also, a number of cities are currently compiling facilities directories. Concerning New York City, see *Spaces. A Directory of Auditoriums and Meeting Rooms, Indoors and Outdoors, Available in the City of New York*, edited by Hannelore Hahn (New York: City of New York Parks, Recreation, and Cultural Affairs Administration, 1975).

Alabama

Birmingham-Jefferson Civic Center
E. A. Jones, Jr., Director
1 Civic Center Plaza
Birmingham, AL 35203
(205) 328-8160
Concert Hall seats 3000; Theater seats 800.

Mobile Municipal Auditorium, Theater And Exposition Hall
W. C. Clewis, Manager
401 Auditorium Drive
Mobile, AL 36602
(205) 438-7261
Arena seats 10,200; Exposition Hall seats 4000; Theater seats 1950.
Musicals, rock, country and western, big band, orchestral concerts.
Available for rental only.

Montgomery Museum Of Fine Arts Auditorium
c/o Museum Manager
440 South McDonough Street
Montgomery, AL 36104
(205) 263-2519
Seats 175.
Chamber concerts.

University Of Alabama
Humanities Auditorium
Dr. Royce Beyer, Director
4701 University Drive, N.W.
Huntsville, AL 35805
(205) 895-6120
Seats 350.
20th century chamber concerts.

University Of South Alabama
University Center Ballroom
Robert Holberg, Director
Mobile, AL 36688
(205) 460-6101
Seats 280.

University Of South Alabama
University Theatre For The Performing Arts
Victor Cook, Manager
North Joachim Street
Mobile, AL 36601
(205) 438-5686
Seats 2000.
Musicals, band concerts.
Available for rental only.

Alaska

Ketchikan High School Auditorium
Mr. Lowry, Principal
2610 Fourth
Ketchikan, AK 99901
(907) 225-2115
Seats 1200.
Available for rental only.

Arizona

Arizona State University
Grady Gammage Auditorium For The Performing Arts
Warren K. Sumners, Manager
Tempe, AZ 85281
(602) 965-5062
Seats 3019.
Tape and playback system.
Available for rental only.

Tucson Community Center
Bob Thompson, Manager
260 South Church
Tucson, AZ 85703
(602) 791-4101
Arena seats 9500; Music Hall seats 2380; Theater seats 535.
Available for rental only.

Arkansas

The Arkansas Arts Center
Townsend Wolfe, Executive Director
Little Rock, AR 72203
(501) 372-4000

Fine Arts Center Of Hot Springs
Col. Haines Hower, Manager
815 Whittington Avenue
Hot Springs National Park
Hot Springs, AR 71901
Seats 150.
Musical comedies, chamber, choral concerts.
Available for rental only.
Alternate address:
P.O. Box 1344
Hot Springs, AR 71901.

California

Brand Library Art Center
E. J. Hagan, Manager
1601 West Mountain
Glendale, CA 91201
(213) 956-2051
Seats 150.
Chamber, new and experimental, vocal concerts.
Available for rental only.

California State University
Marilyn Berglund, Katherine Danner, Concert Managers
Fresno, CA 93740
(209) 487-2654
Recital Hall seats 180: chamber, new and experimental concerts; available for rental only. Union Lounge seats 350: chamber, new and experimental, jazz concerts; available for rental only.

California State University, Sonoma
Ives Hall of Music
Larry Snydek, David Sloss, Directors
1801 East Cotati Avenue
Rohnert Park, CA 94928
(707) 795-2416
Room 119 seats 200; Warren Auditorium seats 275.
Chamber, new and experimental, jazz, ethnic concerts.
Available free to college groups.

Caltech
Beckman Auditorium
c/o Jerry Willis
Pasadena, CA 91109
(213) 795-6811
Seats 1171.
Chamber concerts.

Claremont Colleges
See Pomona College and Scripps College.

College Of San Mateo
1700 West Hillsdale Boulevard
San Mateo, CA 94402
(415) 574-6161
Choral Room seats 200; Main Theatre seats 550.

Concord Pavilion
John Toffoli, Jr., Manager
2000 Kirker Pass Road
Concord, CA 94521
(415) 798-3316
Seats 8000.
Chamber, jazz, rock concerts.
Available for rental only.

Glendale Public Library
Jack A. Ramsey, Manager
222 East Harvard
Glendale, CA 91207
(213) 956-2030
Seats 350.
Chamber, new and experimental, vocal concerts.
Available for rental only.

Harvey Auditorium
Roger Lewis, Manager
1241 G Street
Bakersfield, CA 93301
(805) 324-9841
Auditorium seats 1800; Little Theatre seats 250.
Jazz, orchestral, band, dance concerts.
Available for rental only.

142

The Inner City Cultural Center
C. Bernard Jackson, Manager
1308 South New Hampshire Avenue
Los Angeles, CA 90006
(213) 387-1161
Auditorium Theatre seats 311; Cafe Theatre seats 99; Lodge Theatre seats 175.
Chamber, new and experimental, jazz, ethnic concerts.
Provides free publicity.

Los Angeles County Museum Of Art
Lawrence Morton, Manager
5905 Wilshire Boulevard
Los Angeles, CA 90036
(213) 937-4250
Atrium of Ahmanson Gallery seats 314; Bing Theater seats 602; Gallery seats 100; Outdoor Plaza seats 1000.
Chamber, new and experimental, jazz, ethnic concerts.

Paul Masson Mountain Winery
Edwin J. Schwartz, Producer
Saratoga, CA 95070
(408) 257-4800
Seats 900.
Chamber, jazz concerts.

Mendocino County Museum
Herbert E. Pruett, Director
400 East Commercial Street
Willits, CA 95490
(707) 459-2736
Seats 120.
Chamber, folk concerts.

Mills College
Center For Contemporary Music
Robert Ashley, Director
Mills College
Oakland, CA 94613
(415) 632-2700 Ext. 337
New and experimental concerts.
2 synthesizers, eight-track recording studio available.

Music Center Of Los Angeles
Jack Present, Booking Manager
135 North Grand Avenue
Los Angeles, CA 90012
(213) 626-5781
Ahmanson Theatre seats 2071; Dorothy Chandler Pavilion seats 3217; Mark Taper Forum seats 742.

Musicals, chamber, new and experimental, jazz concerts.

Occidental College
Thorne Hall
Phyllis J. Warschaw, Manager
1600 Campus Road
Los Angeles, CA 90041
(213) 259-2738
Seats 960.
Chamber, orchestral concerts.
Available for rental only.

Pasadena Historical Museum
Dorothy Tucker, Manager
470 West Walnut
Pasadena, CA 91103
(213) 577-1660
Indoor hall seats 60; outdoor area seats 300.
Chamber, new and experimental concerts.
Available for rental only.

Pasadena Public Library
Robert Conover, Library Director
285 East Walnut Street
Pasadena, CA 91101
(213) 577-4041
Seats 225.
Chamber, new and experimental, jazz concerts.
Available free to performing groups.

Pomona College
c/o Music Department
Claremont, CA 91711
(714) 626-8511 Ext. 3266
Balch Hall seats 250; Pattison Hall seats 150.
Chamber, new and experimental concerts.
Electronic studio.

Redding Civic Auditorium And Convention Center
Roy A. Montgomery, Manager
P.O. Drawer P
Redding, CA 96001
(916) 246-0239
Seats 2022.
Jazz, country and western, rock concerts.
Available for rental only.

Scripps College
Little Bridges Hall
c/o Music Department
Claremont, CA 91711
(714) 626-8511 Ext. 3266
Seats 450.

Chamber, new and experimental concerts.

Theatre Vanguard
Judith Stark, Manager
9014 Melrose Avenue
Los Angeles, CA 90069
(213) 278-0641
Seats 199.
Chamber, new and experimental, jazz, electronic concerts.

University Art Museum
Jerrold Ballaine, Manager
2626 Bancroft
Berkeley, CA 94720
(415) 642-1207
Seats 250.
Chamber, new and experimental, jazz concerts.
Provides free publicity.

University of California
Committee For Arts And Lectures
Betty Connors, Manager
Berkeley, CA 94720
(415) 642-3691
Hertz Hall seats 714; Zellerbach Auditorium seats 2000; Zellerbach Playhouse seats 500.
Chamber, new and experimental, jazz, orchestral concerts.

University of California at San Diego
Center for Music Experiment and Related Research
Dr. Roger Reynolds, Director
P.O. Box 109
La Jolla, CA 92037
(714) 452-4383
Seats 150.
New and experimental concerts.

University of California at San Diego
Mandeville Center
Alan Johnson, Manager
Mail Code B-026
La Jolla, CA 92037
(714) 452-2380
Mandeville Auditorium seats 500 to 850; Mandeville Recital Hall seats 200.
Chamber, new and experimental, orchestral concerts.
Four-channel playback system available.

Westwood Playhouse
D. Combs, Manager
10886 Le Conte Avenue
Los Angeles, CA 90024
(213) 479-4107
Seats 500.
Chamber, new and experimental, jazz, dance concerts.

Colorado

Sangre De Cristo Arts And Conference Center
Darrell Bohlsen, Director
210 North Santa Fe Avenue
Pueblo, CO 81003
(303) 543-0130
Seats 500.
Chamber, new and experimental, jazz, orchestral, folk, rock concerts.
Provides free publicity.

Connecticut

Horace Bushnell Memorial Hall
Mr. L. Leverett Wright, Managing Director
Lafayette Circle
166 Capitol Avenue
Hartford, CT 06106
(203) 527-3123
Orchestral, choral, popular, operatic, dance concerts.
Available for rental only.

Educational Center For The Arts
Lynne Karsten, Manager
55 Audubon Street
New Haven, CT 06510
(203) 865-0506
Seats 300.
Chamber, new and experimental, jazz, orchestral concerts.
Available for rental only.

Hartford Civic Center
Byron A. Trimble, Manager
One Civic Center Plaza
Hartford, CT 06103
(203) 566-6588
Assembly Hall seats 1800; Coliseum seats 12,000.
Rock, folk concerts.
Available for rental only.

Kent Memorial Library
Maxine Beckwith, Director
50 North Main Street
Suffield, CT 06078
(203) 668-2325
Seats 70.
Available free to performing groups for concerts.

New Haven Coliseum
Loris Smith, Director
275 South Orange Street
New Haven, CT 06508
(203) 772-4200
Seats 10,200.
Available for rental only.

Post Junior College
Paul Duling, Director of Public Affairs
800 Country Club Road
Waterbury, CT 06708
(203) 755-0121
Cafeteria seats 300 to 400; Campus Center Lounge seats 50 to 100; Lower Library Auditorium seats 300 to 400.
Chamber concerts.

Public Circuit Of New Haven
Carl Nastri, Director
Parks Department
P.O. Box 1416
New Haven, CT 06506
(203) 562-0151 Ext. 454
Contact this agency regarding available parks for summer concerts.

The Stamford Museum And Nature Center
Ezio Pinza Theater
Louise Spirer, Manager
39 Scofieldtown Road
Stamford, CT 06903
(203) 322-1646
Seats 1500.
Chamber, folk concerts.
Provides free publicity.

The Theatre And The Space
John Barringer, Director
148 Orange Street
New Haven, CT 06510
(203) 865-8368
Seats 30.
Chamber, new and experimental, jazz, folk concerts.

Unitarian Church
Reverend Edward Lane, Director
Lyons Plains Road
Westport, CT 06880
(203) 227-7205
Seats 300.
Chamber concerts.
Friends of Music Concert Series presents 6 to 7 concerts per season featuring guest composers and pre-concert lecture-demonstrations for Friends of Music members.

University Of Bridgeport
William Nowcand, Concert Manager
Bernard Arts and Humanities Center
Bridgeport, CT 06602
(203) 576-4404
Mertens Theatre seats 900, Recital Hall seats 200.
Chamber, new and experimental, jazz, operatic concerts.

University Of Connecticut
William Benton Museum
Paul Rovetti, Director
Storrs, CT 06268
(203) 486-4520
Seats 150 to 200.
Chamber, new and experimental, jazz concerts.

Wadsworth Atheneum Theatre
Harrison Cromer, Program Director
25 Atheneum Square North
Hartford, CT 06103
(203) 278-2670
William Pearson, Theatre Manager
Seats 308.
Chamber, new and experimental concerts.
Provides free publicity.

Westport Public Library
Joan Turner, Director
19 East State Street
Westport, CT 06880
(203) 227-8411
Seats 100.
Chamber concerts.

Delaware

University Of Delaware
Anthony Loudis Recital Hall
Henry Lee, Chairman of Music Department
Amy E. DuPont Music Building
Newark, DE 19711
(302) 738-2577
Seats 500.

District of Columbia

American University
McDonald Recital Hall
Dr. Lloyd Ultan, Manager
Kreeger Music Building
Washington, D.C. 20016
(202) 686-2162
Seats 164.
Chamber, new and experimental concerts.

John F. Kennedy Center For The Performing Arts
Office Of Special Events
Washington, D.C. 20566
(202) 254-3600 or 872-0466
Concert Hall seats 2700; Eisenhower Theater seats 1100; Opera House seats 2200.
Musicals, chamber, orchestral, operatic concerts.

Library of Congress
Coolidge Auditorium
c/o Chief, Music Division
Washington, D.C. 20540
(202) 426-6321
Seats 500.
Chamber, new and experimental concerts.
Provides free publicity.

National Gallery Of Art
Richard Bales, Music Director
6th Street and Constitution Avenue
Washington, D.C. 20565
(202) 737-4215
Auditorium seats 300; East Garden Court seats 500.
20th century chamber, new and experimental, 20th century orchestral, choral, and vocal concerts.

The National Shrine Of The Immaculate Conception
Joseph Michaud, Director
4th and Michigan Avenue, N.E.
Washington, D.C. 20017
(202) 526-8300
Seats 2600.
Chamber, new and experimental, organ, choral concerts.
Two organs available.
Provides free publicity.
Available free to performing groups.

George Washington University
Lisner Auditorium
Francis J. Early, Manager
730 21st Street, N.W.
Washington, D.C. 20006
(202) 676-6800
Seats 1500.
Chamber, new and experimental, jazz, dance concerts.
Available for rental only.

Florida

Miami Beach Convention Center
Performing Arts Theater
Norman Litz, Manager
1700 Washington Avenue
Miami Beach, FL 33139
(305) 673-7311
Seats 3000.
Orchestral concerts.
Available for rental only.

Museum Of Fine Arts
Lee Malone, Director
255 Beach Drive North
St. Petersburg, FL 33701
(813) 896-2667
Seats 200.
Chamber concerts.

Georgia

Georgia Southern College
Foy Fine Arts Building
c/o Dr. David Mathew
Statesboro, GA 30458
(912) 681-5600 Ext. 396
Seats 350.
Chamber, new and experimental concerts.
Available free to performing groups.

Island Art Center
Mrs. W. C. Hendrix, Executive Director
P.O. Box 673
Demere Road
St. Simons Island, GA 31522
(912) 638-8770
Construction nearly completed as of April, 1975.
Will seat 150 to 200.
Chamber, new and experimental, jazz concerts.
Will provide free publicity.

The University Of Georgia Chapel
Dr. Olin G. Parker, Manager
Athens, GA 30602
(404) 542-3737
Seats 430.
Chamber, new and experimental concerts.

Illinois

Fine Arts Center Of Clinton
Robin McNeil, Director
119 West Macon
Clinton, IL 61727
(217) 935-5055
Seats 65.
Chamber, new and experimental, jazz concerts.
Available free to performing groups.

Grant Park Music Shell
Stanley M. Ackerman, Manager
Grant Park
Chicago, IL 60605
(312) 294-2420 or 294-4590
Lawn seats 50,000; Music Shell seats 8000.
Orchestral, operatic, choral concerts.
Available for rental only.

Illinois Wesleyan University
Westbrook Auditorium
William Hipp, Director
School of Music
Bloomington, IL 61701
(309) 556-3061
Seats 600.
Chamber, new and experimental, jazz, orchestral,
operatic concerts.
ARP 2600 synthesizer available.

Northwestern University
Lutkin Hall
Jan Whitlock, Concert Manager
School of Music
Evanston, IL 60201
(312) 492-5441
Seats 400.
Chamber, new and experimental, jazz concerts.
Available free to performing groups sponsored by
the school.

Ravinia Park
Edward Gordon, Director
Highland Park, IL 60035
Concert Pavilion seats 3303; Murray Theatre seats
850.
Chamber, orchestral, popular concerts.

Southern Illinois University
Shryock Auditorium
Jo Mack, Manager
Carbondale, IL 62901
(618) 536-2176
Seats 1250.
Chamber, new and experimental, jazz, orchestral,
popular, operatic concerts.

University of Chicago
Mandel Hall
c/o University Theatre Manager
Chicago, IL 60637
(312) 753-3591
Seats 1066.
Chamber, new and experimental, jazz, orchestral,
choral concerts.
Buchla synthesizer available.
Available for rental only.

University Of Illinois
Krannert Center for the Performing Arts
Michael Brotman, Director
Urbana, IL 61801
(217) 333-6700
Festival Theater seats 950; Great Hall seats 2100;
Outdoor Theater seats 560; Playhouse seats 675;
Studio Theater seats 150.
Chamber, new and experimental, jazz concerts.

147

University Of Illinois
School of Music
Robert E. Bays, Director
Urbana, IL 61801
(217) 333-2620
Auditorium in Music Building seats 250; Recital Hall in Smith Music Hall seats 900.
Chamber, new and experimental, jazz concerts.

Waukegan Public Library
Elvera A. Lake, Coordinator
128 North County Street
Waukegan, IL 60085
(312) 623-2041
Seats 300.
Chamber concerts.
Available free to non-profit groups.

Indiana

DePauw University Performing Arts Center
Donald H. White, Director, School of Music
Greencastle, IN 46135
(317) 653-9721
Concert Hall seats 1500; Recital Hall seats 250; Theater seats 440.
Chamber, new and experimental, jazz, orchestral, choral, operatic concerts.
Provides free publicity.
Available free to performing groups.

Indiana University Auditorium
Lawrence L. Davis, Manager
1200 East Seventh Street
Bloomington, IN 47401
(812) 337-0170
Seats 3803.
Chamber, orchestral concerts.
Pipe organ available.

Indiana University
Musical Arts Center
Bloomington, IN 47401
(812) 337-9053
Seats 1460.
Chamber, new and experimental, jazz, orchestral, choral, operatic concerts.

Monroe County Public Library Auditorium
Bob Trinkle, Director
303 East Kirkwood
Bloomington, IN 47401
(812) 339-2271
Seats 144.

Chamber, new and experimental, jazz concerts.
Available free to non-profit groups.

Saint Mary's College
O'Laughlin Auditorium
Mary A. Gerber, Director of Programming
Notre Dame, IN 46556
(219) 284-4176
Seats 1310.
Chamber concerts.

Iowa

Clinton Park And Recreation Department
Ronald D. Cuppy, Director
1401 11th Avenue North
Clinton, IA 52732
(319) 243-1260
Ericksen Community Center has a multi-purpose gymnasium with a stage; Showboat Theatre seats 275.

Des Moines Art Center
James T. Demetrion, Director
Greenwood, Park
Des Moines, IA 50312
(515) 277-4405
Seats 225.
Chamber, new and experimental, jazz concerts.

Flora Park Barn
Michael J. Rice, Manager
Department of Recreation
Bunker Hill
Dubuque, IA 52001
(319) 556-3661
Seats 160.
Musicals, chamber, choral concerts.
Provides free publicity.

Charles MacNeider Museum
Richard Leet, Director
303 2nd Street, S.E.
Mason City, IA 50401
(515) 423-9563
Seats 100.
Chamber, jazz concerts.

Municipal Auditorium
Harold C. Hansen, Manager
Gordon Drive
Sioux City, IA 51101
(712) 279-6157
Seats 4400.

Available for rental only.

William Penn College
Ware Recital Hall
John O. Westlund, Manager
McGrew Fine Arts Center
Oskaloosa, IA 52577
(515) 673-8311 Ext. 260
Seats 140.
Chamber, jazz concerts.
Tape and recording system available.
Provides free publicity.

University Of Iowa
Electronic Music Studio
Peter Tod Lewis, Executive Director
Iowa City, IA 52240
(319) 353-4313
Seats 1956.
New and experimental concerts.

West High School
Ed Kirchenbrock, Manager
Ridgeway and Baltimore
Waterloo, IA 50701
(319) 234-3521
Seats 1735.
Orchestral concerts.
Available free to performing groups.

Witter Art Gallery
Gordon D. Linge, Director
609 Cayuga Street
Storm Lake, IA 50588
(712) 732-2125
Seats 100.
Provides free publicity.
Available free to performing groups.

Kansas

Bethel College
Krehbiel Auditorium
J. Harold Moyer, Manager
Fine Arts Center
North Newton, KS 67117
(316) 283-2500
Seats 450.
Available for rental only.

Topeka Public Library
Robert H. Daw, Manager
1515 West 10th Street
Topeka, KS 66604
(913) 235-2307
Auditorium seats 200; Gallery of Fine Arts seats 100 to 150.
Chamber, new and experimental concerts.
Provides free publicity.
Available free to performing groups.

Washburn University
White Concert Hall
Dr. John Iltis, Manager
Topeka, KS 66621
(913) 235-5341 Ext. 481
Seats 1200.
Chamber, new and experimental, jazz, orchestral concerts.

Louisiana

Louisiana State University
Bill Hite, Concert Manager
Baton Rouge, LA 70803
Colonnade Theater seats 300; University Theater seats 475; University Union Theater seats 1330.

Municipal Auditorium
Richard R. Dixon, Manager
1201 St. Peter Street
New Orleans, LA 70116
(504) 586-4203
Seats 8000.
Available for rental only.

New Orleans Museum Of Art
E. John Bullard, Director
P.O. Box 19123 City Park
New Orleans, LA 70179
(504) 488-2631
Seats 227.
Chamber, jazz concerts.

New Orleans Public Library
Helen Levy Auditorium
Mr. M. E. Wright, Manager
219 Loyola Avenue
New Orleans, LA 70140
(504) 523-4602
Seats 100.
Chamber, jazz, band, choral concerts.
Available free to performing groups.

Southeastern Louisiana University
University Auditorium
David C. McCormick, Manager
Hammond, LA 70401
(504) 549-2211
Seats 750.
Chamber, new and experimental, jazz concerts.

Maryland

The Baltimore Museum Of Art
William Bigel, Manager
Art Museum Drive
Baltimore, MD 21218
(301) 396-7100
Seats 400.
Chamber, new and experimental, jazz concerts.
Available free to performing groups.

Essex Community College
James Duffy, Arno Drucker, Concert Managers
Baltimore, MD 21237
(301) 682-6000
Community Center Theatre seats 412; Recital Hall seats 126.
Chamber concerts.

Hampton National Historic Site
John Miller, Administrator
535 Hampton Lane
Towson, MD 21204
(301) 823-7054
Seats 150.
Chamber, choral concerts.
Originally a private home which became a museum site in 1948. Now owned by the National Park Service.

Massachusetts

Brockton Art Center - Fuller Memorial
Marilyn Friedman Hoffman, Director
Oak Street
Brockton, MA 02401
(617) 588-6000
Seats 300.
Chamber, jazz, rock concerts.

Harvard University
Fogg Art Museum Courtyard
Seymour Slive, Director
32 Quincy Street
Cambridge, MA 02138
(617) 495-2397

Janet Cox, Public Relations
Seats 300.
Chamber concerts.
Free concert series in 3-story marble enclosed courtyard.

Harvard University
Loeb Drama Center
Robert Chapman, Director
64 Brattle Street
Cambridge, MA 02138
(617) 495-2668
Seats 550.

Lenox Arts Center
Lyn Austin, Francis Thorne, Directors
Wheatleigh Estate
P.O. Box 1787
Lenox, MA 02140
(413) 637-2242
Seats 125.
Chamber concerts.

Longy School Of Music
Edward Pickman Hall
Johanna Giwoski, Manager
1 Follen Street
Cambridge, MA 02138
(617) 876-0956
Seats 275.
Chamber concerts.
Available for rental only.

Medford Public Library
Frank Lavine, Director
111 High Street
Medford, MA 02155
(617) 395-7950
Seats 100.
Available free for non-profit purposes.

Museum Of Fine Arts
Musical Instrument Collection
Barbara Lambert, Curator
Huntington Avenue
Boston, MA 02115
(617) 267-9300 Ext. 340
20th century chamber, new and experimental concerts, and concerts on historical instruments from the Collection.

Museum Of Fine Arts
Jeffrey R. Brown, Director
49 Chestnut Street
Springfield, MA 01103
(413) 732-6092
Seats 315.
Chamber concerts.
Available for rental only.

Springfield Civic Center
Jerry Healy, Manager
1277 Main Street
Springfield, MA 01103
(413) 781-7080
Seats 10,152.
Chamber, new and experimental, jazz, rock concerts.
Available for rental only.

Tufts University
Cohen Fine Arts Center
Peter Cokkinias, Manager
Music Department
Talbot Avenue
Medford, MA 02155
(617) 628-5000 Ext. 282
Seats 500.
Chamber, new and experimental concerts.

Wellesley College
Margaret C. Lafferty, Coordinator of Special Events
Wellesley, MA 02181
(617) 235-0320 Ext. 688
Alumnae Hall Auditorium seats 1500; Jewett Auditorium seats 320.
Chamber, dance concerts.
Available by invitation or approval by a committee.

Michigan

Calvin College
Fine Arts Center Auditorium
Harold Geerdes, Manager
1801 East Beltline Avenue
Grand Rapids, MI 49506
(616) 949-4000
Seats 1011.
Available for rental only.

Henry Ford Centennial Library Auditorium
16301 Michigan Avenue
Dearborn, MI 48126
(313) 271-1000
Seats 278.
Chamber concerts.
Provides free publicity.
Available for rental only.

Hope College
Morrette Rider, Dean
East 12th and College
Holland, MI 49423
(616) 392-5111 Ext. 2223
DeWitt Hall seats 500, flexible seating, electronic equipment; Dimnent Hall seats 1100, two organs; Wichers Hall seats 225, electronic equipment.
Chamber, new and experimental, jazz concerts.
Provides free publicity.

Midland Center For The Arts
Don Jaeger, Executive Director
1801 West St. Andrews
Midland, MI 48640
(517) 631-5930
Auditorium seats 1538; Little Theatre seats 386.
Chamber, new and experimental, jazz, orchestral, dance concerts.
Available for rental only.

Western Michigan University
Oakland Recital Hall
Carl Doubleday, Manager
Kalamazoo, MI 49008
(616) 383-0910
Seats 350.
Chamber, new and experimental concerts.
Electronic music studio.
Available for rental only.

Minnesota

College Of St. Catherine
O'Shaughnessy Auditorium
James Wennblom, Manager
St. Paul, MN 55105
(612) 698-0768
Seats 1747.
Chamber, new and experimental, jazz concerts.
Available for rental only.

151

College Of St. Thomas
Division Of Fine Arts
Francis N. Mayer, Chairman
St. Paul, MN 55105
(612) 647-5285
Foley Theatre; Murray Hall Lounge, flexible
seating; O'Shaughnessy Educational Center
Auditorium seats 350 on main floor and 300 in
balcony.
Chamber, choral concerts.

Guild Of Performing Arts
Jim Kerr, Manager
504 Cedar Avenue
Minneapolis, MN 55404
(612) 333-8269
Seats 100.
Chamber, new and experimental, jazz, folk, ethnic
concerts.
Available for rental only.

Orchestra Hall
Barry Hoffman, Manager
1111 Nicollet Mall
Minneapolis, MN 55403
(612) 339-2244
Seats 2753.
Chamber, orchestral concerts.
Available for rental only.

The Unitarian Center Auditorium
Uri Barnea, Music Director
900 Mt. Curve Avenue
Minneapolis, MN 55403
(612) 377-6608
Seats 600.
Chamber, new and experimental, vocal concerts.
Piano and organ available.

University Of Minnesota
Marshall Performing Arts Center
Dr. Pat McDonough, Manager
Duluth, MN 55812
(218) 726-8550
Seats 650.
Chamber, new and experimental, jazz, orchestral,
choral concerts.

Walker Art Center Auditorium
Suzanne Weil, Coordinator of Performing Arts
Vineland Place
Minneapolis, MN 55403
(612) 377-7500
Seats 350.

Chamber, new and experimental, jazz, rock
concerts.
Provides free publicity.
Available through sponsorship by Walker Art
Center.

West Bank Firehouse
Phil Raher, Manager
1501 South 4th Street
Minneapolis, MN 55404
Seats 120.
Chamber, new and experimental, jazz, folk
concerts.

Missouri

Nelson Gallery Of Art
Atkins Auditorium
June Finnell, Secretary
4525 Oak Street
Kansas City, MO 64111
(816) 561-4000
Seats 700.
Chamber concerts.
Available for rental only, subject to approval.

Saints Auditorium
Ken Howler, Manager
River and Walnut Streets
Independence, MO 64050
(816) 833-1000
Seats 5800; Lower Auditorium seats 1000.
Choral, orchestral concerts.
Organ available.
Available for rental only.

The School Of The Ozarks
John L. Moad, Public Relations
Point Lookout, MO 65726
(417) 334-6411
Chapel seats 1000; College Center seats 400;
Jones Auditorium seats 1000; Jordan Auditorium
seats 70; Memorial Fieldhouse seats 4000.
Chamber, jazz concerts.

Montana

Montana State University
Recital Hall
Creech Reynolds, Manager
Creative Arts Complex
Bozeman, MT 59715
(406) 994-3561
Seats 300.

Chamber, new and experimental, jazz concerts.
Recording and playback system available.

Nebraska

Fort Robinson
Vance Nelson, Museum Curator
P.O. Box 304
Crawford, NE 69339
(308) 665-2852
Auditorium seats 85; Howard Dodd Hall seats
300; Post Playhouse seats 163.
Musicals, band concerts.

Nevada

University Of Nevada
Robert Burgan, Director
4505 Maryland Parkway
Las Vegas, NV 89154
(702) 739-3360
Judy Bayley Theatre seats 556; Humanities
Auditorium seats 300.
Chamber, new and experimental concerts.

New Hampshire

Arts And Science Center
Ronald Deane, Director
14 Court Street
Nashua, NH 03060
(603) 883-1506
Seats 250 to 275.
Chamber concerts.

Center For Chamber Music At Apple Hill
Dan Savage, Manager
Apple Hill Farm
Nelson, NH 03445
(603) 847-3362
Seats 100.
Chamber concerts.
Available free to performing groups.

Gilford Middle High School
c/o School Principal
Belknap Mt. Road
Gilford, NH 03246
Seats 800.
Chamber, new and experimental, orchestral,
choral concerts.

Interlakes High School
c/o School Principal
Route 25
Meredith, NH 03253
Seats 500.
Chamber, new and experimental, orchestral,
choral concerts.

Phenix Hall Theatre
Kate Torres, Director
40 North Main Street
Concord, NH 03301
(603) 225-6911
Seats 200.
20th century chamber music presented in the
Noon-Time Concert Series on 20 Fridays each
season.

Sharon Arts Center Gallery
Carl Jackson, Director
Route 123
Sharon, NH 03458
(603) 924-3582
Seats 50.
Chamber, jazz concerts.

New Jersey

Clinton Historical Museum
Gloria Lazor, Manager
56 Main Street
Clinton, NJ 08809
(201) 745-4101
Seats 800.
Chamber, jazz, folk concerts.
Outdoor concert stage, with cliffs forming a
natural setting.
Available free to performing groups.

Drew University Theatre
Ellen Barry, Director of Public Relations
Madison, NJ 07940
(201) 377-5330
Seats 238.
Chamber, jazz concerts.
Available for rental only.

Monmouth Arts Center
c/o Monmouth Arts Council
Eduardo Garcia, Executive Director
99 Monmouth Street
Red Bank, NJ 07701
(201) 842-9000
Seats 1546.

Orchestral, choral, operatic concerts.

Monmouth County Library
John Livingstone, Director
25 Broad Street
Freehold, NJ 07728
(201) 431-4000
Chamber, jazz concerts.
Available free to performing groups.

Monmouth County Library, Eastern Branch
Morey R. Berger, Manager
State Highway 35
Shrewsbury, NJ 07701
(201) 842-5995
Seats 500.
Chamber, jazz concerts.
Provides free publicity.
Available free to performing groups.

Monmouth Museum
Milton Bloch, Director
761 Newman Springs Road
Lincroft, NJ 07738
(201) 747-2266
Seats 150.
Chamber concerts.

Montclair Public Library
Arthur Curley, Director
50 South Fullerton
Montclair, NJ 07042
(201) 744-0500
Seats 75.
Chamber concerts.
Available free to performing groups.

Museum Of Glass
Barry Taylor, Manager
Wheaton Village
Millville, NJ 08332
(609) 825-6800
Seats 150.
Chamber concerts.

The Newark Museum
Mrs. William H. Fredricks, Supervisor of
Programs
49 Washington Street
Newark, NJ 07101
(201) 733-6647
Seats 350.
Chamber, jazz concerts.
Available free to performing groups.

Paterson Free Public Library
Leo Fichtelberg, Executive Director
250 Broadway
Paterson, NJ 07501
(201) 279-4200
Seats 175.
Chamber, new and experimental concerts.

Van Riper Hopper House
Donna Grey, Resident Guide
533 Berdan Avenue
Wayne, NJ 07470
(201) 694-7192
Outdoor seating.
Chamber, choral concerts.
Originally built as a farmhouse. Now owned by
Township and maintained as an historical
museum.

YM-YWHA Of Metropolitan New Jersey
Maurice Levin Theater
Stanley Weinstein, Director
760 Northfield Avenue
West Orange, NJ 07052
(201) 736-3200
Seats 487.
Chamber, new and experimental, jazz, electronic,
dance concerts.

New Mexico

Santa Fe Public Library
Mary H. Handerson, Librarian
P.O. Box 2247
Santa Fe, NM 87501
(505) 982-3824
Seats 60.
Provides free publicity.
Available to non-commercial groups, on Monday
and Wednesday nights only.

New York State

Excluding New York City

**Adirondack Center Museum And Colonial
Garden**
James Bailey, Director
Essex County Historical Society
Elizabethtown, NY 12901
(518) 873-6466
Seats 200.
Chamber, folk concerts.

Albright-Knox Art Gallery Auditorium
Robert Buck, Jr., Director
1285 Elmwood Avenue
Buffalo, NY 14222
(716) 882-8700
Christopher Crossman, Assistant Director of Education
Seats 345.
New and experimental concerts.

Artpark
Jane Ward, Manager
P.O. Box 371
Lewiston, NY 14092
(716) 745-3377
Entire park dedicated to the arts.
Amphitheater seats 300. A carved earthwork structure facing the Niagara River and Gorge.
Artel. A flexible work space for visual and performing artists with an elevated L-shaped platform partially covered by an arched roof. Enclosures for artists available.
Theater seats 2400. Has computerized Century Strand lighting, adjustable stage, removable wall for exposure to outside seating lawn, orchestra pit.

The Arts Center
Recital Hall
1069 New Scotland Road
Albany, NY 12208
(518) 438-7895
Seats 300.
Sponsors an annual series of 6 concerts of works by contemporary composers in the Composers' Forum in Albany Series.

Brentwood United Presbyterian Church
Reverend James Watson, Director
Second Street and Third Avenue
Brentwood, NY 11717
(516) 273-3152
Seats 90 to 150.
Meet the Composer Jazz Concert Series sponsored by Friends of Brentwood Public Library and International Art of Jazz.

Cayuga Museum Of History And Art
Walter K. Long, Manager
203 Genesee Street
Auburn, NY 13021
(315) 253-8051
Seats 100; Annex seats 220.

Corning Glass Center
John P. Fox, Jr., Director
Corning, NY 14830
(607) 936-6147
Seats 1050.
Jazz, ballet, operatic concerts.

Dansville Public Library
Raymond Curtin, Director
200 Main Street
Dansville, NY 14437
(716) 987-6720
Seats 100.
Chamber, vocal concerts.
Provides free publicity.
Available free to performing groups.

The Emelin Theatre
Norman Kline, Manager
Library Lane
Mamaroneck, NY 10543
(914) 698-3045
Seats 273.
Chamber, new and experimental, jazz concerts.
Available for rental only.

Everson Museum Of Art Auditorium
Lenore Bailey, Public Affairs Assistant
401 South Harrison
Syracuse, NY 13202
(315) 474-6064
Seats 300.
Chamber, new and experimental, jazz concerts.
Available for rental only.

Half Hollow Hills Community Library
Sally Miller, Manager
55 Vanderbilt Parkway
Dix Hills, NY 11746
(516) 421-4530
Seats 120.
Chamber, new and experimental, jazz concerts.
Provides free publicity.
Available free to performing groups.

Hall Of Fame Of The Trotter
Philip A. Pines, Manager
240 Main Street
Goshen, NY 10924
(914) 294-6330
Seats 200.
Chamber concerts.
Available free to performing groups.

155

Hempstead Town Hall Pavilion
Roger A. Malfatti, Jr., Manager
Town Hall Plaza
Hempstead, NY 11550
(516) 489-5000
Seats 250.
Chamber, new and experimental, jazz, operatic, choral concerts.
Available free to performing groups.

Hofstra University Playhouse
Dr. Donald H. Swinney, Director
1000 Fulton Avenue
Hempstead, NY 11550
(516) 560-3283
Seats 1135.
Chamber, choral, rock concerts.

Holy Trinity Lutheran Church
Frank A. Novak, Manager
1080 Main Street, near North
Buffalo, NY 14209
(716) 886-2400
Church Sanctuary seats 900; Fellowship Room seats 130.
Chamber, vocal concerts.
Piano, harpsichord, pipe organ available.

Hudson River Museum At Yonkers Auditorium
Mrs. Crawford, Program Director
511 Warburton Avenue
Yonkers, NY 10701
(914) 963-4550
Seats 300.
Chamber concerts.
Sponsors free concerts on Saturday and Sunday.

Island Park Public Library
Rosemarie Baratta, Manager
99 Radcliffe Road
Island Park, NY 11558
(516) 432-0122
Seats 50.
Chamber concerts.
32' by 18' room available for informal concerts, with audience surrounding performers. No piano available.
Provides free publicity.

Belle Levine Art Center
c/o Director
P.O. Box 156
Mahopac, NY 10541
(914) 628-3664
Seats 125.
Chamber concerts.

Levittown Public Library
Robert N. Sheridan, Director
1 Blue Grass Lane
Levittown, NY 11793
(516) 731-5728
Seats 200.
Chamber, new and experimental, jazz concerts.
Provides free publicity.
Available free to performing groups.

Manhasset Public Library
c/o Sylvia Levin
30 Onderdonk Avenue
Manhasset, NY 11030
(516) 627-2300.
Seats 60 to 80.

Nazareth Arts Center
Joseph Baranowski, Director
4245 East Avenue
Rochester, NY 14610
(716) 586-2420
Room A13 seats 198; Auditorium seats 1153.
Chamber, jazz concerts.
Available for rental only, unless sponsored by Nazareth College of Rochester.

Niagara Art Center
M. Jacquie Allen, Director
1022 Main Street
Niagara Falls, NY 14301
(716) 284-8881
Seats 206.
Chamber, new and experimental, jazz concerts.
Available free to performing groups.

Northport Public Library
Victoria Wallace, Executive Director
151 Laurel Avenue
Northport, NY 11768
(516) 261-6930
Seats 135.
Chamber, new and experimental, jazz, folk concerts.

Parrish Art Museum
M. Blocker, Education Coordinator
25 Job's Lane
Southampton, NY 11968
(516) 283-2118
Seats 200.
Chamber concerts.

Patterson Library
James M. Wheeler, Manager
40 South Portage Street
Westfield, NY 14757
(716) 326-2154
Art Gallery seats 60; Library seats 120.
Chamber concerts.
Provides free publicity.
Available free to performing groups.

Reisinger Arts Center
Geraldine Gomes, Manager
Sarah Lawrence College
Bronxville, NY 10708
(914) 337-0700
Seats 425.
Chamber, new and experimental, jazz concerts.
Available for rental only.

Rensselaer Polytechnic Institute
Rensselaer Newman Chapel And Cultural Center
Charles Saile, Executive Director
Student Union
Troy, NY 12181
(518) 274-7793
Chamber, new and experimental, jazz concerts.

Rochester Museum And Science Center
Richard C. Shultz, Executive Director
657 East Avenue
Rochester, NY 14603
(716) 271-4320
Eisenhart Auditorium seats 400; Strasenburgh Planetarium seats 240.
Chamber, new and experimental, jazz concerts.
Available for rental only.

Michael C. Rockefeller Art Center
See State University of New York, Fredonia

St. Paul's Cathedral
Frederick Burgomaster, Manager
128 Pearl Street
Buffalo, NY 14202
(716) 853-6668
Seats 800.

Chamber, new and experimental, choral, organ concerts.
Available free to performing groups.

Sears-Harkness Theater
Roberson Center
Keith Martin, Director
30 Front Street
Binghamton, NY 13905
(607) 772-0660
Seats 296.
Chamber, jazz concerts.
Available for rental only, subject to approval.

South Huntington Public Library
Peter Draz, Director
2 Melville Road
Huntington Station, NY 11746
(516) 549-4411
Community Room seats 122; Reading Room seats 225; outdoor area also available.
Chamber, jazz, rock concerts.

State University Of New York
Performing Arts Center
Michel Sheehan, Manager
Albany, NY 12222
(518) 457-8608
Numerous auditoriums, seating from 100 to 500.
Chamber, new and experimental concerts.
Available free to performing groups.

State University Of New York
Baird Recital Hall
Terry Charles Schwarz, Director
Buffalo, NY 14226
(716) 831-3408 or 831-3425
Seats 185 to 225.
Chamber, new and experimental, jazz concerts.
Available to University affiliates only.

State University Of New York
Michael C. Rockefeller Arts Center
Edward A. DeDee, Manager
Fredonia, NY 14063
(716) 673-3217
Arena Theatre seats 200; Concert Hall seats 1200; Experimental Theatre seats 60; Proscenium Theatre seats 401; Recital Hall seats 225.
Chamber, new experimental, jazz, orchestral concerts.

Studio Arena Theatre
Neal DuBrock, Executive Producer
681 Main Street
Buffalo, NY 14203
(716) 856-8025
Seats 509.

Syracuse University
Crouse College Auditorium
Barbara Perretta, Manager
Syracuse, NY 13210
(315) 423-2193
Seats 744.
Chamber, orchestral, choral concerts.

Utica College
Strebel Auditorium
c/o Dominick B. Sicilia
Burrstone Road
Utica, NY 13502
(315) 792-3038
Seats 300.

WBFO Radio
Studio A
Terry Gross, Library Coordinator
3435 Main Street
Buffalo, NY 14214
(716) 831-5393.
Seats 25.
New music, jazz, folk concerts.

White Plains Public Library
Dr. May V. K. Valencik, Manager
100 Martine Avenue
White Plains, NY 10601
(914) 946-8700
Seats 140.
Available for rental only, unless sponsored by the Library.

New York City

Bronx

The Bronx County Historical Society
Gary D. Hermalyn, Executive Director
3266 Bainbridge Avenue
Bronx, NY 10467
(212) 881-8900
Outdoor seating.
Chamber, jazz concerts.

Congregational Church Of North New York
Reverend Allison Phillips, Manager
411 East 143rd Street
Bronx, NY 10454
(212) 669-3339
Auditorium seats 1000; Gymnasium seats 500.

Davidson Community Center Auditorium
c/o Mrs. Vazquez, Director
2034 Davidson Avenue
Bronx, NY 10453
(212) 294-0134
Seats 50 to 150.
Available for rental only.

Mosholu-Montefiore Community Center
Jay Roth, Assistant Director
3450 De Kalb Avenue
Bronx, NY 10467
(212) 882-4000
Seats 150 to 200.
Available for rental only.

The New York Botanical Garden Auditorium
Roger Biringer, Director
Bronx Park, NY 10458
(212) 933-9400
Seats 100.
Available for rental only.
Outdoor seating also available.

New York City Mission Society Cadet Corps
Frank Jones, Business Manager
14 West 170th Street
Bronx, NY 10452
(212) 681-2361
Auditorium seats 50 to 150; Gymnasium seats 300 to 500.
Orchestral concerts.
Available for rental only.

Parks, Recreation, And Cultural Affairs
Bronx Borough Office
Administration Building
Bronx Park East and Brichall Avenue
Bronx, NY 10462
(212) 822-4711
Apply to Borough Office for permit to perform in public areas.

158

Riverdale-Yonkers Society For Ethical Culture
Mrs. Arnold S. Louis, Executive Secretary
4450 Fieldston Road
Bronx, NY 10471
(212) 548-4445
Seats 140.
Chamber concerts.
Available for rental only.

Brooklyn

Brooklyn Academy Of Music
Harvey Lichtenstein, Executive Director
30 Lafayette Avenue
Brooklyn, NY 11217
(212) 636-4100
Lepercq seats 400; Music Hall seats 1200; Opera
House seats 2100.
Chamber, new and experimental, jazz, folk, rock
concerts.

The New Muse
Charlene Van Derzee, Acting Director
1530 Bedford Avenue
Brooklyn, NY 11216
(212) 774-2900
New and experimental, jazz concerts.

Manhattan

Academy Of Music Theatre
14th Street and 3rd Avenue
New York, NY 10003
(212) 895-7100
Seats 3400.
Available for rental only.

**American Foundation On Automation And
Employment, Inc.**
c/o W. Tyminsky
49 East 68th Street
New York, NY 10021
(212) 628-1010
Seats 60 to 120.

The American Museum Of Natural History
Florence Stone, Community Relations
Central Park West at 79th Street
New York, NY 10024
(212) 873-1300
Auditorium seats 1200; Education Hall seats 300;
People Center seats 80.
Chamber, new and experimental, jazz, ethnic
concerts.

American Theatre Laboratory, Inc.
Suanne Shirley, Administrative Director
219 West 19th Street, 2nd Floor
New York, NY 10011
(212) 691-6500
Seats 80.

Barbizon Plaza Hotel
Richard Bishopp, Director of Sales
106 Central Park South
New York, NY 10019
(212) 247-7000
Seats 505.
Available for rental only.

Beacon Theatre
74th Street and Broadway
New York, NY 10023
(212) 686-6670
Seats 2650.
Orchestral, rock concerts.
Available for rental only.

Vivian Beaumont Theatre
See Lincoln Center for the Performing Arts

Bethune Senior Center
1949 Amsterdam Avenue
New York, NY 10032
(212) 862-6700
Seats 83.
Available for rental only.

Bloomingdale House Of Music
c/o David Greer
323 West 108th Street
New York, NY 10025
(212) 663-6021
Seats 70.
Available for rental only.

The Book Gallery
240 West 72nd Street
New York, NY 10023
(212) 873-0670
Seats 100.

The Buckley School
C. Brett Babcock, Headmaster
113 East 73rd Street
New York, NY 10021
(212) 397-6981
Available for rental only.

CAMI Hall
Robert C. Vacanti, Manager
165 West 57th Street
New York, NY 10019
(212) 397-6981
Seats 260.
Chamber, solo concerts.
Available for rental only.
Formerly Judson Hall.

Carnegie Hall
Julius Bloom, Executive Director
154 West 57th Street
New York, NY 10019
(212) 247-1350
Seats 2800.
Chamber, new and experimental, jazz, orchestral,
rock concerts.
Available for rental only.

Carnegie Recital Hall
Julius Bloom, Executive Director
154 West 57th Street
New York, NY 10019
(212) 247-1350
Seats 298.
Chamber, new and experimental, jazz concerts.

Chambers Memorial Baptist Church Sanctuary
219 East 123rd Street
New York, NY 10035
(212) 348-0420
Seats 150.
Available for rental only.

Church Of All Nations
c/o Philip West
9 2nd Avenue
New York, NY 10003
(212) 477-4155
Chapel seats 116; Gymnasium seats 250.
Available for rental only.

City Center Of Music And Drama, Inc.
c/o Robert A. Lorelli
130 West 56th Street
New York, NY 10019
(212) 586-2828 Ext. 46 or 58
Seats 2934.
Available for rental only.

Columbia University
McMillin Theater
Mrs. Flynn, Concert Manager
Broadway and West 116th Street
New York, NY 10027
(212) 280-3238
Seats 1200.
Chamber, new and experimental, jazz concerts.

Columbia University Teachers College
Horace Mann Auditorium
Mina Kragler, Manager
520 West 120th Street
New York, NY 10027
(212) 678-3707
Seats 650.
Chamber, new and experimental, jazz concerts.
Available for rental only.

Cooper Union Great Hall
Henry C. Alter, Manager
Third Avenue at Seventh Street
New York, NY 10003
(212) 254-6300
Seats 910.
Chamber, new and experimental, jazz, operatic,
orchestral, choral concerts.

Courtyard Playhouse
c/o Bob Stark
39 Grove Street
New York, NY 10014
(212) 765-9540
Seats 75 to 100.
Available for rental only.

Dalcroze School
Dr. Hilda M. Schuster, Director
161 East 73rd Street
New York, NY 10021
(212) 879-0316
Auditorium seats 300; Small Hall seats 150.
Chamber concerts.

The Dance Gallery
J. Antony Siciliano, Manager
242 East 14th Street
New York, NY 10003
(212) 685-5972
Seats 260.
Available for rental only.

Dance Theatre Workshop
c/o Judith Scott
215 West 20th Street
New York, NY 10011
(212) 929-8772
Loft space seats 60.
Available for rental only.

East Bethal Baptist Church
c/o Reverend Jacob Hillary
4-6 West 131st Street
New York, NY 10021
Seats 75 to 100.
Available for rental only.

Environ
Jay Clayton, Booking Agent
476 Broadway, 11th Floor
New York, NY 10013
(212) 226-7408 or 966-6013
Multi-media, new and experimental, jazz, chamber concerts.

Experimental Intermedia Foundation
Elaine Summers, Director
537 Broadway, 5th Floor
New York, NY 10012
(212) 966-3367
Seats 100.
Experimental, electronic, multi-media, film, dance concerts.
Meditations With Music Series includes composer-performers.

Avery Fisher Hall
See Lincoln Center for the Performing Arts

The Solomon R. Guggenheim Museum Auditorium
Thomas M. Messer, Director
1071 Fifth Avenue
New York, NY 10028
(212) 369-5110
Seats 299.
Chamber, new and experimental, jazz concerts.

Hamilton Grange National Memorial
c/o Mr. James
287 Convent Avenue
New York, NY 10031
(212) 283-5154 or 666-1640
Seats 40 to 50; outdoor seating 400.
Concerts on Sundays.
Available free to performing groups.

The Hispanic Society Of America
Theodore S. Beardsley, Jr., Director
155th Street and Broadway
New York, NY 10032
(212) 926-3602
Museum Court seats 150; Museum Terrace seats 1500.
Spanish and Caribbean music, chamber concerts.

Hudson Guild
c/o John A. Sanchez
441 West 26th Street
New York, NY 10010
(212) 524-6700
Auditorium seats 139; Meeting rooms seat 240.
Available for rental only.

Hunter College
c/o Renting Director
695 Park Avenue
New York, NY 10021
(212) 360-2432(3)
Assembly hall seats 2187; Playhouse seats 692.
Chamber, rock concerts.
Available for rental only.

Jazzmania Society's Yardbird Suite
Michael Morgenstern, Manager
14 East 23rd Street
New York, NY 10010
(212) 677-1737 or 852-2722
Living room seats 100.
Jazz concerts.

Judson Hall
See CAMI Hall

Juilliard School
Juilliard Theater
Joe Pacitti, Manager
Lincoln Center Plaza
New York, NY 10023
(212) 799-5000
Seats 1000.
Orchestral, operatic, dance concerts.

The Kitchen
Robert Stearns, Manager
59 Wooster Street
New York, NY 10012
(212) 925-3615
Seats 300.
New and experimental concerts.
Four-channel amplification system, video-tape equipment, movable seating.

161

Available free to performing groups.

Lenox Hill Neighborhood Association Auditorium
c/o David J. Stern
331 East 70th Street
New York, NY 10021
(212) 744-5022
Seats 250.
Available for rental to non-profit groups only.

Lincoln Center For The Performing Arts
Delmar D. Hendricks, Booking Manager
Lincoln Center Plaza
Broadway at 65th Street
New York, NY 10023
(212) 874-4000
Vivian Beaumont Theatre seats 1140; Avery Fisher Hall seats 2836: orchestral, jazz, rock concerts; Metropolitan Opera House seats 3784; New York State Theater seats 2729; Alice Tully Hall seats 1096: chamber concerts.
Available for rental only.

Madison Avenue Presbyterian Church
John Weaver, Music Director
Madison Avenue at 73rd Street
New York, NY 10021
(212) 288-8924
Seats 750.
Chamber, choral concerts.

Manhattan School Of Music
Louis J. Brunelli, Director for Performance
120 Claremont Avenue
New York, NY 10027
(212) 749-2802
John C. Borden Auditorium seats 988; Hubbard Recital Hall seats 325.
Chamber concerts.

The Mannes College Of Music Auditorium
c/o Forrest Miller
157 East 74th Street
New York, NY 10021
(212) 737-0700
Seats 150 to 160.
Available for rental from October to May only.

Marymount Manhattan College
Rita Goldman, College Events
221 East 71st Street
New York, NY 10021
(212) 861-4200 Ext. 477
Auditorium seats 500; Theater seats 250.

Available for rental only.

Metropolitan Opera House
See Lincoln Center for the Performing Arts

M R Studios
Bill and Anne Martin, Managers
251 West 30th Street
New York, NY 10001
(212) 947-7521
Theater seats 60. Rehearsal halls and sound studios available.
Chamber, new and experimental, jazz concerts.
Hammond organ, pianos available.

New School For Social Research
Allan Austill, Dean
66 West 12th Street
New York, NY 10011
(212) 741-5630
Seats 512.
Chamber, new and experimental concerts.

New York Jazz Museum
Howard Fischer, Manager
125 West 55th Street
New York, NY 10019
(212) 765-2150
Seats 250.
Jazz concerts.
Available for rental only.

The New York Public Library
The New York Public Library has branches in Manhattan, Bronx, and States Island. A number of the libraries have auditoriums or performing space.
For children's concerts contact:
New York Public Library
Office of Children's Services
6th Floor
8 East 40th Street
New York, NY 10016
(212) 790-6442
For teenage concerts contact:
New York Public Library
Office of Young Adult Services
6th Floor
8 East 40th Street
New York, NY 10016
(212) 790-6467
For adult concerts contact:
New York Public Library
Office of Adult Services

6th Floor
8 East 40th Street
New York, NY 10016
(212) 790-6492
See also separate listings for New York Public Library Donnell Library Center and The New York Public Library At Lincoln Center.

The New York Public Library
Donnell Library Center Auditorium
Sally Helfman, Manager
20 West 53rd Street
New York, NY 10019
(212) 790-6447
Seats 278.

The New York Public Library At Lincoln Center
Library and Museum of the Performing Arts Auditorium
Dr. Robert M. Henderson, Chief
111 Amsterdam Avenue
New York, NY 10023
(212) 799-2200 Ext. 250
Seats 212.
Chamber, new music concerts.

New York Society Of The New Church
Mrs. Clayton Priestnal, Director
112 East 35th Street
New York, NY 10016
(212) 685-8967
Auditorium seats 65.
Chamber concerts.
Available for rental only, except during the summer.

New York State Theater
See Lincoln Center for the Performing Arts

New York University
Loeb Student Center
Thomas Romich, Assistant Director
566 La Guardia Place
New York, NY 10012
(212) 598-2022
Steve Polniaszek, Concert Manager
Coffee House seats 70; Eisner and Lubin Auditorium seats 728, movable seating in orchestra; South Lobby seats 200 to 250, movable seating; Top of the Park seats 140, terrace with movable seating.
Chamber, orchestral, rock concerts.

North Presbyterian Church
Reverend Robert Kelley, Pastor
525 West 155th Street
New York, NY 10032
(212) 926-5162
Chapel seats 1000; Lecture Room seats 200.
Vocal, chamber concerts.

Pace University
Schimmel Center for the Arts Auditorium
Jess Adkins, Director
1 Pace Plaza
New York, NY 10038
(212) 285-3398
Seats 668.
Available for rental only; application in writing required.

Park Avenue Synagogue Sanctuary
Cantor David Putterman, Director
50 East 87th Street
New York, NY 10028
(212) 369-2600
Seats 1800.
20th century liturgical concerts.

Parks, Recreation, And Cultural Affairs
Manhattan Borough Office
655 Madison Avenue, 8th Floor
New York, NY 10022
(212) 593-8282
3 spaces available: Bandshell, East Meadow, Great Lawn.
Apply to Borough Office for permit to perform in these areas.

The Riverside Church Theater
Arthur Bartow, Artistic Director
490 Riverside Drive
New York, NY 10027
(212) 749-7000
Seats 250.
Chamber concerts.
Available for rental only.

Theodore Roosevelt Birthplace
National Historic Site
Anne Guarnieri, Manager
28 East 20th Street
New York, NY 10003
(212) 673-5151
Seats 160.
Chamber, new and experimental, jazz concerts.
Available free to performing groups.

Saint Stephen's Episcopal Church
120 West 69th Street
New York, NY 10023
(212) 787-2755
Seats 260.
Chamber, orchestral, chamber opera concerts.
Available for rental only.

William Sloane House YMCA
Sloane Room
c/o Ronald R. Graham
356 West 34th Street
New York, NY 10001
(212) 695-5000 Ext. 28
Seats 200.
Available for rental only.

Steinway Concert Hall
Mr. Johann, Manager
111 West 57th Street
New York, NY 10019
(212) 586-0040
Seats 200.
Available for rental only.

Studio Museum In Harlem
c/o Edward S. Spriggs
2033 Fifth Avenue
New York, NY 10035
(212) 427-5959
Seats 100 to 150.
Jazz, gospel, traditional African concerts.

Studio Rivbea
Sam and Bea Rivers, Managers
24 Bond Street
New York, NY 10012
(212) 473-9936
Seats 150.
Jazz concerts.
Provides free publicity.

Studios 58 Playhouse, Inc.
G. B. Bramson, Manager
150 West 58th Street
New York, NY 10019
(212) 265-9018 or 581-7238
Seats 85 to 100.
Chamber, new and experimental, jazz concerts.
Available for rental only.

Sunrise Studio
Michael Mahaffay, Director
122 2nd Avenue
New York, NY 10003
(212) 533-4030
Seats 150.
New and experimental, jazz concerts.

Third Street Music School Settlement Auditorium
David Cooper, Associate Director
235 East 11th Street
New York, NY 10003
(212) 777-3240
Seats 300 in the round.
Available for rental only.

Town Hall
Jesse Reese, Director
123 West 43rd Street
New York, NY 10036
(212) 582-2424
Seats 1504.
Chamber, new and experimental, jazz concerts.
Available for rental only.

Alice Tully Hall
See Lincoln Center for the Performing Arts

The Universalist Church Of New York City Auditorium
Edith Hull, Director of Program and
Administration
4 West 76th Street
New York, NY 10023
(212) 595-8410
Seats 300.
Available for rental only.

Washington Square Church
Paul Abels, Executive Director
135 West Fourth Street
New York NY 10012
(212) 777-2528
Martha Chamberlain, Program Coordinator
Chamber, new and experimental, jazz, folk,
ethnic, liturgical concerts.

John Weber Gallery
John Weber, Manager
420 West Broadway
New York, NY 10012
(212) 966-6115
New and experimental concerts.
Available free to performing groups

Dwight York Preparatory School Auditorium
c/o R. Stewart
116 East 85th Street
New York, NY 10028
(212) 628-1220
Seats 140.
Available for rental only.

Young Men's Christian Association, McBurney Branch Auditorium
c/o Mr. Zeek
215 West 23rd Street
New York, NY 10011
(212) 243-1982
Seats 250.
Available to non-profit groups and YMCA groups only.

92nd Street YMHA Auditorium
Linda Greenberg, Office Manager
1395 Lexington Avenue
New York, NY 10028
(212) 427-6000
Seats 850.
Chamber concerts.
Available for rental after June 1976.

Queens

The Over Look
Queens Borough Office
Parks, Recreation, Cultural Affairs
Union Turnpike and Park Lane
Kew Gardens, NY 11415
(212) 520-5311
Groups must apply for permit to perform.

Staten Island

Clover Lakes Park
c/o Special Events Permit
Staten Island Borough Office
1150 Clove Road
Staten Island, NY 10301
(212) 442-7640
Groups must apply for permit to perform.

North Carolina

North Carolina School Of The Arts
Robert Suderberg, Chancellor
P.O. Box 4657
Winston-Salem, NC 27107
(919) 784-7170
Crawford Hall seats 650; De Mille Theatre seats 250; Dome Theatre seats 50.
Chamber, new and experimental, jazz, multimedia concerts.

North Carolina State University
Stewart Theatre
Maggie Klekas, Manager
University Student Center
Raleigh, NC 27607
(919) 737-3105
Seats 816.
Chamber, jazz, folk, rock concerts.
Available free to performing groups.

Public Library Of Charlotte And Mecklenburg County Auditorium
Arial A. Stephens, Manager
310 North Tryon Street
Charlotte, NC 28202
(704) 374-2530
Seats 200.
Jazz concerts.

North Dakota

City Auditorium And Civic Center
George J. Smith, Manager
P.O. Box 1075
Bismarck, ND 58501
(701) 223-8010
City Auditorium seats 1200; Civic Center seats 7500.
Chamber, new and experimental, jazz concerts.
Available for rental only.

Ohio

Allen County Museum
Folsom Auditorium
Joseph Dunlap, Curator
620 West Market Street
Lima, OH 45801
(419) 222-9426
Seats 150. Movable seating.
Chamber, folk concerts.
Available for rental only.

Bowling Green State University
Recital Hall
c/o David Pope, Assistant Dean
College of Musical Arts
Bowling Green, OH 43403
(419) 372-2181
Seats 350.
Chamber, new and experimental concerts.
Available free to performing groups.

Cleveland Public Library
Ervin J. Gaines, Manager
325 Superior Avenue
Cleveland, OH 44114
(216) 241-1020
Seats 345.
Provides free publicity.
Available free to performing groups on Saturday afternoons.

Dayton Art Institute
Bruce Evans, Director
Forest and Riverview Avenues
Dayton, OH 45406
(513) 223-5277
Auditorium seats 500; outdoor cloisters also available.
Chamber concerts.
Available for rental only.

Ohio Theatre
Donald R. Streibig, Manager
29 East State
Columbus, OH 43215
(614) 469-1045
Seats 2897.
Jazz, orchestral concerts.
Available for rental only.

Ohio University
R. F. Stevens, Concert Manager
Athens, OH 45701
(614) 594-5341
Auditorium seats 2575; Recital Hall seats 250.
Chamber, new and experimental, jazz concerts.
Available for rental only, unless affiliated with Ohio University Artist Series.

The Park Of Roses
Leo Gaffin, Commission Chairman
4048 Roselea Place
Columbus, OH 43214
(614) 261-6551
Amphitheater and gazebo seat 800; bleachers seat 900.
Jazz, band concerts.
Available free to performing groups.

Peninsula Library
B. J. Reymond, Librarian
6105 Riverview Road
P.O. Box 236
Peninsula, OH 44264
(216) 657-2291
Seats 100; outdoor seating unlimited.
Jazz concerts.
Available free to performing groups.

Springfield Art Center
Patricia D. Catron, Director
107 Cliff Park Road
Springfield, OH 45501
(513) 325-4673
Seats 200.
Chamber, new and experimental concerts.
Available for rental only.

University Of Cincinnati
College Conservatory Of Music
c/o Chairman, Music Department
University Of Cincinnati
Cincinnati, OH 45221
Corbett Auditorium seats 725; Patricia Corbett Theatre seats 400.
Chamber, new and experimental, jazz, orchestral, choral concerts.

The Wagnalls Memorial
Jerry W. Neff, Manager
150 East Columbus Street
Lithopolis, OH 43136
(614) 837-4765
Seats 428.
Chamber, new and experimental, jazz, choral concerts.

Oklahoma

Alva Public Library
Lorene Devery, Librarian
504 Seventh Street
Alva, OK 73717
(405) 327-1833
Seats 150.
Chamber concerts.

Oklahoma Historical Society
Bruce E. Joseph, Manager
2100 North Lincoln
Oklahoma City, OK 73105
(405) 521-2491
Seats 350.
Chamber, folk, ethnic concerts.
Available free to performing groups.

Oklahoma Theater Center, Inc.
Russ Walton, Business Manager
400 West Sheridan
Oklahoma City, OK 73102
(405) 239-6884
Arena Theater seats 240; Thrust Theater seats 592.
Musicals, orchestral concerts.
Available for rental only.

Ponca City Indian Museum And Cultural Center
Delia Castor, Maxine Luntz, Managers
1000 East Grand Avenue
Ponca City, OK 74601
(405) 762-6123
Seats 100. Large gardens and patio for outdoor concerts also available.
American Indian Music, chamber, new and experimental, jazz concerts.

Oregon

Maude Kerns Art Center
John Connor, Director
1910 East 15th Avenue
Eugene, OR 97403
(503) 345-1126
Seats 100.
Chamber, new and experimental concerts.

Oregon State University
Horner Museum
Thyrza Anderson, Curator
Corvallis, OR 97331
(503) 754-2951
Carriage Gallery seats 150; Seen Room seats 70.
Chamber concerts.
Available free to performing groups.

Pittock Mansion
Mary Alice Snead, Manager
3229 North West Pittock Drive
Portland, OR 97210
(503) 248-4469
Seats 50.
Chamber concerts.
Available for rental only.

Southern Oregon Fine Arts Center
Maria De Rungs, Executive Director
3347 Old Stage Road
Central Point, OR 97501
(503) 664-4919
Chamber concerts.

Pennsylvania

Allentown Art Museum
Richard N. Gregg, Director
Fifth at Court Street
Allentown, PA 18105
(215) 342-4333
Seats 200.
Chamber concerts.
Provides free publicity.
Available for rental only.

Drexel University
Mandell Theatre
Michael L. Rabbitt, Manager
Philadelphia, PA 19104
(215) 895-2428
Seats 484.
Chamber, new and experimental, jazz, orchestral, operatic concerts.

Edinboro State College
Memorial Auditorium
Dr. D. L. Panhorst, Manager
Department of Music and Drama
Edinboro, PA 16444
(814) 732-2555
Seats 876.
Chamber, new and experimental, jazz concerts.

Free Library Of Philadelphia
Central Library
Shirley Drayton, Executive Secretary
Logan Square
Philadelphia, PA 19103
(215) 686-5400
Lecture Hall seats 400; Skyline Room seats 100.
Chamber concerts.
Available free to non-profit groups that are not
politically or religiously oriented. Concerts during
library hours only.

The Main Point
Emmet Robinson, Manager
874 Lancaster Avenue
Bryn Mawr, PA 19010
(215) 525-5825
Seats 270.
Chamber, jazz, folk, rock concerts.
Provides free publicity.
Available for rental only.

University Of Pennsylvania
University Museum
Joseph A. Minott, Jr., Manager
Philadelphia, PA 19174
(215) 386-7400
Harrison Auditorium seats 800; Rainey
Auditorium seats 200.
Chamber, new and experimental, folk, ethnic
concerts.
Available for rental only; discount for University
of Pennsylvania affiliates.

West Chester State College
Swope Auditorium
c/o Charles Sprenkle, Dean
West Chester, PA 19380
(215) 436-2739
Seats 400.
Chamber, new and experimental, jazz concerts.
Available free to performing groups.

Puerto Rico

Casa Blanca Small Hall
St. Sebastian Street
Old San Juan, PR 00902
(809) 724-0700
Seats 300.

Rhode Island

University of Rhode Island
Recital Hall
Dr. Albert C. Giebler, Manager
Fine Arts Center
Kingston, RI 02881
(401) 792-2431
Seats 525.
Chamber, new and experimental, jazz, orchestral,
choral concerts.

South Carolina

College Of Charleston
Physician's Memorial Auditorium
c/o Fine Arts
Charleston, SC 29401
(803) 722-0181
Seats 400.
Chamber concerts.
Available free to performing groups.

Converse College
Daniel Recital Hall
Henry Janiec, Manager
Spartanburg, SC 29301
(803) 585-6421
Seats 340.
Available for rental only.

Myrtle Beach Convention Center
Glenn Arnette, III, Manager
P.O. Box 1828
Myrtle Beach, SC 29577
(803) 448-7166
Seats 2100.
Chamber; rock concerts.
Available for rental only.

South Dakota

Mitchell Public Library
Janus Olsen, Director
221 North Duff
Mitchell, SD 57301
(605) 996-6693
Seats 100.
Chamber, new and experimental, jazz concerts.
Provides free publicity.
Available free to performing groups.

South Dakota State University
South Dakota Memorial Art Center
Joseph Stuart, Director
Brookings, SD 57006
(605) 688-5423
Seats 147.
Chamber concerts.
Available free to South Dakota State University groups; others are reviewed by the University Music Department.

University Of South Dakota
Shrine to Music Museum
Andre' P. Larson, Museum Director
Vermillion, SD 57069
(605) 677-5306
Concert Hall seats 2000; Recital Hall seats 200; Salon seats 75 to 100; Theater seats 450.
Chamber, jazz concerts.
Provides free publicity.

Texas

Austin Memorial Center Auditorium
Barbara Smith, Manager
220 South Bonham Street
Cleveland, TX 77327
(713) 592-3920
Seats 130.
Provides free publicity.

Convention Center
Francis W. Vickers, Manager
Market and Alamo
San Antonio, TX 78205
(512) 225-6351
Arena seats 11,000; Theatre seats 2800.
Orchestral, operatic, rock concerts.
Available for rental only.

Dallas Museum Of Fine Arts Auditorium
Eugene W. Mitchell, Assistant Director
P.O. Box 26250
Dallas, TX 75226
(214) 421-4187
Seats 250.
Chamber concerts.

Dallas Public Library
Lillian Bradshaw, Librarian
1954 Commerce Street
Dallas, TX 75201
(214) 748-9071
Seats 215.

Chamber, new and experimental concerts.
Provides free publicity.
Availabe free to performing groups.

Del Mar College
Hugh Cagle, Concert Manager
Corpus Christi, TX 78404
(512) 882-6231
Del Mar Auditorium seats 1800; Wolfe Recital Hall seats 300, chamber concerts.

Eastfield College Performance Hall
John D. Stewart, Manager
3737 Motley Drive
Mesquite, TX 75149
(214) 746-3132
Seats 500.
Chamber, new and experimental, jazz concerts.

Fort Worth Art Museum
Richard Koshalek, Director
1309 Montgomery
Fort Worth, TX 76107
(817) 738-9215
Solarium seats 100; several galleries with varied seating also available.
Chamber, new and experimental, jazz, rock concerts.

Incarnate Word College
c/o Sister Judith Ann Gibson
San Antonio, TX 78209
(512) 828-1261
Auditorium seats 1000; Recital Hall seats 88.
Chamber, jazz, orchestral, choral concerts.

Kimbell Art Museum
Richard F. Brown, Director
Will Rogers Road West
Fort Worth, TX 76107
(817) 332-8451
Auditorium seats 200; gallery areas have movable seating.
Chamber, new and experimental, choral concerts.
Provides free publicity.
Available free to performing groups.

La Villita
Charlotte A. Kearney, Manager
416 Villita
San Antonio, TX 78205
(512) 227-0521
Arneson River Theatre seats 1000; Bolivar **Hall** seats 200; Cos House seats 100; Juarez **Plaza seats**

700; National Plaza seats 400; Plaza Nueva seats 1500.
Chamber, jazz, Mexican music, country and western concerts.
Available for rental only.

Memorial Auditorium
Donald M. Burkman, Manager
1300 Seventh
Wichita Falls, TX 76307
(817) 322-5611
Seats 2718.
Chamber, country and western, folk concerts.
Available for rental only.

The Museum Of Fine Arts
Brown Auditorium
Clare B. Gordon, Manager
1001 Bissonnet at Main
Houston, TX 77005
(713) 526-1361
Seats 342; outdoor sculpture garden also available.
Chamber, new and experimental, jazz concerts.

Texas A & I University
Dr. Thomas C. Pierson, Raymond Clark, Jr., Concert Managers
Kingsville, TX 78363
(512) 595-2803 or 595-3401
Jones Auditorium seats 1440: musicals, jazz, orchestral concerts; Music Department Recital Hall seats 350: chamber, new and experimental, jazz concerts.
Provides free publicity.

Virginia

Arlington County Public Library Auditorium
Caroline Arden-Bull, Coordinator of Public Services
1015 North Quincy Street
Arlington, VA 22201
(703) 527-4777
Seats 130; outdoor lawn seats 250.
Chamber, new and experimental, folk concerts.
Provides free publicity.
Available free to non-profit groups.

Mosque Auditorium-Theatre
Leslie D. Banks, Manager
Laurel and Main Street
Richmond, VA 23220
(804) 772-8226
Seats 3732.
Chamber, new and experimental, jazz, orchestral, musicals, rock concerts.
Available for rental only.

Washington

Fort Wright College
Sister Flavia Bauer, Chairman of Music Department
West 4000 Randolph Road
Spokane, WA 99204
(509) 328-2970
Commons seats 500; Little Theatre seats 300; Music Hall seats 175.
Chamber, new and experimental concerts.

Pacific Lutheran University
Dr. Richard Jungkuntz, Provost
Tacoma, WA 98447
(206) 531-6900
Eastvold Auditorium seats 1200; Chris Knutzen Hall seats 400.
Chamber concerts.

Spokane Public Library Auditorium
Betty W. Bender, Director
West 906 Main Street
Spokane, WA 99201
(509) 838-3361
Seats 130.
Musicals, chamber, jazz, choral concerts.
Quadraphonic sound system.
Provides free publicity.
Available free to performing groups sponsored by library.

University of Washington
Meany Theater
Mea Hartman, Manager
Seattle, WA 98195
(206) 543-4880
Seats 1259.
Chamber, jazz, orchestral, operatic concerts.
Computerized lighting.

Valley Art Center, Inc.
Mrs. Harold Rosenberger, Manager
842 6th Street
Clarkston, WA 99403
(509) 758-8331
Seats 125.
Chamber concerts.
Available for rental only.

Washington State University
Performing Arts Coliseum Theatre
James B. Crow, Manager
Pullman, WA 99163
(509) 335-3525
Seats 2600.
Chamber, new and experimental concerts.
Available for rental only.

Whatcom Museum Of History And Art
Susan H. L. Barrow, Director
121 Prospect Street
Bellingham, WA 98225
(206) 676-6990 or 676-6981
Seats 225.
Chamber, new and experimental, chamber opera
concerts.

West Virginia

Concord College
Alexander Center for the Creative and
Performing Arts
Dr. Duchen Cazedessus, Manager
Athens, WV 24712
(304) 384-3115
Seats 780.
Chamber, jazz, choral concerts.
Provides free publicity.

Wisconsin

Charles Allis Art Library
Margaret A. Rahill, Librarian
1630 East Royall Place
Milwaukee, WI 53202
(414) 278-3010
Seats 99.
Chamber, new and experimental, jazz concerts.
Available free to performing groups.

**John Nelson Bergstrom Art Center And
Museum**
Anthony V. Garton, Director
165 North Park Avenue
Neenah, WI 54956
(414) 722-2912
Seats 150.
Chamber concerts.
Provides free publicity.

Milwaukee Art Center
Tracy Atkinson, Director
750 North Lincoln Memorial Drive
Milwaukee, WI 53202
(414) 271-9508
Seats 250 to 500.
Chamber concerts.
Provides free publicity.
Available free to performing groups.

University Of Wisconsin
Elvehjem Art Center
Virginia Merriman, Curator of Education
800 University Avenue
Madison, WI 53706
(608) 263-2246
Seats 230.
Chamber concerts.
Available free to performing groups, subject to
approval.

University of Wisconsin Union
Linda Nieft, Manager
2200 East Kenwood Boulevard
Milwaukee, WI 53211
(414) 963-5524
Fireside Lounge seats 300; Union Ballroom seats
200; Wisconsin Room seats 1000.
Chamber, new and experimental, jazz, rock, folk
concerts.
Provides free publicity.

University of Wisconsin
College of the Arts
Recital Hall
Lorraine Gross, Concert Manager
Whitewater, WI 53545
(414) 472-4869
Seats 500.

Wyoming

University Of Wyoming
Fine Arts Center Concert Hall
David Tomatz, Director
Department of Music
Laramie, WY 82071
(307) 766-5242

Seats 700.
Chamber, new and experimental, jazz concerts.
Walcker pipe organ, stage accommodates 200
performers, 2 concert grand pianos, audio
equipment for performance recordings and
playback system available.

Concert Series And Festivals

The concert series and festivals listed here were selected because they present 20th century music. While some events listed concentrate solely on contemporary music, others present music of many centuries, including this one. For a more general listing of concert series and festivals, consult the *Musical America 1975 International Directory of the Performing Arts* (Great Barrington, Massachusetts: Billboard Publications, 1975) and *The American Music Handbook*, by Christopher Pavlakis (New York: The Free Press, 1974).

Most of the entries below include the number of concerts presented per season. Since this number varies yearly, it is meant only as a general guide.

Events listing first concert dates have been initiated this year and are meant to recur. Contact the directors of these events concerning future plans.

Alabama

Huntsville Chamber Music Guild Student Auditions
Mrs. Robert Shuck, Director
University of Alabama
Humanities Auditorium
Huntsville, AL 35805
(205) 539-2592
Chamber music of all eras.
4 to 6 annual concerts in March and April, sponsored by the Huntsville Chamber Music Guild.
Participants: University of Alabama student ensembles.

Mobile Jazz Festival, Inc.
Jack Maples, Director
Mobile Municipal Theatre
401 Auditorium Drive
Mobile, AL 36602
Jazz.
Annual 3 day fesitival in June, sponsored by the Allied Arts Council of Mobile.
Participants: student and professional ensembles.

Alaska

Alaska Festival Of Music
Robert Shaw, Director
West High School
P.O. Box 325
Anchorage, AK 99510
(907) 272-3022
Chamber music, jazz, orchestral music.
15 annual concerts in June.
Participants: student and professional ensembles.

Sitka Summer Music Festival
Paul Rosenthal, Music Director
P.O. Box 907
Sitka, AK 99835
Chamber music.
Annual 17 day festival in June, sponsored by Sheldon Jackson College and Sitka Concert Association.
Participants: Sitka Festival Ensemble.

Arizona

Arizona State University
Warren K. Sumners, Director
Gammage Auditorium
Tempe, AZ 85281
(602) 965-5062
Various series, such as the Fine Arts Series and the Celebrity Series, presenting chamber music, new and experimental music, jazz.
Participants: student and professional ensembles.

California

Annual Festival Of American Music
Richard Bunger, Director
California State College
Music Department
Dominguez Hills, CA 90747
(213) 532-4300 Ext. 293
8 annual concerts and lectures in the spring, featuring works by American composers.
Participants: student and professional ensembles.

Bring Your Own Pillow Concert Series (BYOP)
Grapestake Gallery
2876 California Street
San Francisco, CA 94115
(415) 931-0779
20th century chamber music, emphasizing new works.
3 annual concerts.
Participants: San Francisco Contemporary Music Players.
Establishes direct contact between audience and performers by creating a casual setting in which the audience is seated on the floor.

Cabrillo Music Festival
Lynette Lytle, Director
Cabrillo College
6500 Soquel Drive
Aptos, CA 95003
(408) 475-6000 Ext. 297
Chamber music, new and experimental music, jazz.
10 annual concerts in August.
Participants: student and professional ensembles.

California State University Spring Festival Of Contemporary Music
Peter Gena, Director
Recital Hall
Fresno, CA 93740
(209) 487-2654
20th century chamber music, new and experimental music, multi-media.
Participants: student ensembles.

Center For Contemporary Music Series
Robert Ashley, Director
Mills College
Oakland, CA 94613
(415) 635-7620
New and experimental music, electronic music, theater.
30 weekly workshops per season.
Participants: student and professional ensembles.

Claremont Music Festival
Giora Bernstein, Director
Pomona College
Claremont, CA 91711
(714) 626-8511 Ext. 2242
Chamber music, orchestral music.
Annual summer festival.

Coleman Chamber Concerts Series
George Heussenstamm, Manager
Beckman Auditorium
1201 East California
Pasadena, CA 91109
Chamber music.
6 concerts per season.
Participants: professional ensembles.
Alternate address:
202 South Lake Avenue, Suite 201
Pasadena, CA 91109
(213) 793-4191.

Concord Summer Festival
John Toffoli, Director
Concord Pavilion
1950 Parkside Drive
Concord, CA 94519
(415) 682-6600
Chamber music, jazz, orchestral music.
9 annual concerts during July and August.
Participants: professional ensembles.

Festival Players Of California Series
Dr. Dorye Roettger, Director
KPFK Auditorium
3729 Cahuenga Building West
North Hollywood, CA 90606
(213) 877-2711
Chamber music of all eras.
8 concerts per season.
Participants: Festival Players of California.

Los Angeles Chamber Orchestra Series
Neville Marriner, Director
Music Center of Los Angeles
Mark Taper Forum
Los Angeles, CA 90069
(213) 657-5883
Chamber orchestra music of all eras.
4 concerts per season.
Participants: Los Angeles Chamber Orchestra.

Monday Evening Concerts Series
Dorrance Stalvey, Director
Los Angeles County Museum of Art
5905 Wilshire Boulevard
Los Angeles, CA 90036
(213) 937-4250
Chamber music, new and experimental music, contemporary choral and vocal music.
12 to 20 concerts per season.
Participants: professional ensembles.

174

Montclair Starlite Series
Harve Edwards, Director
Montclair High School Auditorium
4725 Benito Avenue
Montclair, CA 91763
20th century chamber music, dance, drama, musical theater.
5 free concerts per season, sponsored by the city of Montclair, Department of Recreation.
Participants: student and professional ensembles.
Alternate address:
2064 Magnolia Avenue
Ontario, CA 91761
(714) 629-8341.

Music At The Vineyards Series
Sandor Salgo, Director
P.O. Box 97
Saratoga, CA 95070
(408) 257-7800
Chamber music, new and experimental music.
6 concerts per season.
Participants: professional ensembles.
Alternate address:
Ed Schwartz
3325 Jackson
San Francisco, CA 94118
(415) 929-7119.

Music Here And Now Festival
Gail Kubik, Director
Scripps College
Music Department
Claremont, CA 91711
(714) 626-8511 Ext. 3266
20th century chamber music, new and experimental music.
6 annual concerts during May and June.
Participants: student and professional ensembles.

Ojai Festival
Michael Tilson Thomas, Music Director
P.O. Box 185
Ojai, CA 93023
(805) 646-2094
20th century chamber music, new and experimental music, jazz,
Annual festival during May and June.
Participants: professional ensembles.

Percussive Arts Society Festival
California Chapter
David Levine, President
P.O. Box 34
Northridge, CA 91324
(213) 345-5380
20th century chamber music, new and experimental music, jazz.
Annual spring festival.

Redwood Empire Stage Band Festival
Gloria and Walt Oster, Directors
California State University, Sonoma
Ives Hall of Music
Rohnert Park, CA 94928
(707) 795-2235 or 795-2416
Jazz.
Annual festival in November.
Participants: student ensembles.

San Mateo County Chamber Music Society Artists-In-Residence Concert Series
Helen Beyer, Executive Director
730 Winchester Drive
Burlingame, CA 94010
(415) 347-9315
Chamber music.
4 concerts per season, featuring one work by a resident composer per concert.

Symposium Of Contemporary Music
Dr. Matt Doran, Director
Mount St. Mary's College Theater
12001 Chalon Road
Los Angeles, CA 90049
(213) 272-8791
New and experimental music.
Annual 1 day festival in March, promoting contemporary music and composers.
Participants: student and professional ensembles.

University Of California, Los Angeles (UCLA) Contemporary Music Festival
Edmond G. Harris, Director
405 Hilgard
Los Angeles, CA 90024
(213) 825-4084
Henri Lazarof, Artistic Director
20th century chamber music, new and experimental music.
Annual series of concerts presented from October through April, featuring 20th century composers.
Participants: professional ensembles.

175

University of California, Riverside
Contemporary Music Festival
John Crawford, Coordinator
Music Department
Riverside, CA 92502
(714) 787-3141
20th century chamber music, new and experimental music.
Annual 3 day festival in March.
Participants: student and professional ensembles.

University Of California, Santa Cruz Concert Series
Committee on Arts and Lectures
Dorothy Kimble, Manager
Santa Cruz, CA 95064
(408) 429-2826
Chamber music, new and experimental music, jazz, multi-media.
7 to 10 concerts per season.
Participants: student and professional ensembles.

Colorado

Aspen Conference On Contemporary Music
Richard Dufallo, Director
Aspen Amphitheater
P.O. Box AA
Aspen, CO 81611
(303) 925-3254
20th century chamber music, new and experimental music, orchestral music, vocal music.
A 3 week annual series during July and August, presenting lectures, films, and concerts of contemporary music, featuring eminent composers-in-residence. This is part of the 9 week Aspen Music Festival (see below).
Participants: student and professional ensembles.
Winter address:
1860 Broadway
New York, NY 10023
(212) 581-2196.

Aspen Music Festival
Gordon Hardy, Director
Aspen Amphitheater
P.O. Box AA
Aspen, CO 81611
(303) 925-3254
Chamber music, new and experimental music, orchestral music, choral music.
Annual 9 week festival from late June through August, offering seminars, workshops, master classes, and performances of music of all eras. The

Aspen Music School has a faculty of prominent performing artists and ensembles, conductors, and composers. Festival conferences include The Aspen Choral Institute, Aspen Conference on Contemporary Music (see above), and The Aspen Music Critics Conference.
Winter address:
1860 Broadway
New York, NY 10023
(212) 581-2196.

University Of Colorado Artist Series
Mildred W. Coffin, Manager
University of Colorado
Macky Auditorium
Boulder, CO 80302
(303) 492-7425 or 492-8008
Chamber music.
6 concerts per season.
Participants: professional ensembles.

Connecticut

Connecticut Traditional Jazz Club Annual Series
P.O. Box 30
Wethersfield, CT 06109
(203) 529-4845
Jazz.
8 concerts per season.
Participants: professional ensembles.

Festival Of Contemporary Music
Dr. Harrison R. Valante, Director
University of Bridgeport
Mertens Theatre
Bridgeport, CT 06602
(203) 576-4404
20th century chamber music, orchestral music, choral music.
Annual 3 day festival in March honoring one contemporary composer per year.
Participants: student and professional ensembles.

Friends Of Music Concert Series
Reverend Edward Lane, Director
Unitarian Church
Lyons Plains Road
Westport, CT 06880
(203) 227-7205
Chamber music.
6 to 7 concerts per season, featuring guest composers and pre-concert lecture-demonstrations for Friends of Music members.

Greater Hartford Civic And Arts Festival
Catherine Wysmuller, Director
250 Constitution Plaza
Hartford, CT 06103
(203) 525-4451 Ext. 263
20th century chamber music, new and experimental music, jazz, popular music, choral music.
1 week of free annual public concerts from May through June.
Participants: student and professional ensembles.

Institute Of Contemporary American Music
Dr. Norman Dinerstein, Director
Hartt College of Music
200 Bloomfield Avenue
West Hartford, CT 06117
(203) 243-4439
20th century music.
2 concerts per season.
Participants: student and professional ensembles.

Music Mountain
Urico Rossi, Director
Gordon Hall
Falls Village, CT 06031
(203) 824-7126
Chamber music.
11 annual concerts from June through August.
Participants: Berkshire Quartet.

Silvermine Guild Of Artists Chamber Music Center Series
Mrs. M. E. Grunewald, Chairman
Gifford Hall
1037 Silvermine Road
New Canaan, CT 06820
(203) 966-5617
20th century chamber music.
4 annual summer concerts from July through August.
Participants: professional ensembles.

Starlight Festival Of Chamber Music
J. Scheir, D. Green, Directors
Yale Law School Courtyard
P.O. Box 6065
Hamden, CT 06517
(203) 624-6405
Chamber music, jazz.
5 annual summer concerts during June and July.
Participants: professional ensembles.

Summer Chamber Music Concert Series
Joseph Mulready, Director
Hartt College of Music
200 Bloomfield Avenue
West Hartford, CT 06117
(203) 243-4454
20th century chamber music.
5 annual summer concerts during July and August.
Participants: professional ensembles.

The Theatre And The Space Open Music Series
John Baringer, Director
148 Orange Street
New Haven, CT 06510
(203) 865-8368
20th century chamber music, new and experimental music, jazz.
A weekly series in an intimate setting.
Participants: student and professional ensembles.

The Theatre And The Space Saturday Series
Leo Smith, Director
148 Orange Street
New Haven, CT 06510
(203) 865-8368
20th century chamber music, new and experimental music, jazz.
Weekly concerts on Saturdays.

Twentieth Century Arts Festival
Howard Tuvelle, Director
Western Connecticut State College
Ives Concert Hall
Danbury, CT 06810
(203) 792-1400 Ext. 338
20th century chamber music, new and experimental music.
Annual spring festival.
Participants: professional ensembles.

Yale Music At Norfolk Series
Keith Wilson, Director
c/o Yale Summer School of Music and Art
Norfolk, CT 06058
(203) 542-5537
20th century chamber music.
10 annual concerts from June through August.
Participants: professional ensembles.

Delaware

Concerts In The Parks Series

Ralph Cryder, Executive Director
New Castle County Department of Parks and
Recreation
3300 Faulkland Road
Wilmington, DE 19808
(302) 571-7730
20th century chamber music, new and
experimental music, jazz, folk music, band music.
16 to 20 annual summer concerts.

District of Columbia

Inter-American Music Festival Of Washington

Guillermo Espinosa, Director
Organization of American States
Washington, D.C. 20006
(202) 381-8353
Harold Boxer, Managing Director
20th century chamber music, new and
experimental music, contemporary orchestral
music.
Triennial festival from April through May,
sponsored by the Organization of American States
and the Inter-American Music Council. Features
composers from the Americas.
Participants: professional ensembles.

National Gallery Of Art American Music Festival

Richard Bales, Music Director
6th Street and Constitution Avenue
Washington, D.C. 20565
(202) 737-4215
20th century American chamber music, new and
experimental American music.
8 free Sunday evening concerts in the spring.

Smithsonian Institution Jazz Concert Series

Martin Williams, Director
Constitution Avenue
Washington, D.C. 20560
(202) 381-6523
7 to 9 concerts per season, featuring American
jazzmen who have made important contributions
to music. Jazz Heritage Tours offered in
conjunction with the concerts.

Washington Ethical Society Third-Monday Concert Series

Nan Goland, Music Chairman
7750 16th Street, N.W.
Washington, D.C. 20012
(202) 882-6650
20th century chamber music, new and
experimental music, multi-media.
9 free public concerts presented on the third
Monday of each month September through May.
Features works by living composers. Presents
premieres and rarely heard pieces. First concert:
September 16, 1974.
Participants: The Contemporary Music Forum.

Florida

New College Summer Music Festival

Paul C. Wolfe, Musical Director
P.O. Box 1898
Sarasota, FL 33578
(813) 355-2116
Arthur R. Borden, Jr., Administrative Director
Chamber music.
Annual 3 week festival in June, featuring master
classes, ensemble instruction, and concerts.
Participants: student and professional ensembles.

Georgia

Contemporary Arts Festival

Thomas Weaver, Director
University of Georgia
Fine Arts Auditorium and University Chapel
Athens, GA 30602
(414) 542-3737
20th century chamber music, new and
experimental music.
Annual festival.
Participants: student and professional ensembles.

Golden Isles Arts Festival

Mrs. W. C. Hendrix, Director
c/o Glynn Art Association
P.O. Box 673
St. Simons Island, GA 31522
(912) 638-8770
20th century chamber music, jazz.
Annual 1 week festival in October.
Participants: student and professional ensembles.

New Music Concert Festival
Dr. David Mathew, Director
Georgia Southern College
Foy Fine Arts Building
Statesboro, GA 30458
(912) 681-5600 Ext. 396
New and experimental music.
Annual 1 day festival in May.
Participants: student and professional ensembles.

Illinois

Festival Of Contemporary Performing Arts
Ben Johnston, Director
University of Illinois
Krannert Center for Performing Arts
Urbana, IL 61801
(217) 333-2588
20th century chamber music, new and experimental music, jazz, operatic music, orchestral music, 20th century choral music.
Participants: student and professional ensembles.

Mississippi River Festival
Lyle Ward, Managing Director
Southern Illinois University
P.O. Box 67
Edwardsville, IL 62025
(618) 692-2300
20th century chamber music, new and experimental music, jazz, orchestral music.
Annual 2 month festival from late June through August.
Participants: professional ensembles.

Ravinia Festival
Edward Gordon, Director
Highland Park
22 West Monroe Street
Chicago, IL 60603
(312) 273-3500 or 782-9626
20th century chamber music, jazz.
Annual 4 month festival from June through September.
Participants: professional ensembles.

Symposium Of Contemporary Music
Illinois Wesleyan University
Westbrook Auditorium
Bloomington, IL 61701
(309) 556-3061
Annual 2 day festival in March sponsored by the University School of Music.

Indiana

Contemporary Music Festival
Donald H. White, Director
DePauw University
DePauw Performing Arts Center
Greencastle, IN 46135
(317) 653-9721
20th century chamber, choral, and orchestral music, new and experimental music, jazz.
Annual 3 day festival in April.
Participants: student and professional ensembles.

Festival Of New Music
Cleve L. Scott, Director
Ball State University
University Hall
Muncie, IN 47306
(317) 285-7072
20th century chamber music, new and experimental music.
6 annual concerts in January.
Participants: student and professional ensembles.

Festival Of New Sounds
Barton McLean, Director
Indiana University Auditorium
Northside Boulevard
South Bend, IN 46615
(219) 237-4101
20th century chamber music, new and experimental music, electronic music, multi-media.
4 to 5 concerts per season.
Participants: student and professional ensembles.

South Bend Chamber Music Society Series
Zeal Fisher, Director
Schuyler Colfax Auditorium
2920 Kettering Drive
South Bend, IN 46635
(219) 232-4606
Chamber music.
6 to 8 free concerts per season.
Participants: New Wind Quintet, South Bend String Quartet, and guest artists.

University Of Notre Dame Collegiate Jazz Festival
Reverend George Wiskirchen, Director
University of Notre Dame
Stepan Center
Notre Dame, IN 46556
(219) 283-7136
Jazz.

179

Annual 3 day festival in April.
Participants: student and professional ensembles.

Iowa

Cornell Music Festival
Cornell College
Music Department
Mount Vernon, IA 52314
(319) 895-8811
Music of all eras, including the works of major contemporary composers and performances by ensembles specializing in 20th century music.

Kansas

Festival Of 20th Century Music
Peter Ciurczak, Director
Emporia Kansas State College
Beach Hall
Emporia, KS 66801
(316) 343-1200
Chester L. Mais, Composer-In-Residence
20th century chamber, orchestral, choral, and band music.
Annual 2 day festival in April.
Student and faculty ensembles from a number of Kansas state colleges perform works written for them by resident composers of the Kansas Cooperative College Composers Project as well as other 20th century works.

Louisiana

Louisiana State University Festival Of Contemporary Music
Dinos Constantinides, Chairman
School of Music
Baton Rouge, LA 70803
(504) 388-3261
Annual 1 week festival during January and February.
Participants: student and professional ensembles.

Maine

Augustana Music Society Jazz Series
Myrtle D. Willey, President
P.O. Box 2105
Augustana, ME 04330
(207) 582-5350
Jazz.
Monthly concerts of jazz of all eras. Concerts include performances by Society members and hired groups.

Bowdoin College Contemporary Music Festival
Elliott Schwartz, Director
Bowdoin College
Brunswick, ME 04011
(207) 725-8731
Chamber music.
9 annual summer concerts.
Participants: Aeolian Chamber Players, and guest artists.

Massachusetts

Castle Hill Festival Series
Thomas Kelly, Director
Agilla Road
Ipswich, MA 01938
(617) 356-4070
Contact Mrs. Terry
20th century chamber music.
Annual series during July and August.
Participants: professional ensembles.

Festival Of Contemporary Music At Tanglewood
Gunther Schuller, Director
Berkshire Music Center
Lenox, MA 01240
(413) 637-1600
20th century chamber music, new and experimental music.
Annual 1 week festival in August. The Festival is a culmination of a summer music study program at the Berkshire Music Center. Student musicians from throughout the U.S.A. receive fellowships to study with prominent composers, conductors, and performers of contemporary music. The Festival features performances of works by guest composers, premieres, and works commissioned by the Berkshire Music Center and the Fromm Music Foundation. The event is co-sponsored by the Berkshire Music Center and the Fromm Music Foundation at Harvard.

Fogg Art Museum Concert Series
Seymour Slive, Director
Harvard University
32 Quincy Street
Cambridge, MA 02138
(617) 495-2397
Janet Cox, Public Relations
Chamber music.

Several annual series, each consisting of free concerts. Programs depend on availability of artists and suitability of instruments to acoustics. Artist payment varies.

Fromm Music Foundation At Harvard Concert Series
Elliot Forbes, Director
Harvard University
Department of Music
Cambridge, MA 02138
(617) 495-2791
20th century chamber music.
3 free public concerts per season, featuring premieres.
Participants: professional ensembles.

Lenox Arts Center Concert Series
Lyn Austin, Francis Thorne, Directors
Wheatleigh Estate
Lenox, MA 01240
(413) 637-2242
Chamber music.
6 annual concerts during July and August.

Museum Of Fine Arts Collage Series
Barbara Lambert, Curator
Musical Instrument Collection
Huntington Avenue
Boston, MA 02115
(617) 267-9300 Ext. 340
20th century chamber music, new and experimental music.
2 concerts per season, featuring Collage - The Contemporary Music Ensemble of Boston.

Outstanding Artists Chamber Music Series
Christopher Yavelow, Director
c/o Creative Media, Inc.
P.O. Box 74
Nahant, MA 01908
(617) 354-1139
Chamber music.
5 concerts per season, emphasizing Debussy and composers preceding him.

Southeastern Massachusetts University Institute And Festival
Margaret May Meredith, Managing Director
Southeastern Massachusetts University
North Dartmouth, MA 02747
(617) 997-9321
Josef Cobert, Music Director

Chamber music, orchestral music, music education workshops, operatic music.
Annual festival during June and July.

South Mountain Concerts
Mrs. Willem Willeke, Director
P.O. Box 23
Pittsfield, MA 01201
(413) 443-6517
20th century chamber music.
Several annual concerts in a summer series; numerous public school concerts per season.
Participants: professional ensembles.

Summerthing Festival
Betty Cook, Director
Mayor's Office of Cultural Affairs
One City Hall Plaza
Boston, MA 02201
(617) 722-4100
Music, dance, theater.
Annual festival from June through August.
Participants: student and professional ensembles.

Michigan

Meadow Brook Music Festival
Mr. Dearth, Director
Oakland University
Music Department
Rochester, MI 48063
(313) 377-2030
Chamber music.
Annual festival from late June through August.
Participants: professional ensembles.

National Music Camp
Dr. George Wilson, Director
Interlochen, MI 49643
(616) 276-9221
An educational facility for students of the arts, from elementary through university level. The Composers Forum features performances and discussions of student works.
20th century chamber music, new and experimental music, jazz.
370 annual concerts from June through August.
Participants: student and professional ensembles.

181

New Structures In Sound Series
C. Curtis-Smith, Director
Western Michigan University
Oakland Recital Hall
Kalamazoo, MI 49008
(616) 383-2320
20th century chamber music, new and
experimental music, jazz.
4 concerts per season.
Participants: student and professional ensembles.

Minnesota

Capital Series
M. Janet McNeill, Director of Public Relations
75 West 5th Street
St. Paul, MN 55101
(612) 291-1144
20th century chamber music.
Participants: St. Paul Chamber Orchestra

The Divertimento Recital Series
Uri Barnea, Director
First Unitarian Center
900 Mt. Curve Avenue
Minneapolis, MN 55403
(612) 377-6608
20th century chamber music, new and
experimental music, vocal music, solo music.
3 to 5 concerts per season, sponsored by the First
Unitarian Society.
Participants: student and professional ensembles.

Minnesota Black Composers Symposium
C. Edward Thomas, Executive Director
Orchestra Hall
1111 Nicollet Avenue
Minneapolis, MN 55403
(612) 339-2244
20th century chamber music, new and
experimental music, jazz, choral music.
Annual 1 week festival in May, sponsored by the
Afro-American Music Opportunities Association,
Inc. and the Minnesota Orchestra.
Participants: student and professional ensembles.

Minnesota Composers Forum New Music Series
Steven Paulus, Elizabeth Larsen, Directors
Walker Art Center
Vineland Place
Minneapolis, MN 55402
(612) 377-7500
20th century chamber music, new and
experimental music, jazz, theater music.

3 to 6 concerts per season of new works by
Minnesota composers.

Perspectives Series
Walker Art Center
Vineland Place
Minneapolis, MN 55402
(612) 377-7500
Features contemporary works for small ensembles,
with composer interviews and explanations.
Participants: The Saint Paul Chamber Orchestra.

Plymouth Music Series
Philip Brunelle, Director
Plymouth Congregational Church
1900 Nicollet Avenue
Minneapolis, MN 55403
(612) 871-7400
Contemporary religious music.
5 concerts per season.
Participants: professional ensembles.

University Of Minnesota Jazz Festival
John Smith, Director
Marshall Performing Arts Center
Duluth, MN 55812
(218) 726-8000
First concert: Spring 1975.
Participants: student ensembles.

Missouri

Central Missouri State University Jazz Festival
Robert M. Gifford, Director
Hendricks Hall and Utt Music Building
Warrensburg, MO 64093
(816) 429-4909
Annual festival in February. First concert:
February 7, 1975. Provides clinics, concerts, and
contact with professional jazz musicians for
college and public school students. Includes a jazz
band composition contest.
Participants: student and professional ensembles.

Montana

Annual Contemporary Music Festival
Alan Leech, Glen Johnston, Directors
Montana State University
Music Building, Recital Hall
Bozeman, MT 59715
(406) 994-3561
20th century chamber music, new and
experimental music.

4 concerts in April. First concert: April 21, 1975.
Participants: student and professional ensembles.

Annual Jazz Festival
Glen Johnston, Director
Montana State University
Music Building, Recital Hall
Bozeman, MT 59715
(406) 994-3561
1 annual jazz concert in January.
Participants: student ensembles, and guest faculty artists.

Nevada

Annual Contemporary Music Festival
Virko Baley, Director
University of Nevada
Judy Bayley Theatre
Las Vegas, NV 89154
(702) 739-3332
20th century chamber music, new and experimental music, operatic music.
Annual festival lasting approximately 10 days during January and February. Includes guest professional ensembles and soloists performing in 7 concerts and 7 lecture-demonstrations. Listening facilities for electronic music available. Participants also perform in the community during the Festival.

Pipers Opera House Series
Mrs. M. F. Driggs, Director
P.O. Box 131
Virginia City, NV 89440
(702) 847-0344
20th century chamber music.
Annual summer series.
Participants: professional ensembles.

Reno International Jazz Festival
Dr. John Carrico, Director
Pioneer Theatre Auditorium
Reno, NV 89502
(702) 747-1317
New and experimental music, jazz.
Annual festival during March and April.
Participants: student and professional ensembles.

University Of Nevada, Las Vegas, Jazz Festival
Frank Gagliardi, Chairman
Department of Music
4505 Maryland Parkway
Las Vegas, NV 89154
(702) 739-3332
Annual 3 day festival in March, featuring professional jazz musicians who live and work in the Las Vegas area.

New Hampshire

Apple Hill Chamber Players Series
Apple Hill Farm
East Sullivan, NH 03445
(603) 847-9706
Chamber music.
56 concerts per season.
Participants: Apple Hill Chamber Players.

Arts And Science Center Series
Ronald Deane, Director
14 Court Street
Nashua, NH 03060
(603) 883-1506
Chamber music.
5 concerts per season, sponsored by the Arts and Science Center and the Nashua Symphony Association.
Participants: student and professional ensembles.

New Hampshire Music Festival
Tom Nee, Director
P.O. Box 147
Center Harbor, NH 03226
(603) 253-4331
20th century chamber music, new and experimental music.
Annual festival of approximately 17 concerts during July and August.
Participants: professional ensembles.

Phenix Hall Theatre Noon-Time Concerts Series
40 North Main Street
Concord, NH 03301
(603) 225-6911
20th century chamber music.
20 Friday concerts per season.

The Strawberry Banke Chamber Music Festival
Frank S. Dodge, Director
P.O. Box 300
Portsmouth, NH 03801
(603) 436-8010
Chamber music, new and experimental music, operatic music.
Annual festival from June through August.

New Jersey

Annual Pee Wee Russell Memorial Stomp
Martinsville Inn
Martinsville, NJ 08836
(201) 356-1941
Jazz.
Annual event, sponsored by the New Jersey Jazz Society.
Participants: professional ensembles.

Concerts In The Park
James R. Marsh Park
Clinton Historical Museum
Clinton, NJ 08809
(201) 735-4101
Jazz, ethnic music.
6 concerts per season, sponsored by the Clinton Historical Museum.
Participants: student and professional ensembles.

Paterson Free Public Library Always On Sunday Series
Sylvia Jaroslow, Program Coordinator
250 Broadway
Paterson, NJ 07501
(201) 279-4200
20th century chamber music, new and experimental music, film, poetry.
Events every other Sunday from Ocober through May.

Paterson Free Public Library Chamber Music Series
Sylvia Jaroslow, Program Coordinator
250 Broadway
Paterson, NJ 07501
(201) 279-4200
Chamber music.
1 concert in the fall and 1 in the summer.

YM-YWHA Of Metropolitan New Jersey Series
Stanley Weinstein, Director
Maurice Levin Theater
760 Northfield Avenue
West Orange, NJ 07052
(201) 736-3200
20th century chamber music, new and experimental music, jazz.
6 to 12 concerts per season.
Participants: student and professional ensembles.

New Mexico

Santa Fe Chamber Music Festival
Sheldon Rich, Director
Museum of New Mexico
P.O. Box 853
Santa Fe, NM 87501
(505) 983-2075
Chamber music, new and experimental music.
14 summer concerts.
Participants: professional ensembles.

Taos School Of Music Series
Chilton Anderson, Director
Taos Community Auditorium
P.O. Box 1879
Taos, NM 87571
(505) 776-2388
Chamber music.
8 concerts from June through August.
Participants: student and professional ensembles.

New York State

Excluding New York City

Caramoor Festival
Michael Sweeley, Director
Katonah, NY 10536
(914) 232-3246
Chamber, orchestral, and operatic music.
19 annual summer concerts.
Participants: professional ensembles.

Chamber Music At Sarah Lawrence Series
Michael Rudiakov, Director
Sarah Lawrence College
Reisinger Auditorium
Bronxville, NY 10708
(914) 337-0700
Chamber music.
7 concerts per season.

Participants: professional ensembles.

Chautauqua Institution Summer Festival
The Amphitheater
Chautauqua, NY 14722
(716) 357-4411
Chamber music, jazz, orchesral music, operatic music.
21 annual summer concerts.
Participants: student and professional ensembles.

Composers' Forum In Albany Series
Julie Schwartz, Director
The Arts Center
1069 New Scotland Road
Albany, NY 12208
(518) 438-7895
20th century chamber music, new and experimental music.
5 to 6 concerts per season, sponsored by the Arts Center in Albany.
Participants: professional ensembles.

County Of Nassau Office Of Cultural Development June Arts Festival
John W. Maerhofer, Director
Northern Boulevard
P.O. Box D
Roslyn, NY 11576
(516) 484-9333
Chamber and orchestral music, art exhibits.
5 annual free public concerts in June.
Participants: professional ensembles.

Creative Music Festival
Dr. Karl Hans Berger, Director
P.O. Box 671
Woodstock, NY 12498
(914) 679-9245 or 679-6031
New and experimental music, jazz.
Annual festival in June, sponsored by the Creative Music Foundation, Inc.
Participants: student and professional ensembles.

Eastman School Of Music
Robert Freeman, Director
Kilbourn Hall and Eastman Theatre
26 Gibbs Street
Rochester, NY 14604
(716) 275-3037
20th century chamber music, new and experimental music, vocal music, band music.
60 concerts per season, sponsored by the Eastman School of Music.

Participants: Eastman School of Music ensembles.

An Evening Of Music At Yaddo
Curtis Harnack, Director
Yaddo Mansion
P.O. Box 395
Saratoga Springs, NY 12866
(518) 584-0746
20th century chamber music.
First concert: September 26, 1975.
Participants: professional ensembles.

Evenings At Eight-Thirty Series
c/o Student Activities and Special Sessions Department
Long Island University
South Hampton, NY 11968
(516) 283-4000
Chamber music, jazz.
7 annual summer concerts.
Participants: professional ensembles.

Evenings For New Music Series
Albright-Knox Art Gallery
1285 Elmwood Avenue
Buffalo, NY 14222
(716) 882-8700
New and experimental music.

Everson Museum Of Art Series
401 South Harrison
Syracuse, NY 13202
(315) 474-6064
Chamber music, new and experimental music, electronic music.
5 concerts per season presented by the Museum, and The Society For New Music, Syracuse. 1 concert per season is devoted to regional composers.

Free Music Store Series
Joel Chadabe, Director
State University of New York
Performing Arts Center
Albany, NY 12222
(518) 457-2147
20th century chamber music, new and experimental music, jazz, electronic music, multimedia.
6 to 10 concerts per season.
Participants: student and professional ensembles.

Friends Of The Westchester Conservatory Of Music, Inc. Series
Michael Pollon, Director
Westchester Conservatory
30 Burling Avenue
White Plains, NY 10605
(914) 761-3715
6 concerts per season.
Participants: student and professional ensembles.

Hofstra University Annual Jazz Clinic And Festival
Dr. Donald Swinney, Director
John Cranford Adams Playhouse
1000 Fulton Street
Hempstead, NY 11550
(516) 560-3283
New and experimental music, jazz.
First concert: March 21, 1975.
Participants: student and professional ensembles.

Holy Trinity Sunday At 5 Series
Frank A. Novak, Director
Holy Trinity Lutheran Church
1080 Main Street
Buffalo, NY 14209
(716) 886-2400
20th century chamber music, vocal music.
7 concerts per season.
Participants: student and professional ensembles.

International Art Of Jazz, Inc. Series
Ann H. Sneed, Director
5 Saywood Lane
Stony Brook, NY 11790
(516) 246-6125
10 to 12 jazz concerts per season.
Participants: professional ensembles.

Saratoga Performing Arts Festival
Craig Hankenson, Director
Saratoga Performing Arts Center
Saratoga Springs, NY 12866
(518) 584-9330
Chamber music, jazz, orchestral music, ballet, film, popular music.
Annual summer festival.
Participants: professional ensembles.

Sleepy Hollow Community Concerts Association Series
44 Whitetail Road
Irvington, NY 10533
(914) 591-7404
Chamber music, solo performers.
4 annual concerts, produced by the Sleepy Hollow Community Concerts Association, to be attended by subscriber members.

Tappan Zee Concerts
Abba Bogin, Musical Director
Rockland Center for the Arts
Old Greenbush Road
West Nyack, NY 10994
(914) 358-0877
Chamber music.
Annual series produced by the Tappan Zee Concert Society, featuring American chamber ensembles performing contemporary and earlier works. At least one American work is performed per concert.

Westchester Chamber Music Society Series
50 Coralyn Avenue
White Plains, NY 10605
(914) 948-8165
Chamber music.
5 concerts per season.
Participants: professional ensembles.

New York City
Bronx

Bronx Arts Ensemble Concert Series
William Scribner, Director
Riverdale-Yonkers Society for Ethical Culture
4450 Fieldston Road
Bronx, NY 10471
(212) 548-4445
Chamber music.
10 concerts per season.
Participants: Bronx Arts Ensemble.

Brooklyn

Meet The Moderns Series
Brooklyn Academy of Music
30 Lafayette Avenue
Brooklyn, NY 11201
20th century chamber music, new and experimental music, jazz.
4 concerts per season, featuring composer-conductors and composer interviews.

Theater-In-The-Back Series

Charlene Victor, Chuck Reichenthal, Directors
Brooklyn Museum
200 Eastern Parkway
Brooklyn, NY 11238
(212) 783-4469
20th century chamber music, new and experimental music, jazz.
20 annual summer concerts, sponsored by the Brooklyn Arts and Culture Association, Inc.
Participants: student and professional ensembles.

Manhattan

American Landmark Festival Composers' Concerts

Francis L. Heilbut, Director
Theodore Roosevelt Birthplace
28 East 20th Street
New York, NY 10003
(212) 673-5151
20th century chamber music, new and experimental music, jazz.
12 concerts per season.
Participants: professional ensembles.

Chamber Music Society Of Lincoln Center Series

Charles Wadsworth, Director
c/o Columbia Artists Management, Inc.
165 West 57th Street
New York, NY 10019
(212) 397-6900
Chamber music.
Approximately 14 concerts per season in Alice Tully Hall, Manhattan.
Participants: Chamber Music Society of Lincoln Center, and guest performing ensembles.

Clarion Concerts

The Clarion Music Society, Inc.
John L. Hurley, Jr., Executive Director
415 Lexington Avenue, Room 1110
New York, NY 10017
(212) 697-3862
Chamber music.
4 concerts per season, featuring works from the 17th and 18th centuries. One contemporary work is performed per season, often commissioned by the Society.

Composers' Forum

William Hellermann, General Manager
111 Amsterdam Avenue
New York, NY 10023
(212) 666-8307
20th century chamber music, new and experimental music.
6 concerts per season at WBAI Free Music Store, Manhattan.

Composers' Showcase

Charles Schwartz, Director
Whitney Museum
Madison Avenue at 75th Street
New York, NY 10021
20th century chamber music, new and experimental music, jazz, dance, operatic music, multi-media, electronic music.
4 to 5 concerts per season, featuring works by composers who are often present to explain or conduct them.
Participants: professional ensembles.

The Composer Speaks

Sheldon Soffer, Executive Director
Sheldon Soffer Management, Inc.
130 West 56th Street
New York, NY 10019
(212) 757-8060
20th century chamber music, new and experimental music.
6 concerts per season, featuring composers who introduce and discuss premiere performances of their works.

Concert Artists Guild Concert Series

154 West 57th Street, Studio 136
New York, NY 10019
(212) 757-8344
Contact the Guild concerning various series that it presents throughout New York City.

Cooper Union Forum Series

Henry C. Alter, Director
Cooper Union Great Hall
Third Avenue at 7th Street
New York, NY 10003
(212) 254-6300
20th century chamber music, new and experimental music, jazz, operatic, orchestral, and choral music.
18 concerts per season.
Participants: student and professional ensembles.

187

Creative Music Festival
Dr. Karl Hans Berger, Director
Artists House
131 Prince Street
New York, NY 10012
New and experimental music, jazz.
Annual event.
Participants: student and professional ensembles.

Dalcroze Faculty Concert Series
Dr. Hilda M. Schuster, Director
Dalcroze School of Music
161 East 73rd Street
New York, NY 10021
(212) 879-0316
Chamber music.
Participants: Dalcroze Faculty Ensemble.

Environ Thursday Night Concert Series
Jay Clayton, Booking Agent
The Environmental Community Arts Corporation
476 Broadway, 11th Floor
New York, NY 10013
(212) 966-6013
Chamber music, experimental music, jazz, dance, multi-media.
New series, beginning July 1975.
Participants: professional ensembles.

Free Life Communication Jazz And Brunch
Michael Moss, Director
Sunrise Studios
122 2nd Avenue, 3rd Floor
New York, NY 10003
(212) 533-4030
20th century chamber music, new and experimental music, jazz, ethnic music.
12 concerts per season.
Participants: professional ensembles.

Hear America First Series
Joseph Fennimore, Director
5th Avenue Presbyterian Church
7 West 55th Street
New York, NY 10019
American music.
Minimum of 6 concerts per season.
Participants: student and professional ensembles.
Alternate Address:
463 West Street, Apartment 350D
New York, NY 10014
(212) 691-1347.

International Computer Art Festival
Sema Marks, Director of Academic Computing
City University of New York
Graduate School and University Center
33 West 42nd Street
New York, NY 10019
(212) 794-5685
Charles Dodge, Music Director
Computer music.
An annual festival in June.

International Festival Series
Evelyn Johnson, President
c/o Harvey Publications
15 Columbus Circle
New York, NY 10023
(212) 582-2244
20th century chamber music.
3 concerts per season performed by Thruston Johnson, violin, and David Garvey, piano. Each concert has a theme, such as works from a chosen country or by a particular composer. At the concerts are relevant exhibits, tapes, and photographs. Future plans include American Composers' Listening Concerts, featuring contemporary composers.

Jazz Composers Orchestra Association Series
Michael Mantler, Executive Director
6 West 95th Street
New York, NY 10025
(212) 749-6265
Series of 5 jazz workshops where the works of participating composers are rehearsed and performed. Composers included have been Karl Berger, Gunter Hampel, David Izenzon, Frederic Rzewski.

Jazzmania Society, Inc. Series
Michael Morgenstern, Director
14 East 23rd Street
New York, NY 10010
(212) 677-1737 or 852-2722
Jazz.
90 public jam sessions held twice weekly, open to professional and amateur performers who are members of the Society.

Jewish Music Festival
Irene Heskes, Executive Director
Jewish Music Council
15 East 26th Street
New York, NY 10010
(212) 532-4949

Annual celebration of Jewish Music Month, lasting from Purim to Passover. The Jewish Music Council promotes active national participation in Jewish music by encouraging commissioning projects, concerts, lectures, and displays in American communities.

League-ISCM Concerts Series
Hubert S. Howe, Jr., President
Carnegie Recital Hall
7th Avenue and 57th Street
New York, NY 10019
(212) 247-1350
20th century chamber music, new and experimental music, electronic music.
5 concerts per season, sponsored by League-International Society for Contemporary Music, U.S. Section.

May Festival Of Contemporary American Music
John Watts, Director
Composers Theatre
25 West 19th Street
New York, NY 10011
(212) 989-2230
20th century chamber music, new and experimental music, electronic music, orchestral music.
2 annual May concerts, presenting contemporary works by American composers of a wide variety of styles.
Participants: Composers Festival Orchestra.

Meditations With Music Series
Philip Corner, Director
Experimental Intermedia Foundation
537 Broadway, 5th Floor
New York, NY 10012
(212) 966-3367
New and experimental music, electronic music, multi-media.
9 concerts per season, featuring composer-performers.

Music From Marlboro Series
c/o Columbia Artists Management, Inc.
Michael Ries, Personal Director
165 West 57th Street
New York, NY 10019
(212) 397-6900
Chamber music.
Touring series, featuring performers from the Marlboro Music Festival, Vermont.

Music In Our Time Series
Max Pollikoff, Producer
25 West 68th Street
New York, NY 10023
(212) 873-8152
Experimental music, electronic music, mixed-media.
5 concerts per season.

New And Newer Music Series
Dennis Russell Davies, Director
Alice Tully Hall
1941 Broadway
New York, NY 10023
(212) 362-1900
20th century chamber music, new and experimental music.
4 concerts per season.
Participants: The Ensemble.

Newport Jazz Festival New York
George Wein, Producer
P.O. Box 1169 Ansonia Station
New York, NY 10023
(212) 787-2020
Annual 10 day jazz festival in July.

New Wilderness Events
Charles Morrow, Director
Washington Square Church
135 West Fourth Street
New York, NY 10012
(212) 777-2528
New and experimental music.
7 to 9 concerts per season.
Participants: professional ensembles.

The New-York Historical Society Concert Series
Joyce M. Crawford, Director
The New-York Historical Society
170 Central Park West
New York, NY 10024
(212) 873-3400
Chamber music.
28 concerts per season.
Participants: student and professional ensembles.

New York Jazz Repertory Company Series
George Wein, Executive Director
c/o Herbert Barrett Management
1860 Broadway
New York, NY 10023
(212) 245-3530

15 jazz concerts per season.
Participants: New York Jazz Repertory Company.

New York Musicians Jazz Festival
James Du Boise, Director
193 Eldridge Street
New York, NY 10002
(212) 260-1211
Jazz.
Annual 1 week festival in June.
Participants: professional ensembles.

Park Avenue Synagogue Sanctuary Annual May Service
Cantor David Putterman, Director
50 East 87th Street
New York, NY 10028
(212) 369-2600
New liturgical music.
Annual service of works commissioned and premiered at Park Avenue Synagogue.

The Performers' Committee For Twentieth-Century Music Composers' Retrospective Concerts
Cheryl Seltzer, Joel Sachs, Directors
333 West End Avenue, Apartment 16C
New York, NY 10023
20th century chamber music, 20th century chamber orchestra music, vocal music.
Several concerts per season, featuring the works of one major 20th century composer per concert. The concerts present representative works from many periods of the composer's life. Performances are held at McMillin Theatre of Columbia University, Manhattan.

St. Stephens Series
Wendy Sharp, Administrator
c/o Concert Artists Guild, Inc.
154 West 57th Street, Studio 136
New York, NY 10019
(212) 757-8344
Chamber music.
Sunday afternoons at 4:00 at St. Stephen's Church, 120 West 69th Street, New York, NY.

Studio Rivbea Evening Concert Series
Sam Rivers, Director
24 Bond Street
New York, NY 10012
(212) 473-9936
Jazz, new and experimental music.
Participants: student and professional ensembles.

Studio Rivbea Summer Music Festival
Sam Rivers, Director
24 Bond Street
New York, NY 10012
(212) 473-9936
Jazz, new and experimental music.
Annual festival during June and July.
Participants: student and professional ensembles.

Summergarden
c/o Elizabeth Shaw
Museum of Modern Art
8 West 54th Street
New York, NY 10019
(212) 956-7298 or 956-7501
20th century chamber music, new and experimental music, jazz.
36 free summer concerts in the Sculpture Garden of the Museum.
Participants: student and professional ensembles.

Uptown Concerts Series
Gregg Smith, Director
c/o Gomer Rees
325 Riverside Drive, Apartment 3
New York, NY 10025
(212) 865-7035
20th century vocal chamber music.
8 concerts per season.
Participants: Gregg Smith Singers.

Queens

Jamaica Arts Center Chamber-Jazz Series
Mike Siegel, Director
161-04 Jamaica
Jamaica, NY 11432
(212) 658-7400
Chamber music, jazz.
10 concerts of chamber music from the 17th to 20th centuries, sponsored by the Jamaica Arts Center.

North Carolina

Eastern Music Festival
Sheldon Morgenstern, Music Director
Guilford College
Dana Auditorium
Greensboro, NC 27405
(919) 274-3444
20th century chamber music, new and experimental music.
38 summer concerts.
Participants: student and professional ensembles.

Ohio

Blossom Music Center Festival
Michael Maxwell, Director
Blossom Music Center
1145 West Steel's Corner Road
Cuyahoga Falls, OH 44223
(216) 929-3048 or 861-5674
Over 60 annual concerts from June to September, featuring all the performing arts.
Participants: professional ensembles.
Year-round address:
1037 National City Bank Building
Cleveland, OH 04114.

The Cincinnati Contemporary Music Series
Ellsworth Milburn, Director
University of Cincinnati
College-Conservatory of Music
Cincinnati, OH 45221
20th century chamber music, new and experimental music.
4 concerts per season, sponsored by the University of Cincinnati.
Participants: student and professional ensembles.

Civitan Sunday Evening Concerts Series
Don Hollenback, Director
The Park of Roses
4048 Roselea Place
Columbus, OH 43214
(614) 261-6551
20th century chamber music, new and experimental music, jazz, band and choral music.
13 concerts per season, sponsored by the Columbus Park of Roses Foundation, North Civitan Club, and Greater Columbus Arts Council.
Participants: student and professional ensembles.

Composers' Forum
Dr. Kenley Inglefield, Director
Bowling Green State University
College of Musical Arts
Bowling Green, OH 43403
(419) 372-2181
20th century chamber music, new and experimental music.
1 annual concert, presenting new works, followed by a question and answer period between the audience and composers.
Participants: New Music Ensemble, New Music Singers.

Lima Symphony Orchestra Series
Joseph Firszt, Director
Memorial Hall
P.O. Box 1651
Lima, OH 45802
(419) 222-5701
20th century chamber music, new and experimental music, jazz, folk music.
20 concerts per season, sponsored by the Lima Symphony Association, and Allen County Historical Society.
Participants: student and professional ensembles.

Music Arts Festival
Betsy Bodurtha, Director
Cleveland Music School Settlement
11125 Magnolia Drive
Cleveland, OH 44106
(216) 421-5806
20th century chamber music, new and experimental music, jazz, arts and crafts.
10 concerts per season. First concert: September 19, 1975.
Participants: student and professional ensembles.

Music-At-Antioch
Antioch College
Kelly Hall
Yellow Springs, OH 45387
20th century chamber music, new and experimental music, jazz.
Participants: student and professional ensembles.

New Directions Series
c/o Chairman, New Music Committee
Oberlin College Conservatory of Music
Warner Concert Hall
Oberlin, OH 44074
(216) 774-1221
New and experimental music.
12 to 18 concerts per season.
Participants: student and professional ensembles.

Ohio Theatre Concert Series
Donald Streibig, Director
29 East State Street
Columbus, OH 43215
(614) 469-1045
Jazz.
5 concerts per season, sponsored by the Columbus Association for the Performing Arts.
Participants: professional ensembles.

Ohio University Artist Series
Richard F. Stevens, Director
Ohio University Memorial Auditorium
Athens, OH 45701
(614) 594-4667
20th century chamber music, new and experimental music, theater, dance.
11 to 13 concerts per season.
Participants: student and professional ensembles.

Oklahoma

Oklahoma Historical Society Series
B. E. Joseph, Director
2100 North Lincoln
Oklahoma City, OK 73105
(405) 521-2491
20th century chamber music.
10 concerts per season.
Participants: student and professional ensembles.

Oregon

Peter Britt Gardens Music And Arts Festival
John Trudeau, Director
Music Pavilion and U.S. Hotel
P.O. Box 669
Jacksonville, OR 97520
(503) 779-0847
20th century chamber music, new and experimental music, orchestral music.
Annual festival in August.
Participants: student and professional ensembles.

Chamber Music Northwest Festival
c/o Concert Manager
Reed College Commons
P.O. Box 751
Portland, OR 97207
(503) 229-4079
20th century chamber music, new and experimental music.
14 annual summer concerts, featuring a resident composer.
Participants: professional ensembles.

North Coast Friends Of Music Concert Series
Coaster Theater
Cannon Beach, OR 97108
Chamber and orchestral music.
6 concerts per season.
Participants: North Coast Chamber Orchestra.

Portland Composers Concerts
John Trudeau, Music Director
Portland State University
P.O. Box 751
Portland, OR 97207
(503) 229-3011
Annual 3 day community presentation of works by Portland composers.
First concert: February 25, 1975.

Pennsylvania

Colloquium For Contemporary Music
Wayne Slawson, Director
Carnegie Music Hall
Forbes and Bellefield
Pittsburgh, PA 15213
(412) 624-4126
20th century chamber orchestra music.
2 concerts per season.
Participants: student and professional ensembles.

Evenings Of New Music Series
Larry Nelson, Director
West Chester State College
Swope Auditorium
West Chester, PA 19380
(215) 436-2739
20th century chamber music, new and experimental music.
4 to 8 concerts per season.
Participants: student and professional ensembles.

Festival Of The Avant-Garde
Larry Nelson, Director
West Chester State College
Swope Auditorium
West Chester, PA 19380
(215) 436-2739
New and experimental music.
Annual festival in April. First concert: April 4, 1975.
Participants: student and professional ensembles.

Muhlenberg College Series
Charles S. McClain, Acting Dean
Allentown, PA 18104
Chamber music.
10 to 15 concerts per season, emphasizing contemporary American works.

Penn Contemporary Players Concert Series
Nancy Adams Drye, Performance Coordinator
University of Pennsylvania
Harold Prince Theatre
Philadelphia, PA 19174
(215) 243-6244
20th century chamber music, new music.
3 concerts per season, featuring contemporary works and new pieces by University of Pennsylvania composers.
Participants: Penn Contemporary Players.

Pennsylvania Composers Project
c/o Fleischer Music Collection
The Free Library of Philadelphia
Logan Square
Philadelphia, PA 19103
(215) 686-5313
20th century orchestral music, 20th century chamber orchestra music.
4 concerts per season, presenting works by Pennsylvania composers. Works performed are selected from compositions submitted to a panel of judges. Scores and performance materials are prepared by the Edwin A. Fleischer Collection of Orchestral Music in The Free Library of Philadelphia. First series: March 9 through June 1, 1975 at Drexel University.
Participants: The Orchestra Society of Philadelphia.

Philadelphia Musical Academy Electronic Music Symposium
Andrew Rudin, Director
313 South Broad Street
Philadelphia, PA 19107
(215) 735-9635
Electronic music, jazz, theater, multi-media.
Annual symposium, presenting lectures, performances, and demonstrations of electronic music, including computer music and live electronics, jazz, theater, and multi-media. Emphasizes composers from New York, Washington D.C., and Philadelphia.
Participants: professional ensembles.

Philarte Quartet Concert Series
Nancy Adams Drye, Performance Coordinator
University of Pennsylvania
Harold Prince Theatre
Philadelphia, PA 19174
(215) 243-6244
20th century string quartets.
3 concerts per season.

Participants: The Philarte Quartet.

Temple University Music Festival
David Kanter, Director
Temple University
Philadelphia, PA 19122
(215) 787-8318
Jazz, operatic music, orchestral music, popular music.
56 annual summer concerts.
Participants: professional ensembles.

Puerto Rico

Casals Festival
University of Puerto Rico
G.P.O. 2350
San Juan, PR 00931
(809) 767-3206
Chamber music.
Annual festival in June.
Alternate address:
1290 Avenue of the Americas
New York, NY 10019
(212) 245-1961.

Rhode Island

Newport Music Festival
Glen Sauls, Director
5 Hozier Street
Newport, RI 02840
(401) 846-1133
20th century chamber music, operatic music.
27 to 30 annual summer concerts.
Participants: professional ensembles.

Rhode Island College Fine Arts Series
Billie Ann Burrill, Director
600 Mt. Pleasant Avenue
Providence, RI 02908
(401) 931-6600
20th century chamber music, new and experimental music, jazz.
1 to 2 concerts per season.
Participants: professional ensembles.

South Carolina

Contemporary Music Festival
Henry Janiec, Director
Converse College
Daniel Recital Hall
Spartanburg, SC 29301
(803) 585-6421
Participants: student and professional ensembles.

Tennessee

Memphis State University New Music Festival
Don Freund, Director
Memphis State University
Department of Music
Memphis, TN 38152
(901) 454-2553
20th century chamber music, solo music.
Participants: student and professional performers.

Oak Ridge Civic Music Association Chamber Series
Mrs. A. E. Cameron, Executive Director
P.O. Box 271
Oak Ridge, TN 37830
(615) 483-7037
Chamber music.
4 concerts per season at Oak Ridge Community Playhouse.

Oak Ridge Civic Music Association Coffee Concerts
Mrs. A. E. Cameron, Executive Director
P.O. Box 271
Oak Ridge, TN 37830
(615) 483-7037
Free Sunday evening concerts, performed by local musicians. Refreshments served.

Tennessee Technological University Composer Festival
Robert Jager, Director
Derryberry Hall
Cookeville, TN 38501
(615) 528-3161
20th century chamber music, new and experimental music, jazz, choral, band, and orchestral music.
Annual festival.
Participants: student and professional ensembles.

Texas

Contemporary Music Festival
William A. Schroeder, Director
Del Mar College
Corpus Christi, TX 78404
(512) 882-6231
20th century chamber music, choral music.
Annual festival in February.
Participants: student and professional ensembles.

Dallas Public Library Composer Festival
George Henderson, Director
1954 Commerce Street
Dallas, TX 75201
(214) 748-9071
20th century chamber music, new and experimental music.
Occurs once every few years.
Participants: Dallas Symphony Orchestra and Dallas Chamber Music Society.

Festival Of 20th Century Music
Dr. John D. Stewart, Director
Eastfield College
3737 Motley Drive
Mesquite, TX 75149
(214) 746-3132
20th century chamber music, new and experimental music, jazz.
Annual festival, presenting 20th century music in lecture-demonstrations, discussions, and master classes.
Participants: student and professional ensembles.

Symposium Of Contemporary Music
Dr. Mary Jeanne van Appledorn, Director
Texas Tech University
P.O. Box 4239
Lubbock, TX 79409
(806) 742-1121
20th century chamber music, new and experimental music, jazz.
Annual festival lasting approximately 10 days in December.
Participants: student and professional ensembles.

Utah

University Of Utah Festival
Charles Bestor, Director
University of Utah
Salt Lake City, UT 84112
(801) 581-6765
20th century chamber music, new and
experimental music, jazz.
Annual festival in January.
Participants: student and professional ensembles.

Vermont

Bennington Chamber Music Conference And Composers Forum Of The East
Alan Carter, Director
Bennington College
Music Department
Bennington, VT 05201
(802) 442-5401
Chamber music.
Annual event in August.
Participants: student and professional ensembles.

Festival Of The Arts
Arthur Jones, Director
Southern Vermont Art Center
Manchester, VT 05254
(802) 362-1405
Chamber music.
8 annual summer concerts.
Participants: professional ensembles.

Marlboro Music Festival
Rudolph Serkin, Artistic Director
Marlboro, VT 05344
(802) 254-8163
Chamber music.
Annual summer festival.
Participants: student and professional ensembles.

St. Michael's College Concert Series
Dr. William Tortolano, Director
St. Michael's College
McCarthy Arts Center
Winooski, VT 05404
(802) 655-2000
20th century chamber music, new and
experimental music.
2 to 3 concerts per season.
Participants: student and professional ensembles.

Virginia

Shenandoah Valley Music Festival
John Fishburn, Director
P.O. Box 12
Woodstock, VA 22664
(703) 459-3396 or 459-3567
Chamber music.
Annual summer festival.
Participants: professional ensembles.

Wolf Trap Farm Park For The Performing Arts Festival
John M. Ludwig, General Director
Filene Center
1624 Trap Road
Vienna, VA 22180
(703) 938-3810
Chamber music, new and experimental music,
jazz, operatic music, ballet, popular music.
Annual summer festival, sponsored by the Wolf
Trap Foundation for the Performing Arts.
Participants: student and professional ensembles.

Washington

The Contemporary Group Series
William Bergsma, William O. Smith, Directors
University of Washington
102 Music Building
Seattle, WA 98195
(206) 543-1200
20th century chamber music, new and
experimental music.
8 to 10 concerts per season, sponsored by the
University of Washington School of Music.
Participants: student and professional ensembles.

An Evening Of Contemporary Music Series
David P. Robbins, Director
Pacific Lutheran University
Tacoma, WA 98447
(206) 531-6900
20th century chamber music.
3 concerts per season, sponsored by Pacific
Lutheran University.
Participants: student and professional ensembles.

Tamarack Festival
Dr. Wendal S. Jones, Director
Eastern Washington State College
Pence Union Building
Cheney, WA 99004
(509) 359-7082

Chamber and orchestral music, new and
experimental music, jazz.
2 to 5 annual summer concerts.
Participants: student and professional ensembles.

Wisconsin

Festival Of The Arts
Lorraine Gross, Associate Dean
University of Wisconsin
College of the Arts
Whitewater, WI 53545
(414) 472-4869
6 annual concerts in October.
Participants: student and professional ensembles.

**La Crosse Community Concert Association
Series**
Charles Schmitt, Manager of Arts Centre
Viterbo College
Fine Arts Centre
La Crosse, WI 54601
(608) 782-5661
Chamber music.
4 concerts per season.
Participants: professional ensembles.

Peninsula Music Festival
Katherine S. Wilson, Chairman
Gibraltar Auditorium
Fish Creek, WI 54212
(414) 854-4060
20th century chamber orchestra music.
9 annual concerts for 2 weeks in August.
Participants: professional ensembles.

Pro Musica Nova Series
Tele Lesbines, Vincent McDermott, Directors
Milwaukee Art Center
Milwaukee, WI 53202
20th century chamber music, new and
experimental music.

3 annual concerts per season, sponsored by the
Wisconsin College-Conservatory Women's
League, and Milwaukee Art Center.
Participants: Pro Musica Nova Ensemble.

Summer Evenings Of Music Series
Robert W. Corrigan, Director
University of Wisconsin
Department of Music
Milwaukee, WI 53201
(414) 963-4393
20th century chamber music.
Annual 2 month summer festival.
Participants: professional ensembles.

Wyoming

Grand Teton Music Festival
Ling Tung, Director
Festival Hall
P.O. Box 20
Teton Village, WY 83025
(307) 733-3050
20th century chamber music, new and
experimental music.
27 annual concerts for 6 weeks in the summer.
Participants: professional ensembles.

Western Arts Music Festival
University of Wyoming
Department of Music
Laramie, WY 82071
(307) 766-5242
Annual festival from June through July, featuring
courses in performance and composition
techniques, chamber music workshops, and choral
workshops. During the Festival, one week entitled
*Composers Symposium: New American Music:
Tangents* is devoted to contemporary music,
featuring workshops, lectures, discussions, and
performances.

Bibliography

Hahn, Hannelore, ed. *Spaces. A Directory of Auditoriums and Meeting Rooms, Indoors and Outdoors, Available in the City of New York.* New York: City of New York Parks, Recreation, and Cultural Affairs Administration, 1975.

Handel, Bea; Spencer, Janet; and Turner, Nolanda, eds. *The National Directory for the Performing Arts and Civic Centers.* Dallas: Handel and Co., 1975.

Handel, Bea; Spencer, Janet; and Turner, Nolanda, eds. *The National Directory for the Performing Arts/Educational.* Dallas: Handel and Co., 1975.

Israel, Barbara B. and Newton, Michael K., eds. *A Guide To Community Arts Agencies.* New York: Associated Councils of the Arts, 1974.

Lewis, Marianna O., ed. *The Foundation Directory.* Edition 5. New York: The Foundation Center, 1975.

Lincoln, Harry B., ed. *Directory of Music Faculties in Colleges and Universities, U.S. and Canada 1972-1974.* Binghamton, New York: The College Music Society, 1972.

Musical America 1975 International Directory of the Performing Arts. Great Barrington, Massachusetts: ABC Leisure Magazines, 1975.

Noe, Lee, ed. *The Foundation Grants Index, 1974.* New York: The Foundation Center, 1975.

Pavlakis, Christopher. *The American Music Handbook.* New York: The Free Press, 1974.

INDEX

200

204

206

212

225